HOMELAND

NEW DIRECTIONS IN TEJANO HISTORY

Alberto Rodriguez and Timothy Paul Bowman,
Series Editors

HOMELAND

Ethnic Mexican Belonging since 1900

AARON E. SÁNCHEZ

UNIVERSITY OF OKLAHOMA PRESS ✷ NORMAN

Library of Congress Cataloging-in-Publication Data

Names: Sánchez, Aaron E., 1985– author.
Title: Homeland : ethnic Mexican belonging since 1900 / Aaron E. Sánchez.
Other titles: Ethnic Mexican belonging since 1900
Description: Norman : University of Oklahoma Press, [2021] | Series: New directions in Tejano history ; volume 2 | Includes bibliographical references and index. | Summary: "Explores how the concept of belonging within the ethnic Mexican community changed over the course of the twentieth century"—Provided by publisher.
Identifiers: LCCN 2020026850 | ISBN 978-0-8061-6843-2 (pbk)
Subjects: LCSH: Mexican Americans—Texas-—Ethnic identity. | Mexican Americans—Texas—History—20th century. | Mexican Americans—Texas—Intellectual life—20th century. | Aztlán. | Chicano movement. | National characteristics, Mexican. | Mexicans—United States—Ethnic identity.
Classification: LCC E184.M5 S2545 2021 | DDC 976.4/0046872—dc23
LC record available at https://lccn.loc.gov/2020026850

Homeland: Ethnic Mexican Belonging since 1900 is Volume 2 in the New Directions in Tejano History series.

The paper in this book meets the guidelines for permanence and durability of the Committee on Production Guidelines for Book Longevity of the Council on Library Resources, Inc. ∞

To Joaquín Adrian and Lucía Kate Sánchez,

That your histories may be recorded and your stories may be written

Contents

Series Editors' Preface

Aaron E. Sánchez's innovative study *Homeland: Ethnic Mexican Belonging since 1900* is the second book in the New Directions in Tejano History series. The work is an important contribution to the emergent field of Chicana/o intellectual history. Sánchez has changed the way Latina/o/x–Chicana/o–Mexican American historians understand ethnic Mexicans' senses of belonging in the United States and Mexico. His work takes the reader on a journey from the Mexican Revolution to the early 1920s, placing ethnic Mexicans at the center of competing ideas on both sides of the border. Sánchez uses belonging to recast citizenship and the Mexican American Civil Rights Movement, linking it to the League of United Latin American Citizens, which led middle-class activism between the 1920s and 1950s while often excluding noncitizens. With the coming of the Red Scare and the Cold War, the ethnic Mexican left became linked with class and belonging based on labor internationalism. During what Sánchez calls the "pre-Chicana/o Movement," visions of belonging took a global perspective, juxtaposing ethnic Mexicans' inequality and discrimination at home and abroad. As the Chicana/o Movement took hold, visions of belonging took a global perspective, juxtaposing ethnic Mexicans' inequality and discrimination at home and abroad. As the Chicana/o Movement took hold in the United States, ethnic Mexicans redefined belonging through art, literature, and poetry, creating a multifaceted intellectual history that shaped many fields of studies for several generations.

Homeland challenges historians to rethink ethnic Mexican agency in terms of citizenship, class, and activism in the United States and Mexico. Sánchez uses the term "belonging" to capture the various combinations of roles that ethnic Mexicans may deploy to define themselves. *Homeland* moves Latina/o–Chicana/o–Mexican American scholarship to a different level and opens new doors to our understanding of the changing world of the ethnic Mexican. No longer are historians limited to labor, migration, racial, and nation-state studies. Sánchez truly shows that a study can incorporate all these components to give a nuanced understanding of the role ethic Mexicans have played in the vital histories of the United States and Mexico. It is a great honor to have such a work in the New Directions in Tejano History series.

Alberto Rodriguez
Series coeditor with Tim Bowman

Acknowledgments

Writing a book is like running an ultra-marathon without being sure where the finish line is. Luckily, I have had the support of wonderful colleagues, friends, and family.

I am lucky to work with the people in the History Department at Mountain View College (MVC). Ken Alfers, Ruben Arellano, Richard Means, Andrew McGregor, Ryan Pettengill, and Jessica Waldrop are excellent scholars who are committed to educating students. I have also been fortunate to work with deans who have supported me and my research. Quentin Wright and, especially, Stephanie Scroggins encouraged me to keep writing even with a full teaching load. Rebecca McDowell and the Department of Professional Development at MVC provided me with funds to continue my research and conference presentations, which has helped me strengthen this monograph and become a better professor.

I can trace back the ideas that inspired this project to undergraduate courses at Trinity University. I arrived on that campus in San Antonio with no intention of graduating, but I was pulled into the world of ideas available to me there. In my work I try to re-create what I learned in the classes of Robert Huesca, Alida Metcalf, David Spener, and Rita Urquijo-Ruiz. While at Trinity I was fortunate to have Arturo Madrid as my mentor. He is kind, generous, and brilliant. He graciously indulged a young undergraduate student who probably took up too much of his time and asked too many questions. In all the conversations we had, while I was focused on answers, he gently guided me to the right questions.

At Southern Methodist University I was privileged to take classes focused on the US West, Southwest, and borderlands. Peter Bakewell, the late Dennis Cordell, Edward Countryman, Benjamin Johnson, Alexis McCrossen, John Mears, and Sherry Smith all shared their strengths as historians with a student interested in Aztlán. My dissertation committee members, Crista DeLuzio, Andrew Graybill, and George Mariscal, all made my dissertation stronger. I was lucky to have John Chávez, an exceptional historian and a kind human being, as a dissertation advisor. I have tried many times over to emulate his incisive questioning and excellent writing skills, and they have shaped this book.

At conferences and in conversations, very many scholars have helped me revise and think through my ideas. I would like to thank Roberto Calderón, Antonia Castañeda, George T. Díaz, Mario T. García, Nicolás Kanellos, Max Krochmal, Jaime Mejía, Natalie Mendoza, Tatcho Mindiola, David Montejano, Stephen Nuño, Michael A. Olivas, Carmen Tafolla, Juan Tejeda, and John Weber.

The Tejas foco of the National Association for Chicana and Chicano Studies (NACCS-Tejas), the Society for US Intellectual History (SUSIH), and the Recovering the US Hispanic Literary Heritage project have been supportive of my project. As a graduate student I was awarded a grant from the Research Grants Program of the Hispanic History of Texas Project that funded nearly all the research for my dissertation. NACCS-Tejas awarded me with the 2014 Dissertation Award, giving me the confidence to continue working on this project. And NACCS and SUSIH have been welcoming forums for my research.

I thank Alberto Rodriguez and Timothy Bowman for supporting this book. It is truly an honor to contribute to the New Directions in Tejano History series. The outside reviewers, Ruben Flores and Cynthia Orozco, gave much time to reading the manuscript and provided extensive comments and notes that made this book much stronger. In addition, Ruben Flores has always been gracious with his time and insights. He is an exceptional intellectual historian who has shaped my understanding of Chicana/o intellectual history. All the shortcomings, of course, are solely mine. The editors at University of Oklahoma Press have been incredible and supportive. Without the help of Steven Baker and Kent Calder, this book would not have been possible. Copyeditor Kirsteen E. Anderson made the book stronger and easier to read. Thank you all so much.

My work as a journalist renewed my faith in the importance of writing. Thank you to Victor Landa at *News Taco*, Julio Ricardo Varela at

National Public Radio's *Latino USA*, and Hector Luis Alamo, then at *Latino Rebels*, for giving me opportunities to report on issues crucial to Latinxs in our contemporary moment. As a columnist for *Sojourners*, I have had the privilege to work with wonderful editors who have allowed me to grow as a writer. Thank you, Daniel José Camacho, Christina Colón, and Sandi Villarreal.

Of course, none of this would have been possible without my family.

The Mowrey/Mortensen family have been very supportive over the years. They have consistently asked about my research and listened as I have expounded at length. Roger, Sharon, and Drew, thank you for letting a stranger who randomly showed up at your house one day into your family. I can't imagine how much of a bother I was then, but you never let me feel that. Your love and support mean the world to me.

The Herrera and Sánchez families are the reasons I became a historian. I am grateful for my grandparents (Monico, Josefina, Carmen, and Lino) and all my tías, uncles, and cousins. Our family stories piqued my curiosity and were my first introduction to primary sources. I am thankful for my parents and their spouses. Dad, during the times when I questioned the value of writing and my degrees, the pride with which you said "este es mi hijo, el doctor" reassured me that I had done something worthwhile. Mom, you heard the quiet words of a six-year-old when I told you I wanted to be a writer. I heard the ways you blended English and Spanish, bending words to your needs. I knew I could do the same if I tried. Sheesha, every day I am grateful to be your little brother. You walked me to class on the first day of school every year until graduate school and helped me find my way. Thanks Sheesha. Jaiden and Kian, you have given me the joy of being an uncle. Sanjay, thank you for joining and growing our family.

Joaquín and Lucía, you two are all the prayers I have ever prayed and all the hope I have ever had. Leah, I still have no idea by what cosmic mistake or miracle of grace you love me, but I am grateful that you do. It is no cliché or stretch of the imagination to say that this project would not have been possible without you. I cannot imagine a different partner in this life.

Note on Terminology

It has become customary to include a short note on terminology in historical works on the transnational ethnic Mexican population.[1] The changes in terms and shifting definitions are not empty exercises in semantics or claims at historiographical novelty. Instead, the growing availability of terms to historians of the ethnic Mexican population demonstrates the academic and intellectual vitality of the field, showing that historians are increasingly focused on using words that accurately reflect the worlds of their historical subjects and the histories they are writing. Various terms can be used to indicate differences in ideas, identities, citizenships, and time periods.

In this work, I use the terms "ethnic Mexicans," Mexican nationals," "US-born Mexicans," "Mexican Americans," and "Chicanas/os." "Ethnic Mexicans" describes the population of Mexican-descent people in the United States, regardless of their citizenship. "Mexican national" refers to a person with Mexican citizenship living in the United States. "US-born Mexican" signifies a person with Mexican descent born in the United States. "Mexican American" describes a person of Mexican descent born in the United States who used that term with intention from the 1920s through the 1960s, a time when the term was not widespread nor politically neutral. "Mexican American" was associated with influential groups that were constructing an important identity as US citizens, and the term was in conversation with prevailing ideas about progress, modernity, race, and belonging.

I use "Chicana," "Chicano," and "Chicana/o" at different points in this work and avoid projecting the term "Chicana/o" into the past. It is largely reserved for people who identified with the myriad of social, political, and ideological projects associated with that term after the 1960s. I use "Chicana/o" and "Chicana" to recognize the agency and presence of Chicanas in places, organizations, and histories that have generally been remembered as overwhelmingly male..

Another important term in this work is "México de Afuera." "México de Afuera" certainly means a community of Mexican exiles living in the United States after 1910. But I use the term with a more capacious definition, as it approaches what I believe to be the more correct denotation of the people using it at the time. México de Afuera was a temporary refugee homeland for Mexican nationals after the Mexican Revolution. It was a space of belonging for those who were torn from their place of birth, a space where all the virtues of the nation were cultivated and sustained in expectation of an imminent and certain return. This refugee homeland was not open to everyone, as chapter 1 will show, and at times I refer to its adherents as "Afuerenses."

The key term in this work is "belonging." Belonging is a complex historical idea that has evolved over time and space as people across the world have constructed identities and tried to give them fixity. Multiple competing and overlapping conceptions of belonging can exist at the same time or over time, as I show. Belonging can be hard to define. The historian Eric D. Weitz, in his history of human rights, urged his readers to understand that rights "constitute in this book an angle of orientation, not a definitional end point."[2] I encourage readers to consider belonging similarly in the following pages.

Acronyms

AAA	Agricultural Adjustment Act
AFL	American Federation of Labor
ASARCO	American Smelting and Refining Company
CIO	Congress of Industrial Organizations
CPUSA	Communist Party USA
CTM	Confederación de Trabajadores Mexicanos
ILA	International Longshoremen's Association
ILGWU	International Ladies Garment Workers Union
IWW	International Workers of the World
LDC	Latino Donor Collaborative
LULAC	League of United Latin American Citizens
MAYO	Mexican American Youth Organization
OSA	Order of Sons of America
PLM	Partido Liberal Mexicano (Mexican Liberal Party)
SPA	Socialist Party of America
UCAPAWA	United Cannery, Agricultural, Packing and Allied Workers of America
WPA	Works Progress Administration

INTRODUCTION
An Intellectual History of Ethnic Mexican Belonging

This is an intellectual history of belonging in ethnic Mexican thought since 1900. Belonging is a complex interwoven collection of ideas that frames the ideological architecture of human interconnectedness. It shapes the contours of responsibilities and obligations humans engage in with and to one another. My task is to untangle how these interwoven ideas intersected with the US-Mexico borderlands. These ideas of belonging had global and national origins that were expressed in transnational and translocal practices. In the twentieth century, ethnic Mexicans adapted, adopted, and abandoned the ideas of belonging that were available to them, for pragmatic, political, and ideological reasons.

Often highly ideological and emotional, belonging is often expressed spatially through a homeland. A homeland is important because it gives the ideas and feelings of belonging fixity; that is, geographical shape, boundaries, borders, and physical roots. Early on, the imagined dimensions of homelands were limited and their physical reach narrow, restricted to a specific river, hunting ground, plain, forest, desert, or watering hole. As they grew and the world became more interconnected, homelands became harder to define. Broadly, historian John R. Chávez has described a homeland as a historical territory that is identified with a distinct ethnic group over time.[1] Cultural geographer Richard L. Nostrand identified three central components to a homeland: "a people, a place, and identity with place."[2] Later, Nostrand and his colleague Lawrence E. Estaville expanded the definition to five characteristics but claimed that the key component to homelands was "bonding with place."[3] As forms of human organization grew, initial homelands became the basis for parts of larger empires and nation-states across the globe.[4]

Homelands were important for envisioning who belonged to a group in a certain area, but the rise of the nation-state as the primary political and organizational unit changed the nature of belonging in the world, and especially in the US-Mexico borderlands. The nation-state built upon homelands but also erased them. In many cases the borders of nation-states cut across and through homelands, dividing and amalgamating people, places, and spaces. The bureaucratically managed nation-state of the late nineteenth and early twentieth centuries ascribed to itself the authority to regulate various actions and rights that adhered previously to individuals or groups, such as the legitimate means of violence.[5]

Of particular importance, and a focus of this book, is the influence of the nation-state and citizenship upon belonging in twentieth-century ethnic Mexican thought. Over the course of the twentieth century, citizenship became not only the determiner of who had rights, but it also became the legitimate means of belonging across the world, and especially in the United States. As other modes of organizing belonging collapsed, citizenship became the defining characteristic of belonging. The twentieth century saw the consolidation of large bureaucratic states in both the United States and Mexico that needed to manage and control their populations. The increasing salience of citizenship would prove problematic for a transnational population that moved back and forth across the border for many reasons. Many ethnic Mexicans—whether US or Mexican born, working class or upper class, rural or urban—deliberated whether or not they could be both Mexican and American. Some even despaired that they were neither. In the twentieth century, ethnic Mexicans reacted and responded to changes in the legitimate means of belonging by creating multiple ideologies that expressed how they viewed their positions in the region, nation, and world and how they understood their responsibilities to other human beings.

Another important point is that although the focus of this book is Texas, I draw several points of comparison to California. I do so not only to avoid the accusations and problems of a parochial perspective, but also to show that similar ideas existed and operated across the Southwest—and especially in the two states with the largest populations of ethnic Mexicans. Nevertheless, while many of these ideas existed across the Southwest, differences, both subtle and extreme, existed in ideas and identities in places like New Mexico, Colorado, and Arizona. Yet, this is not a limited community study. Until the mid-twentieth century, Texas had the largest population of ethnic Mexicans in the United States and was home to some of the largest ethnic Mexican barrios. Ethnic Mexicans' historical persistence and the fact that they comprised a large percentage of urban populations was important in shaping policies, politics, and ideas. Important Mexican American advocacy organizations—such as the League of United Latin American Citizens (LULAC), the American GI Forum, and the Mexican American Legal Defense and Education Fund (MALDEF)—were founded in Texas and spread nationwide. Ideas that originated in Texas spread across the nation over the course of the twentieth century.

CHICANA/O INTELLECTUAL HISTORY

While this book rests at the intersection of cultural, intellectual, and literary history, I have chosen to call it a work of Chicana/o intellectual history. I assert that not only were ethnic Mexicans manual laborers, conquered people, and segregated proletarians, but they were also people who thought deeply and profoundly about their position in the world. I am joining historians in other areas who are trying to make the field of intellectual history more inclusive of people who are not formal intellectuals. As historian Catherine E. Kelly explains, the traditional emphasis of intellectual history on highbrow, elite, and scientific bodies of thought has privileged white males as thinkers, while the ideas of women and communities of color have been reduced to "experiences." White men are not the only people who have thoughts and express ideas. Ethnic Mexicans experienced the world around them, but they also made meaning of this experience intellectually.[6]

Historians of thought have slowly expanded the definition of intellectuals from strictly philosophers and political theorists toward members of popular culture, while continuing to highlight connections to elite or high culture.[7] Historian Donald R. Kelley has claimed that "intellectual history should indeed be concerned with human self-understanding."[8] Even though the broader field has shifted focus, there is still however a relative dearth of Chicana/o intellectual histories.[9] In the field of Chicana/o studies, literary scholars have attempted to fill the lacuna of Chicana/o intellectual history with complex textual studies. As new historicists, they have taken the lead in exploring texts ranging from the works of María Amparo Ruiz de Burton in nineteenth-century California to Jovita González's and Américo Paredes's poetry and novels in the early twentieth century.[10] Efforts like the University of Houston's Recovering the US Hispanic Literary Heritage Project have uncovered, recovered, and digitized a wealth of material previously inaccessible or unknown to scholars. It seems that literary scholars' interdisciplinary approach makes them more comfortable than historians of ideas about using popular culture and performance as sources. Yet, literary scholars may lack training in the historical methodologies that help explain why meanings and ideas arise and wane at certain moments.[11]

A quarter century after the linguistic and postmodern turn caused an existential crisis in the field of intellectual history, historians and new historicists have come to a détente of sorts, working side by side but rarely together. No longer guilty of the extremes of poststructuralist presentism and deconstruction that reduced texts and ideas to detcontextualized abstractions of language with no meaning, new historicist literary scholars have gained surprising insights by connecting literary texts to their historical contexts. This trend has moved literary scholars closer to the history of ideas, but most literary scholars are still uncomfortable with what they see as historians' imposition of narrative and chronology on the past.[12] Literary scholars' historicism extends only so far—usually limited to a brief review of a small selection of historical monographs. Their focus of attention remains the text.

A Chicana/o history of ideas extends beyond literary criticism to show that ethnic Mexicans were in conversation with the prevailing discourses and ideas that were changing the world at the time. Academics, writers, politicians, and journalists are commonly recognized as intellectuals, but humans of all social classes have thoughts and ideas. Every day, they make meaning of their lives. I argue that ethnic Mexicans were not simply passive recipients of the world of ideas that surrounded them but often contributed to it. Ethnic Mexicans were aware of their citizenship long before they fought abroad in two world wars.[13] They were already engaged in an ideological and intellectual global transformation and were responding to the changing notions of belonging surrounding them.

This is not a social history of prominent Mexican American intellectuals.[14] Those studies have been written and written well. Biographies of figures like George I. Sánchez, Carlos Castañeda, Alonso S. Perales, Josefina Fierro de Bright, and Luisa Moreno have dealt directly with the social circulation of their ideas.[15] Those studies provide deeply researched pictures of the individual's life, childhood, education, professional development, and other things. Therefore, in my work I provide limited biographical information. It is not my desire to decontextualize historical actors, but rather to draw attention to their ideas and contextualize them in an intellectual history of ethnic Mexican belonging.

Analyzing the notion of belonging in an intellectual history questions the meaning of citizenship in the twentieth century. An intellectual history of belonging allows us to understand citizenship as not only a political identity, but also as a concept that organizes an individual's relationship and responsibilities to the state, other citizens, and other people in the world. Citizenship is one of many forms of human organization in the history of humankind. In the twentieth century, ethnic Mexicans in Texas contested and acceded to different meanings of citizenship and changing ideas of belonging.

TEXAS, ETHNIC MEXICANS, AND TRANSNATIONAL TRANSFORMATIONS OF BELONGING

Through changes in the mode of economic production, increases in state bureaucracies, the rise of a new passport regime, and the introduction of exclusionary immigration policies—all of which entailed powerful racialized discourses about citizenship—the nation-state became the main arbiter of identity. With the collapse of previous modes of imagining that had organized belonging, citizenship became the legitimate means of belonging by the early twentieth century.[16] By the 1920s the discursive authority of the nation-state—predicated on complex bureaucratic structures and a specialized core of civil servants trained to manipulate them—was beginning to codify the rights and meaning of citizenship. This process was disrupting old and creating new ways of thinking about belonging across the globe.

But what did these national and global changes in citizenship mean for ethnic Mexicans in the United States? Ethnic Mexicans in Texas, and across the nation, wrestled with the meaning of citizenship personally, politically, and ideologically. They reworked or rejected citizenship as a concept that should dictate the responsibilities of people to the state and to each other, while simultaneously fighting for full extension of the rights that citizenship entailed. They grappled with the meaning of citizenship, which rendered their grandparents, uncles, aunts, and cousins who lived across the Rio Grande somehow different.

Texas had had a long history of changing national identities. In the early nineteenth century, Texas sat on the edge of the Spanish empire, playing a much less important role than New Mexico on the northern frontier. After independence from Spain in 1821, Texas sat at the intersection of growing markets and trade routes that led toward both the United States and Mexico. Increasing market interactions with the United States helped push Texas toward the American orbit.[17] At the same time, in the United States, the pressure for extensive and intensive development—meaning territorial expansion and increased industrial development, respectively—brought more Anglo settlers to the Texas region.[18] Increasing market forces combined with a growing state centralization movement in Mexico to fuel the Texas revolution of 1835–36. The Republic of Texas briefly became an independent nation in 1836, before voting for annexation by the United States in 1845.[19] This precipitated the two-year war with Mexico. With the signing of the Treaty of Guadalupe Hidalgo on February 2, 1848, Texas officially became part of the United States, and all Mexican citizens who remained in the state one year later became US citizens. Just a few years later, in 1861, the flag flying over Texas would change once again as Texas joined the Confederacy.

Whereas early nineteenth-century Mexican politics left that country disjointed and controlled by powerful regional caudillos, the 1876 election of Porfirio Díaz as president brought a slate of economic policies that would unite the country as never before. Díaz built railroads that interconnected national markets and connected them to ports for exporting goods.[20] Unfortunately, Porfirian policies also alienated subsistence farmers, industrial workers, and the growing Mexican middle class.[21] Discontent grew across these many segments of the population, until eventually in 1911, Francisco Madero, an elite businessman from the northern state of Coahuila, began the revolution that ended Díaz's presidency.

The Mexican Revolution was a product of uncertain cross-class alliances and competing, often contradictory class goals.[22] These class and regional cleavages underlined the uneven sense of national identity that existed in Mexico. Many Mexican nationals felt a sense of belonging to their *patria chica*, instead of the larger nation. The Mexican Revolution quickly devolved into a decade-long civil war. By its end, hundreds of thousands of Mexicans had perished in the violence,[23] and more than 1.5 million Mexican nationals had taken refuge in the US Southwest, the majority of them in Texas. Ethnic Mexicans in the state found themselves embroiled in two nationalizing projects.

In the new revolutionary Mexican state, government agencies, bureaucrats, poets, and artists were trying to rebuild a country from the ashes of a very violent decade. Muralists such as Diego Rivera, José Clemente Orozco, and David Alfaro Siqueiros painted grand narratives of the new state, with indigenous peasants and urban workers in the foreground. Secretary of Education José Vasconcelos organized rural schools with the goal of educating the entire nation. The schools played a crucial role in extending the administrative power of the state into areas it had never reached before.[24] Out of this revolutionary cauldron came modern Mexican nationalism, a force aimed at uniting its citizens and its growing diaspora through a reimagined shared past.[25] Many expatriate Mexicans felt proud to be Mexican, inspired by the ideas of the Revolution and the rebuilding of their nation. The anti-Americanism of the revolution was a powerful force in modern Mexican nationalism. The Mexican consular corps, nearly all of them located in the United States, contributed to promoting Mexican nationalism through sponsored patriotic festivals and organizations. These extensions of the Mexican state brought the nationalization project to ethnic Mexicans in the United States.

Meanwhile, the United States was busy incorporating the semi-peripheral region of the Southwest into the nation.[26] In addition, during the first decades of the twentieth century, the forces of racism and nationalism fused into a very powerful form of racial nationalism. In this context, ethnic Mexicans in Texas tried to negotiate citizenship, belonging, and identity. The tensions between Mexican nationals and US-born Mexicans during this period were expressed in debates over what historian Emilio Zamora calls "evolving homeland politics."[27] That is, they disagreed over and debated the meaning of Mexicanness and the extent of Mexican belonging in the United States. The exile and refugee Mexican nationals brought with them pre-revolutionary and post-revolutionary ideas of Mexicanness and patriotism. Though living in the United States, they waxed sentimental about their country, composing patriotic and sentimental poetry and songs about their beloved Mexico. Through rose-tinted lenses they remembered an idyllic utopia that never existed. These notions colored their views of the United States as a nightmarish place of greed, selfishness, moral decay, and racism. Americanness was the opposite of Mexicanness, they reasoned. True Mexicans, thus, did not belong or want to stay in the United States. They watched US-born Mexicans closely for signs of American infections and affectations—such as speaking English, smoking American cigarettes, and wearing American fashions—that proved their Mexicanness had been compromised. To Mexican nationals, the Mexicanness of US-born Mexicans was devolving and their Americanness was in arrested development; they were a sad people without a country and without belonging. In many cultural forms, Mexican nationals appropriated authentic Mexicanness for themselves and resisted belonging to the United States. The post-revolutionary Mexican state coopted the hyper-patriotism of unwitting Mexican nationals. The new government insisted that ethnic Mexicans belonged to and in Mexico. In response US-born Mexicans created multiple ideologies that expressed how they viewed their position in the region, nation, and world and how they understood their responsibilities to other human beings.

Homeland is organized both chronologically and thematically. Chapter 1 deals with the onset of the Mexican Revolution in 1910 to the end of the decade of repatriation in the United States in 1940. This chapter explores the ways that pre-revolutionary Mexican nationalism, modern Mexican nationalism, and a conservative form of expatriate Mexican cultural nationalism that developed in Texas influenced ethnic Mexican ideas of belonging in the United States. Mexican expatriates in the United States created an insular community—*México de Afuera* (Mexico outside of Mexico)—based on a limited and deeply conservative understanding of Mexicanness. Over the course of three decades, Mexican nationals effectively expelled US-born Mexicans from México de Afuera.

Chapter 2 details the rise of Mexican Americanism from the 1920s to the mid-1950s. US-born Mexicans in the 1920s believed themselves to be a people without a country, their sense of belonging unmoored. Mexico ignored them while their fellow Americans refused to recognize them as equals. And the increasingly modern, bureaucratized US state had difficulty "seeing" Mexican Americans. The "synoptic view" of the state could not see a significant difference between Mexican nationals and US-born Mexicans.[28] In documents ranging from the 1930 census to city directories, US-born Mexicans and Mexican nationals were classified similarly. The US state was seemingly blind to their presence as anything other than racialized or foreign workers. It was their duty, then, to "ask for a country within our actual country," as one LULAC member explained.[29] Mexican Americanism did not just acknowledge citizenship, but understood it as the legitimate means of belonging. In order to make themselves into citizens, Mexican Americans participated in the racialized language of citizenship, embraced American ideals of middle-class comportment, and engaged with popular ideas about progress, race, and evolution.

Chapter 3 explores how between 1910 and 1942 ethnic Mexican leftists created a consciousness that emphasized class and challenged citizenship. Through labor internationalism, the ethnic Mexican left offered not only opportunities for resisting capitalism but also a new understanding of the relationships among people worldwide. They redrew the boundaries of belonging and refused to be bound by the nation-state or their citizenship. The world they imagined was not separated into nations, but united in a shared vision of workers. These ideas helped ethnic Mexicans resist racism, exploitation, and discrimination by the state. These ideas and institutions declined in part as a product of the Red Scare and the Cold War. However, the shift in the focus of US liberalism away from structural critiques of capitalism and toward economic growth as the primary avenue of social progress also negatively affected the ethnic Mexican left. As the state began to provide many New Deal programs that borderless leftists were demanding, many US-born Mexicans acceded to citizenship.

Chapter 4 explores the shared intellectual space of American liberalism and global liberation in the postwar years leading up to the Chicana/o Movement, highlighting Mexican American liberalism in Texas. Many Mexican Americans who came of age in the mid-twentieth century were caught up in a collection of ideas, policies, and solutions that explained inequality and discrimination through social science models of modernization. For them, as for the larger domestic social science world, American history, American principles, American liberalism, and American capitalism provided a road map for social equality through economic growth at home and abroad. By the late 1960s, however, many of the promises of liberalism had failed to manifest, not just in communities of color in the United States, but also in many former colonies across the world. Younger US-born Mexicans stretched the logic and grammar of liberalism before finding it wanting and ultimately abandoning it. This chapter shows that the chasm between Mexican American and Chicana/o activists and intellectuals was not just generational but also ideological.

Exploring the intellectual history of the Chicana/o Movement in Texas, chapter 5 reveals cultural nationalism to be a diverse body of thought with multiple competing ideas that blurred the line between poetics and protest. Chicana/o art, literature, and poetry helped create new understandings of belonging. US-born Mexican youth used barrio cultural nationalism, Chicano cultural transnationalism, and Chicana feminist transnationalism to challenge citizenship, reject the nation-state in favor of alternate spatial conceptualizations, and reimagine the relationships between people of the world in different ways. The chapter uncovers the multifaceted intellectual history of the Chicano Movement and how young people involved in that movement understood the idea of belonging.

At the heart of my project is the belief that belonging is complex. While citizenship is the most widely acknowledged and recognized form of belonging, this has not always been so. Ethnic Mexicans in the Southwest developed bodies of thought that responded to the intrusion of citizenship. Some adopted while others resisted the concept of citizenship. Not only were ethnic Mexicans engaged in a world of work and manual labor, but they were also engaged in a vibrant and diverse intellectual world.

CHAPTER 1

"*Emigrated Mexico will redeem enslaved Mexico*"

MEXICAN NATIONALS, MÉXICO DE AFUERA, AND LONGING FOR A NATION IN AN AGE OF NATIONALISMS, 1910–1940

In 1920, journalist, exiled politician, and writer Nemesio García Naranjo wrote, "The president [of Mexico] has opened the doors of the nation and the exiles will not delay in returning to their land. There may be a few who stay abroad [in the United States] for an indefinite amount of time, but emigration as a collective entity is now at the point of disappearing."[1] García Naranjo's declaration of the imminent return of the Mexican community in the United States was indeed premature. Nonetheless, for the better part of the twentieth century, writers and journalists like García Naranjo were certain that once political and economic conditions changed, Mexicans living abroad would recognize their political, nationalistic, and cultural responsibilities to return to Mexico without hesitation.

García Naranjo's conviction that Mexicans had a duty and obligation to return to Mexico was a central idea that circulated within ethnic Mexican communities in the first three decades of the twentieth century. Mexican political and economic elites, rural campesinos, and poor urban workers who left Mexico began to see themselves as part of an important community that existed inside the United States but was vital to the spirit, nation, and eventual state of Mexico. They saw themselves as a México de Afuera, or a Mexico outside of Mexico. Their cartographical imagination was not rooted in physical geography or a desire to reconquer lost land. Instead, their México de Afuera was a

"Mexican Flood Refugees" in San Antonio, Texas, being assisted by the Red Cross, September 1921.
Library of Congress, Prints & Photographs Division, American National Red Cross Photograph Collection (LC-DIG-anrc-14340).

complex collection of ideas that explained the essential facets of Mexican culture and the extensive responsibilities of the diaspora.[2]

As political conservatives and radicals found themselves in cities on the US side of the border during and after the Mexican Revolution, various groups and individuals contested the definition of Mexico and what it meant to be Mexican in the United States. Revolutionaries like Francisco Madero launched their revolutionary efforts from Texas, and conservatives who supported Porfirio Díaz left Mexico for the United States after his fall in 1910. Subsequently, upper-class liberals fled the Revolution after Madero's murder and overthrow in 1913. These émigrés generally had significant wealth and stature and preferred to associate with people of their own class.[3] One of these exiles was Ignacio E. Lozano, who left Nuevo León for San Antonio in 1908. In 1913 he founded *La Prensa*, which would become the most important ethnic Mexican newspaper of the first half of the twentieth century and the mouthpiece of México de Afuera, with a national and international readership and correspondents in Paris, Mexico City, and Washington, DC.[4] Affluent exiles like Julio G. Arce (who wrote under the pseudonym Jorge Ulica), Nemesio García Naranjo, Juan Sánchez, and Daniel Venegas took to writing in *La Prensa* in order to convey the responsibilities of los Mexicanos de Afuera.[5]

The elite women of México de Afuera, such as Angela Madero, Sara Madero, Virginia Salinas Carranza, and Leonor Villegas de Magnon, also made their presence felt. While these women primarily socialized amongst themselves, they felt a responsibility to assist the larger community of poor ethnic Mexicans in dealing with social discrimination and economic exploitation.[6] These women often set aside their partisan politics and united through their identity as proper, respectable women and mothers.[7] For them and their husbands, maintaining a pristine Mexican womanhood—at odds with and in contradistinction to Anglo-American womanhood—was central in maintaining a community that was properly Mexican.

As the Revolution progressed, poor Mexican nationals continued to leave Mexico for the United States. Well more than a million Mexicans moved north, finding homes in the barrios of the Southwest. In just a decade, from 1910 to 1920, they outnumbered US-born Mexicans in many communities across Texas and the Southwest. During the 1920s Mexican nationals responded to exile, revolution, industrialization, and discrimination by rethinking the contours and parameters of their imagined community to exclude US-born Mexicans. While poorer Mexican nationals often disagreed politically with the elite Mexicans who had emigrated earlier, both groups agreed that US-born Mexicans were entirely too Americanized and unnaturally effete to be Mexican. Their US-born compatriots were no longer part of the solution, but part of the problem.

Whereas divisions of class and politics separated Mexican nationals in Mexico, the experience of living as foreigners and the ideas of México de Afuera united many of them in the United States. Political upheaval and exile forced Mexican nationals to consider the meaning of patria, patriotism, nation, and nationalism. In *el destierro*, they began to articulate a notion that the nation might be lost, but the national essence—the culture, ideas, and beliefs—could be maintained. In this way, Mexicans involuntarily living abroad were never homeless nor completely nationless, because the national spirit lived within them. Since the nation had been lost, the essence that remained needed to be guarded and maintained. Among the many traits they wanted to keep, the most widely accepted were the need to maintain the Spanish language, male power and performative masculinity, and Mexican femininity. American sexual promiscuity was singled out as a danger, because it led to either moral decline or interracial dating/marriage. Exogamy meant the certain end of the national essence and cultural traits needed to rebirth the nation. Perhaps the most important idea of México de Afuera was that Mexicans needed to return to Mexico eventually. The national essence could not survive uprooted and without native soil forever, nor could it be transplanted or grafted onto some other place.

The ideas, while shared, were not always unanimous. A complicated mix of pre-revolutionary regionalism, conservative Mexican cultural nationalism, and modern Mexican nationalism changed and challenged the perceptions of belonging among ethnic Mexicans in Texas and the United States. As these ideas collided and the importance of the nation-state grew in the borderlands, Mexican nationals came to believe that true Mexicans would not voluntarily stay in the United States. Those who did stay were viewed as culturally, morally, and politically compromised, and their identity as Mexicans was suspect. By 1930, Mexican nationals had pushed many US-born Mexicans outside of México de Afuera.

THE PATRIOTISM AND POLITICS OF HOMELAND

Mexican communities had existed in what became the Southwest before the United States acquired those territories in the Mexican-American War. Strong familial and cultural ties continued to connect communities on both sides of the US-Mexico border well after 1848. Railroads, telegraphs, and the growth of international markets continued to tie binational communities together. In the late nineteenth century, the administration of Porfirio Díaz (1876–1910) sought economic modernization and political stability for Mexico. Industrialization and integration into global markets were profitable for some, but since many industries were dominated by foreign investors, natural resources were extracted and the resulting capital was not reinvested in Mexico.[8] Displaced and underpaid, poor rural and urban workers sought higher wages in northern Mexican cities and in the United States.[9] While workers found slightly better wages in the United States, working conditions remained dangerous and discrimination was widespread.

In the 1890s and early 1900s, ethnic Mexicans worked together to provide themselves with economic protections and protections from discrimination. Ethnic Mexican workers across the United States began to form mutual aid societies, while middle-class border residents formed fraternal organizations.[10] Workers pooled funds to provide burial insurance, disability protections, and other work-related programs. They also created a sense of community, both to insulate themselves from discrimination and to fight it. A "Mexicanist" tradition formed in the late nineteenth century and the first years of the twentieth century. This tradition emphasized Mexican nationals' and US-born Mexicans' ethnic unity as *mexicanos*, regardless of their citizenship, leading to a strong sense of community, ethnic insularity, and nationalism.[11] A shared culture, language, and love of la patria united them. Their place of birth did not matter, only their belonging to an imagined patria.

The high point of this Mexicanist tradition was the 1911 Primer Congreso Mexicanista held in Laredo, Texas. At that meeting, ethnic Mexican reformers from both sides of the border came together to discuss the issues confronting the ethnic Mexican community in Texas and the Southwest, of which discrimination was a primary concern. These reformers focused on the cultural redemption of the working classes. Respectability would unburden workers from the yolk of racist discrimination, and the middle classes, the gente decente, would lead the way.[12] The Mexicanist tradition held until the demographic dislocations and ideological transformations of the Mexican Revolution eroded the foundation of the unifying cultural nationalism on which it was built.

The violence and disruptions of the Revolution caused unprecedented population shifts. Cities like San Antonio, El Paso, Tucson, Albuquerque, and Los Angeles would never be the same. The Mexican Revolution transformed these communities, where cross-border interactions had been common after 1848 and many families on both sides of the border were related.[13] The chaos of the Revolution forced at least a million Mexican nationals out of the country in the decade after its start. In 1910 the ethnic Mexican population in the United States was around 367,510, with 42.5 percent born in Mexico. By 1920, the number had nearly doubled, to 700,541, with more than 65 percent being foreign born. By 1930 the ethnic Mexican population had increased by 103.1 percent, to 1,422,533.[14]

Mexican nativity in the United States reached its nadir in 1920, when less than 35 percent of the ethnic Mexican population was US-born. Mexican nationals outnumbered US-born Mexicans by nearly two to one, compared to only a decade earlier, when their populations were relatively similar. As Mexican nationals unfamiliar with borderlands culture moved into ethnic Mexican neighborhoods across the Southwest, misunderstandings arose between these groups. In cities with long-established US-born Mexican populations, the demographic equilibrium was upset.

In San Antonio, Texas, ethnic Mexicans numbered 41,469 in 1920, accounting for 25.7 percent of the total population. Of these, 27,603 Mexicans, or 66.6 percent, were foreign born, a significant increase from 1910.[15] The influx of Mexican nationals into San Antonio came in three waves, which at times overlapped. The first wave of nearly 25,000 Mexican nationals who entered between 1900 and 1910 were upper-class political refugees. This wave included revolutionaries like Francisco I. Madero and Venustiano Carranza, as well as prominent lawyers and politicians like García Naranjo, Querido Moheno, René Capistrán Garza, Bernardo Reyes, and José E. Santos. The second wave in the late 1920s were likewise affluent refugees, but they were fleeing the violence of the Cristero Revolt, which was a rebellion of Catholic believers against what they thought were unfair impositions of taxes and expropriations of church holdings. Lastly, a wave of poor Mexican peasants sought solace from the violence of the Revolution and better wages in the United States.[16]

Similar waves of migration and changes in the national origin of the ethnic Mexican population occurred in El Paso as well. The total ethnic Mexican population in that city reached 39,571 in 1920, with 76.1 percent being Mexican nationals. For comparison, the same shift happened in Los Angeles. In 1920, the ethnic Mexican population there reached 29,757 people, of whom only 31.7 percent were US-born and the remainder were Mexican nationals.[17]

As US nativity dipped drastically, Mexican nationals acquired the ability to represent Mexicanness in the United States by their sheer majority and their influential positions in newspapers and community organizations. The major newspapers of the time, such as *La Prensa* in San Antonio and *La Opinión* in Los Angeles, were owned and operated by Mexican nationals.[18] *La Prensa*'s Lozano often hired affluent, politically and culturally conservative writers who were fellow exiles.[19] Their most common form of writing was the *crónica*, or chronicle, a short satirical column in which they laid out their México de Afuera ideology of what it meant to be Mexican and in exile. The demographic changes of "Greater Revolutionary Mexico" provided the context for the changing ideas about Mexicanness and belonging in the United States.[20] The overwhelming influx of influential Mexican nationals into US-born Mexican communities upset the Mexicanist tradition that had prevailed since the late nineteenth century and gave rise to quarrels over "homeland politics."[21] These disagreements transformed the Southwest from a "lost land" for all mexicanos into a México de Afuera to which US-born Mexicans did not belong.[22] In that transition, agonizing over Mexico as a *patria ausente*, or a place of origin that was experiencing an existential threat, reflected a larger clash between competing nineteenth-century regionalisms and notions of patriotism in the face of twentieth-century nationalisms and citizenship.[23]

In the 1910s, exiled Mexican nationals and US-born Mexicans both focused on themes of patria and patriotism, but the definitions of these terms were in flux.[24] Various nineteenth-century Mexican presidents, from Antonio López de Santa Anna to Porfirio Díaz, attempted to forge a unifying nationalism but failed. Northern Mexicans, subject to

Indian raids, geographic isolation, draconian economic policies, and enticing American markets, maintained an ambivalent political relationship with the central government and expected a certain degree of autonomy. In the absence of a unifying nationalism, various regionalisms arose across the country, each based on a patria chica, a small geographic area such as a town (like Torreón), a valley, a region, or a state (like Jalisco). Residents held strong loyalties to this immediate area, but most felt limited connections or obligations to a larger national community.[25] These regionalisms grew and found expression in early twentieth-century calls for patriotism.

Mexican nationals fleeing the Revolution arrived in the United States with uneven concepts of national identity.[26] "Patria" did not mean nation-state. "Nation," for them, was still a broad collection of people who shared passions, culture, language, or religion. It was a community of people, not a territorialized, bureaucratically managed, and organized nation-state. When these early-arriving Mexican nationals spoke of patria, they were referring not only to their physical place of birth, but also to an ideological world that gave roots to their existence and meaning to their lives.[27] Patria was a connection to their cultural past and genealogical ancestors. In their calls for patriotism, they drew upon their individual patrias chicas, their regional connections and regionalisms.

As the twentieth century progressed, the discussions surrounding the concepts of patria, patriots, and patriotism narrowed from an ideologically expansive understanding with many possible interpretations toward much more limited and defined understandings of the nation-state, citizenship, and nationalism.[28] Mexican nationals exiled in the United States reworked the definitions and meanings of patria and patriotism in the 1910s. Under this formulation, the patriotism of Mexican exiles was a form of cultural nationalism.[29]

In a 1916 article titled "El Silencio de los Desterrados" (The Silence of the Exiles), journalist Manuel Bonilla responded to a previous article that claimed Mexican nationals living outside Mexico were traitors. He wrote, "We are not traitors. Those who live in refuge under the shadow of a foreign flag . . . are not traitors. . . . The traitors [to Mexico] in all cases are others."[30] Although physically located outside of Mexico,

Bonilla emphasized that he and all other exiled Mexican nationals were proud and loyal patriots, lovers of their patria. The traitors were the crooked politicians in Mexico who were leading the country into chaos. As Bonilla expressed, the politics of the Mexican Revolution uprooted many Mexican nationals—politicians and peasants, conservatives and liberals—and their shared experience of living outside their nation forced many to rethink their position in the region, nation, and world. Because becoming an exile, *un desterrado*, carried with it a connotation of being unearthed and torn from one's native soil, Mexican political factions seemed less important in the United States.[31]

Many articles, books, and writings carried political messages, but the strongest among them expressed a desperate sense of dislocation. It was this dislocation that strongly influenced Mexican cultural nationalism in the United States in the first two decades of the twentieth century. Irrespective of their politics, many exiles began creating a discourse of an idealized, lamentably absent, patria. Being forced out of Mexico caused them to rethink their ideas about their homeland and patriotism.

In the 1916 poem "Sin Patria" (Without Homeland), the author cannot fathom how to exist in the United States:

> How can I sing in a foreign land?
> because my song
> Can be nothing more than a sad moan.[32]

The author of another poem expressed sadness at being exiled from Mexico:

> all of the lands elegantly dressed
> all of them full of light and love
> but you will find my soul sad
> because my heart is sad
> when I sigh without hope
> Oh sweet country! Far from you."[33]

These poets evoked hearts wounded by revolution and exile but kept alive by idyllic images of their homeland. Another poet described Mexico as a "magic Eden," a place upon which his soul depended.[34] Mexican nationals came to terms with their exile by reimagining

Mexico as a nearly utopian and almost lost homeland. In reality a nation that, for nearly forty years under President Porfirio Díaz, had implemented policies that displaced peasants and workers, Mexico in exiles' rendition was a pastoral place where people were free from worry.[35] These images transformed Mexico from an industrializing nation into an Arcadian homeland. The desterrados bemoaned their distance from an idealized Mexico on the verge of nonexistence. Their love poems to their patria expressed their existential despair.

These lyrical verses reflected the idea that the patria was something detached from a bureaucratically managed nation-state. Mexico was an idea, a culture, a story.[36] For this community, patria was not a "crustacean" nation-state, but an idea that laid the ideological foundations for community and belonging.[37] The article, "Pensando en la Patria," written under the telling pseudonym of Juan Sintierra (John without a Home), explained:

> If we exist and have any reality in life it is because we carry within our being all the essential attributes of the patria. Our blood she gave us: we know, because her science nurtured us, we speak words that the patria taught us; the air of the patria molded our character; her misfortunes hurt us, her triumphs filled us with pride . . . the patria belongs to us wholly, we are from her absolutely, while humanity has not found a new form to exist and relate to each other, patriotism will be a necessary and positive sentiment like filial love.[38]

Sintierra insisted his patria was like an element of nature, or one of the humors that affected human behavior. Patriotism was an essential human relationship that connected people to one another. Another San Antonio newspaper writer described patria as "fundamentally the thought, the institutions, the history, your home."[39] In a 1913 *La Prensa* article, the author explained that "our country is not only the land in which we were born: there is something more than the land that we should love, that is our country."[40]

Exiles' cultural nationalism rooted belonging within the patria, which was Mexico. For these patriots that meant although they currently resided in the United States, one day they would have to return to

Mexico. If they became Americans or Americanized, the patria would dissolve into nonexistence. An article written in San Antonio entitled "México emigrado y México esclavo" (Emigrated Mexico and Enslaved Mexico) illustrated the evolution of thought from uprooted Mexicans to true patriots and their movement toward defining themselves as true Mexicans. Underlying each of these intellectual developments was the eventual return to Mexico:

> And comparing our sadness with that of those who have stayed in Mexico, we have to confess that if we suffer from the nostalgia for our land, they suffer the inconsolable nostalgia for the national spirit. They are uprooted in their own land, and they wait in their villages and cities for the soul of the Patria to return to the Patria. They do well, those poor people, in waiting for Mexico to return to Mexico. We, for our part, should consider our return to the Patria as a duty and not a desire. We represent the national thought in its essence and the energies and incoherent aspirations of a nationality that waits our return like salvation . . . emigrated Mexico will redeem enslaved Mexico.[41]

The ideas that the exiles and their particular form of Mexicanness were the soul of the homeland, and that they were the true Mexicans who needed to return to Mexico, were becoming increasingly popular among Mexican nationals in the United States. Although their situation of being exiled from their country was unfortunate, their carefully crafted and sustained patriotism was positive. Their loyal patriotism and true Mexicanness would redeem Mexico, or as the title suggested, Mexican émigrés were going to emancipate enslaved Mexicans. The author concluded, "The exiles are going to reconstruct their country. If they do not, they deserve . . . the curse of history for not bequeathing to their sons the inheritance of an intact and autonomous country which they had received from their parents."[42]

In 1918 another writer argued that the true Mexicans had been forced out of Mexico by thieves and crooks, and the exiles would redeem Mexico through their return: "the 16th of September for the exiles will be a day of pain; for the inhabitants of the biggest cities of Mexico it will be a day of desecration." He encouraged his fellow exiles,

"This is not the time to sing, nor the time to give in to vain laments. We must prepare to return to our land; we will restore profaned altars; we will recover our country."[43]

Exiled Mexicans came to see themselves as embodying the essence or spirit of the nation. Even though they were distanced from the place of their birth, they carried within them the means of its rebirth. To ensure the national essence remained, they would need to maintain their Mexican character, culture, and spirit. It was vital to the survival of the patria and the nation that they maintain their Mexicanness in the United States. But for the uprooted, the national essence was on life support. While it could be preserved on foreign soil, it could only thrive in native soil. They would have to return to Mexico.

As more Mexican nationals fled the Mexican Revolution, their ability to define Mexicanness continued to grow. In the process of appropriating Mexicanness, they began to imagine a new community in the Southwest. From a "patria ausente," they began to forge a Mexico outside of Mexico—a México de Afuera. This was more than a simple name that a few bereaved journalists and exiled elites used. México de Afuera was an imagined community with an important attendant nationalism that defined Mexicanness through exclusion. By the late 1920s, US-born Mexicans would find themselves pushed outside of the borders of México de Afuera, an exclusion that would have an important impact on US-born Mexican thought in later decades.

DELIMITING MÉXICO DE AFUERA

Afuerense ideology was reinforced by the creation of an important trope, the pocha/pocho. These were US-born Mexicans or, in some cases, Mexican nationals, who had lost their Mexicanness—linguistically, culturally, materially, and sexually. Afuerense cultural nationalism helped explain an increasingly internationalized, industrialized world to a group of displaced people.[44] Ideals of Mexicanness and Mexico made order of the world, organized relationships and gender roles, and created a sense of belonging that protected this community from feeling lost. Pochas/pochos illustrated to the Mexican-origin community why it was very important that they maintain their Mexicanness. Elite and common Mexican nationals alike participated in this discourse. As working-class Mexican-born migrants fleeing the Revolution moved into ethnic Mexican barrios established during the nineteenth century, more and more of them failed to understand their new neighbors and strange cousins of the north.[45] For many, the US-born Mexicans were odd and characteristically un-Mexican.

The notion of *pochismo* undermined the ethnic Mexican unity that had defined the first decade of the twentieth century. Mexican nationals moving into ethnic Mexican neighborhoods in the 1910s and 1920s quickly discovered that US-born Mexicans were a strange and tragic people, very different from Afuerenses. Author and journalist Conrado Espinoza gave an unflattering portrayal of the US-born Mexican population in his 1926 novel *El Sol de Texas*, describing them as "families that, in terms of appearance, have lost their Mexican identity and are in terms of language (horrible Spanish and horrible English), in terms of their customs (grotesque and licentious), in terms of their desires (futile and fatuous ambition); a hybrid group which adapts itself neither to this country nor to our own."[46] Espinoza was not alone in his assessment, many other journalists felt similarly. The writer of an article entitled "In Edinburg There Are No Mexicans" criticized the US-born Mexican community, "We are an embarrassment! We deny that our parents are or were Mexican, and even though we are recognizable as Mexican, we will with cowardice deny it and with more verve if [we] can stutter a few words in English."[47]

Conflict between Mexican nationals and pochas/os abounded from the 1920s into the early 1930s. The tension was not limited to Texas. Anastacio Torres, a Mexican migrant to the United States who lived in Los Angeles, California, and was originally from León, Guanajuato, described the tense situation in the 1920s: "I don't have anything against the pochos, but the truth is that although they are Mexicans, for they are of our own blood because their parents were Mexicans, they pretend that they are Americans. They only want to talk in English and they speak Spanish very poorly. That is why I don't like them."[48]

Pochas/os' pretentiousness in speaking English caused a good deal of animosity between working-class Mexican nationals and US-born Mexicans. According to Mexicans, pocho culture equated sophistication and social stature with English language proficiency, whereas use of Spanish was often seen as a signifier of the lower class and peasants. The author of an article entitled "Una campaña en pro del idioma español" (A Campaign in Favor of the Spanish Language) resisted the idea that English was becoming "chic" among ethnic Mexicans. He saw this trend as a grave wrong and a danger for Mexicanness.[49] "Vamos aprendiendo ingles" (We Are Starting to Learn English), a poem published in San Antonio, likewise bemoaned the loss of Spanish. US-born Mexicans used false cognates like "marqueta" (market), "traque" (railroad track), "mechas" (matches), and "daimes" (dimes), so-called pochismos. More troublesome for the poet was that most Mexicans learned English in order to pursue Anglo women. The poet rhymed sardonically that Mexicans in the United States were turning into deformed monkeys:

> Now we should not be asses
> no, we should not be
> we are becoming monkeys
> we are learning English!
> Goodness! Isn't it embarrassing?
> when you see in the street
> a little nine-year-old kid
> who tells you as they're passing
> something in English?
> Tell me, isn't it embarrassing?
> to have to see.
> They were born here.
> We have been here for four years, and we only know in English
> "veri güel"
> and even that by chance.
> Isn't it embarrassing, woman?
> Casilda, my God, Casilda:
> We are learning English!
> Ultimately,
> why don't you learn English?
> Because you do not want to be running around with white girls,
> why else would you want to learn [it]?[50]

The notion that pochas/os deformed into barely recognizable Mexicans appeared in many working-class media. For example, the narrative of the pocha/o showed up in corridos (Mexican folk ballads) as well. In "Los mexicanos que hablan ingles," US-born Mexicans were condemned for speaking English. The corrido described Texas in the 1920s as an awful "revoltura" (mix-up, chaos). It was a world turned upside-down, a place where the natural order was upset, where none of the Mexicans spoke Spanish, but instead spoke only English. In this topsy-turvy world there existed no real Mexicans, only pathetic emulations of Americans. Interestingly, this criticism carried gendered connotations, as the singer interacted almost exclusively with pochas who dismissed his advances:

En Texas es terrible
por la revoltura que hay,
no hay quien diga "hasta mañana,"
nomás puro *goodbye.*
Y *jau-dididu mai fren,*
en ayl si yu tumora,
para decir "diez reales"
dicen *dola yene cuora.*
Yo enamore una tejana,
y de esas de sombrilla,
le dije: -Te vas conmigo?-
y me dijo:-*Luque jia*!-
Enamore otra catrina
de esas de garsole
le dije: -Te vas conmigo?-
y me dijo: -*Huachu sei*?-[51]

Mexican nationals across the nation bemoaned the "revoltura" that was occurring. Another corrido, "Los Pochis de California," also addressed the transformation of Mexicanness into pochismo. According to this ballad, the pochas of California only cared to speak English. But underlying this linguistic affiliation lay more troubling cultural changes and affectations:

The pochos of California
No longer know how to eat tortillas
Because now on their tables
They only use bread and butter.

I married a pocha
In order to learn English
And after three days of marriage
I had learned to say yes.[52]

Pochas and pochos were even more suspect because they did not operate under the prescriptive gender roles that defined Mexicanness.[53] Male power was perhaps one of the most important factors in Mexican male identity. In Mexico and the United States, many ethnic Mexicans believed that men rightly controlled women and the family, but in the United States, they perceived that the women controlled the men. This inversion of gender roles called into question not only the masculinity of pocho men—they were not macho and subsequently not "real men"—but also their identity as Mexican.

This theme of patriarchal crisis even made its way into the popular corrido "Desde México he venido" (From Mexico I Have Come):

From Mexico I have come,
just to come and see
that American law that says
the woman is boss."[54]

To this traveling musician it is so strange for women to "mandar" (order) men around that he travels all the way to the United States to describe something that is unknown in Mexico.

Mexican nationals made a point of exposing pochos for the effeminates they were. As one male migrant in Los Angeles explained, "I haven't wanted to get married because the truth is I don't like the system of the women here. They are very unrestrained. They are the ones who control their husband and I nor any other Mexican won't stand for that," adding, "I think that he who lets himself be bossed by a woman isn't a man."[55] Another migrant interviewed in Belvedere, California, described his belief in the norm of an authoritarian patriarch whom women must obey: "here the old women want to run things and a poor man has to wash the dishes while the wife goes to the 'show' and for that reason not even 'for fun would he get hitched to [a US-born Mexican woman].'"[56]

Many within the ethnic Mexican community believed that Mexican femininity was expressed through domesticity, docility, tenderness, passivity, thrift, and care of the family. In fact, many middle-class ethnic Mexican women in the borderlands used the cult of domesticity as a justification for activism and social involvement. Through "patriotic Mexican motherhood" ethnic Mexican women enlarged their roles into society without transgressing the domestic sphere.[57] Women were supposed to be the disseminators of culture, through their central role as mothers in the home. In addition, the true Mexican woman would be a tender partner to her husband, helping him deal with the anguish of el destierro. As one woman explained, the Mexican woman was "divinely chosen to feel sorry for others and to sympathize with them; she is called to make a nest of kindness in her soul: she was born to love, and to love purely, because a man's path is full of traps, he does not heed the voice of misfortune, and does not hear the echo of pain of our less fortunate brothers." She continued, "Whose obligation is it then [to care]? It is the woman's, and more precisely it falls to the Mexican woman in these bitter moments to help and share with the thousands of unfortunate orphans without bread, without a coat, without family, without a home. Those who have nothing but their tears and hurt!"[58]

Guadalupe S. de García Hidalgo, who was living out her exile in Cuba, described the authentic Mexican woman in another article published in El Paso. The home was the woman's proper place in her recounting of Mexican femininity: "the woman is called on to carry out an important role in society, especially in the home, where her virtue and beneficial influence should be felt. She should be a model of self-sacrifice; a heroine who does not stop, who sacrifices herself on the altar of duty, lifting up her husband in his daily battles, and comforting his soul with examples of her moral energy that the privations will not defeat him nor will the multiple pains that come with exile." García Hidalgo concluded of Mexican women in the United States, "We can do little [politically] for our country: but all Mexican women can contribute, we can sweeten the sorrow of our husbands, our sons, and our brothers."[59]

Nationalist Afuerenses saw none of these traits in US-born Mexican women. Middle-class ethnic Mexican reformers saw in pochas dangerous ideas that could undermine their attempts at reform. Pochas were pretentiously gringa in their attitudes and purchases. In the late 1920s Mexican anthropologist Manuel Gamio interviewed many Mexican men who criticized US-born Mexican women especially: a man "criticizes, as well, certain details of American material culture, above all the 'Americanized' Mexican women who dress like Americans and have the customs and habits of American women."[60]

Pochas, according to Mexicanos de Afuera, not only inverted Mexican patriarchy but were licentious. "Las pelonas" (The Flappers), a corrido from 1920s San Antonio, expressed the migrants' perception of pochas as loose women:

> Red bandannas
> I detest,
> And now the flappers
> Use them for their dress.
> The girls of San Antonio
> Are lazy at the metate.
> They want to walk out bobbed-haired,
> With straw hats on.
> The harvesting is finished,
> So is the cotton;
> The flappers stroll out now
> For a good time.[61]

"Las pelonas" reveals that the ideology of México de Afuera portrayed US-born Mexican women as sexually promiscuous (cutting their hair short like promiscuous Anglo women, wearing little more than red bandanas as skirts). Furthermore, they were "lazy at the metate," meaning that they failed to provide food for their family—as the metate was the tool used to make masa for tortillas. Moreover, the moment their paying job let out, US-born Mexican women quickly left to waste their time and money in the streets, instead of returning home to clean the house and behave responsibly like respectable Mexican women.

Even more troubling for Afuerense nationalists, pochas were helping to destroy Mexicanness by dating Anglo men. In the article "Those Who Have Gringo Boyfriends," Benjamín Padilla railed against this situation, which he viewed as tantamount to another invasion of Mexican sovereignty: "the Yankee danger, which has already invaded our mines, merchants, and industries, now threatens something that should be exclusively ours, something intimate that belongs to the country, the virgin hearts of our little chicks: the ineffable love of our Mexican girls."[62] Mexican women's bodies and sexuality belonged to Mexico and Mexican men. Pocha mothers and daughters, according to Padilla, favored American men in sad, ultimately disastrous, attempts to assimilate. The fears of Afuerenses linked cultural with sexual reproduction. Dating or marrying an Anglo threatened Mexican culture because the children would be only half Mexican and most likely would not maintain their Mexican culture or lineage. Even more vexing, young Mexican men had to follow Mexican traditions of dating—chaperoned meetings, supervised visits at home, and vigilant oversight by the father—Americans did not.[63] Pocha women disregarded Mexican morality for a chance at an Anglo man, often leading to a soiled reputation or pregnancy. Padilla concluded with a resounding lesson for pocha mothers and daughters: "Oh women who are partial to Gringos! In your sin you will carry your penitence!"[64]

The pocha, then, was cast in contradistinction to the "good Mexican woman." Miguel Chávez, a resident of Chino, California, described his wife as the ideal Mexican woman: "industrious and good, and not like those gringas who even want to strike their husbands."[65] In such ways, Mexican men equated machismo and traditional gender roles with Mexicanness. Pochos were emasculated men who let their women boss them around, even beat them and, consequently, were neither "real" Mexicans nor men. Pochas were pretentious, immoral, and poor excuses for Mexican women. Their attempts at emulating flappers/American women proved their indecency.

Afuerense novels helped popularize the narrative that pochas/os were sad, degraded non-Mexicans, or in some cases, anti-Mexicans.

The pocha/o trope showed up continually. Authors like Conrado Espinoza, Jorge Ainslie, and Daniel Venegas highlighted pochismo and the difficulty of maintaining Mexicanness outside of the México de Afuera community. Espinoza's *Sol de Texas* (San Antonio, 1926), tells the story of two Mexican families in the United States: the Quijanos and the Garcías. Both are poor families from agricultural areas in Mexico who come to Texas to earn money. The Garcías become pochas/os while the Quijanos remain true Mexicans. In an argument with his wife, Quico, the patriarch of the García family, tells his wife that the United States has been good to them and that "here we'll find everything we've been looking for." To which the wife, Cuca, replies, "Or lose all the things we've ever found."[66]

His wife's hesitancy turns out to be prescient. Quico and Cuca's son becomes an alcoholic who hates work and disrespects his parents. His is the tragedy of becoming a *sin vergüenza*, a person without shame. The daughter is seduced by an American who impregnates her and abandons her rather than marrying her. Her tragedy is the family's downfall; she becomes a *desvergonzada*, a woman forever shamed and indecent. As a man, Quico should have had the ability to recognize what was happening and the power to discipline his children. He fails. Instead, the only person in the family who recognized with certainty that the family would lose everything important to them was Cuca. Thereby, Espinoza offered a direct critique of pocho masculinity. Pocho men had less wisdom than simpleminded women.

At the end of the novel, the honorable Quijanos manage to maintain their Mexicanness and are preparing to return to Mexico. Quico meets them at the train station to recount to them the disasters that occurred to his family. When the Quijanos recommend the Garcías return home, Quico launches into a desperate monologue: "No they would never return. . . . Here they had lost their honor, here they would stay here in order to avoid dying of shame upon retuning to their homeland, and walking among their acquaintances who, [though] very ignorant, very simpleminded, understood it was better to confront their misery than to lose their honor. He would become another Texas Mexican." As the train leaves the station Quico yells to the Quijanos: "Go on! Tell our comrades to take it like men, to stay in their homeland. . . . Here, it's easier to find death and dishonor than money."[67] According to this allegorical account, the ethnic Mexicans who stay in Texas, or the United States, are those who have lost their Mexicanness—meaning honor, respect, family values, manhood, and language. In this understanding, there is no such thing as a Texas Mexican or a Mexican American. There are only Mexicans who have failed, who have become dishonored, who have lost their dignity, who cannot return to Mexico and must stay because they would die of embarrassment in Mexico.

Daniel Venegas's novel *The Adventures of Don Chipote, or when Parrots Breastfeed* (Los Angeles, 1928) presents the life of ethnic Mexicans in the United States in a similar way. On managing to return to Mexico after working *en el traque* (laying railroad track), Don Chipote reminisces about his experiences in the United States. He waxes nostalgic and considers returning to the United States, but then remembers his hardships there. The last sentence is Don Chipote's cynical conclusion in respect to Mexicans in the United States: "he came to the conclusion that the Mexicans would become rich in the United States WHEN PARROTS BREASTFEED."[68] Thereby Venegas expressed his opinion that Mexicans would never succeed in the United States. They could work. They could break their backs in the fields. They could debase themselves by adopting American customs, but they would never be accepted or belong. Their presence in the United States was not only unnatural, like a parrot breastfeeding, but it was also a sadistic exercise in futility.

Pochismo is the central topic of Jorge Ainslie's *Los Pochos* (Los Angeles, 1934). The plot mirrors other Afuerense novels. The Godinez family is displaced by the Revolution and comes to the United States to work. When they get carried away with American culture, the children become sin vergüenzas and *malcriados* (spoiled brats). The family is rescued by a nephew who was born in Mexico, is a true Mexican gentleman, and is sent to return the family to Mexico. The nephew is a cultural foil to the pocho son. Near the end of the novel Ainslie, too, offers his critique of the United States: "We live now in a country [the United States], where under the pretext of civilization, the men have confused liberty with licentiousness. . . . But how many families have suffered, like ourselves, the rigors of exile, and yet they still don't go, or even want to return. They will return when they become convinced that it is better to eat a tortilla with friends than a cut of ham with enemies."[69]

Novels like these fed the nationalism of México de Afuera. Afuerenses could be assured of their true Mexicanness through contrast with the failures and deformations of Americanized Mexicans. They could be assured of their manliness by contrast with the effete pochos. They could be sure of their patriotism because those in Mexico were destroying the country and those outside of Mexico were forgetting it. For Mexican nationals, Afuerense cultural nationalism made meaning of new relationships between people, of an industrializing world, of the internationalization of the borderlands, of modernity, and of encroaching neocolonialism by insulating them against these changes with a secure and limiting sense of belonging. The Mexican state would use this nationalism to its advantage as it rebuilt itself after the worst violence of the Revolution gave way.

FORJANDO PATRIA

The author of the 1916 article "México emigrado y México esclavo" called on Mexicans in the United States to return to Mexico in order to return the national soul to the nation.[70] In a 1931 speech republished in a Texas newspaper, the Mexican consul of Denver used similar language: "beloved compatriots, it is over there [in Mexico] in the ground where the ashes of our grandfathers rest, where our future waits for our children; it is over there, where the promised land awaits us with open arms like a mother who waits for her beloved children, where you will have all the guarantees of a true believer, where our sons will not have to suffer humiliations, and we will live content and happy."[71] Even though both men called for a return to Mexico, the call in 1916 had a different intent than its counterpart in 1931. As Afuerense intellectuals transformed their community from a patria ausente into México de Afuera they wrestled with the meanings of patria and patriotism. Eventually their cultural nationalism helped the Mexican government create a new sense of Mexican nationalism. Unwittingly, the project of México de Afuera—creating true patriots and Mexicans—intersected with the Mexican government's attempt at *forjando patria*—forging a new nation and new citizens—because both efforts relocated Mexican belonging.

The worst violence of the Revolution subsided just as a dramatic global change occurred in the power of the nation-state. The growth of the capitalist world system in the nineteenth century had instigated a remarkable movement towards the free mobility of people.[72] In Mexico, mobile peasants headed to relatively industrialized northern Mexican cities like Monterrey and to cities in the US Southwest that were experiencing huge growth.[73] By the early twentieth century, governments were becoming concerned about distinguishing those who belonged in their nation from outsiders. Nation-states quickly monopolized the authority to regulate movement by granting legitimacy to certain movements of people.[74] The bureaucratic authority to control the documents that allowed movement gave the nation-state much of its power to define identity—or the legitimate means of belonging—through citizenship and its attendant documents.

During the first decades of the twentieth century, Mexico had not been able to create a disciplined citizenry that viewed itself as a national community.[75] The chaos of the Revolution and ongoing changes in political leaders prevented a strong central government from asserting control. But as the violence subsided, Mexico did try to *forjar patria*, forge a new nation. In *Forjando patria* (1916) Mexican intellectual and anthropologist Manuel Gamio commented on the state of nationalism in Latin America: "Except for a very few Latin American countries, the rest do not have the inherent characteristics of a definite and integrated nationalism, nor is there a unique concept nor a unanimous sentiment of what the nation is. There exists only regional ties and local nationalisms."[76] Arguing Mexico's goal in the twentieth century should be to forge a new nation he declared, "Revolutionaries of Mexico seize the mallet and put on the smith's apron so that from the miraculous anvil a new nation made of iron and bronze may spring forth. . . . There is the iron. . . . There is the bronze. . . . Hammer away brothers!"[77] His vision was a new, vibrant Mexican nationalism built on Mexican culture, rather than borrowed European conceits. But because the Revolution had caused such a large exodus of Mexican nationals to the United States, forging a new Mexican nationalism would be difficult. The Mexican state would have to create citizens from refugees. The power of citizenship in defining belonging became increasingly important in this goal of reaching the expatriate population.[78] By 1918, Mexican consuls in the United States were starting to reach out to the ethnic Mexican population again, an effort that only grew in the following years. By 1921 consuls in such cities as San Antonio, Dallas, and Austin formed patriotic commissions (*comisiones honoríficas*) to promote Mexican nationalism and organize *fiestas patrias*.[79] Elite Mexican women exiles who had participated in constructing México de Afuera organized many of these events with the support of the Mexican government.[80]

The lectures and patriotic festivals that Mexican officials sponsored in the United States in the 1920s linked Mexicanness with Mexican citizenship.[81] Because citizenship took precedence over other forms of belonging, Mexicans had to return to Mexico not only because they were the soul of the nation, as they had thought in the 1910s, but because they were Mexican citizens. In other words, they could know for certain they were Mexicans because they were Mexican citizens. This had an important effect on ethnic Mexicans and their conceptions of belonging.

In interviews conducted by Manuel Gamio between 1926 and 1928, the importance of citizenship was readily apparent. Pedro Nazas, originally from Zapotlán, Jalisco, explained "I will never change my citizenship, for that would be to deny the mother who has brought one into the world. That is the way one's country is. We were born there and it is for us to love her always."[82] By virtue of being Mexican citizens, Mexican nationals rooted their belonging in Mexico. As the historian Gabriela F. Arredondo describes, Mexicanos de Afuera as far away as Chicago understood citizenship in a personal, emotional way that affected their understanding of identity. "Changing flags" (changing citizenship) entailed denying their identity as Mexicans.[83] One Mexican national in Chicago described a woman who became a naturalized US citizen as a "traitor to her country!" who "denie[d] her mother because they get more wages and aid here!"[84]

For many Mexican nationals in the United States, death was preferable to renunciation of Mexican citizenship. One author in Texas condemned US-born Mexicans to the darkest corner of hell for being

American citizens: "We have heard it said that my country is where I can have a better life, moreover that I am Mexico-Texan. To conclude, let me say that those who do not love their country do not love God or their home. They are beings from the remotest part of hell."[85] Another journalist in El Paso asked of US-born Mexicans "How can you be a good citizen if you cannot base yourself in the rich tradition of your country because you are not even familiar with your country?"[86] There were similar feelings among Mexican nationals in California, as Elías González expressed: "One thing is sure; I would rather die before changing my citizenship. I was born a Mexican and my parents always told me never to change from being a Mexican citizen because one never ought to deny one's country nor one's blood."[87]

Return, a central idea in México de Afuera, would continue to be an important feature of Mexican nationalism in the 1920s, with the support of the Mexican government. Juan Berzunzolo, a native of Ojos de Agua, Guanajuato, who had lived in both Texas and California, communicated his desire to return: "Although my children are already grown up I don't want their children to be pochos. That is why we are all going [back to Mexico] so that their children will be born over there and they will be brought up good Mexicans."[88]

After his initial call for a new Mexican nationalism and sense of belonging, and after interviewing ethnic Mexicans in the United States, Gamio concluded that US-born Mexicans were "semi-Mexican" and people "without a country."[89] Later he stated, "[A Mexican] does not find that country [the United States] a true homeland even when he [or she] becomes naturalized."[90] The Mexican consul in San Antonio, Enrique Santibáñez, agreed with Gamio's conclusion. He wrote, "Some [US-born Mexicans] are conceited, living with a sense of superiority that they are American citizens. I think that they show it more than they feel it."[91] In a 1930 editorial in the Spanish newspaper *La Prensa*, Santibáñez directed harsh criticism at US-born Mexicans: "allow me to say to the Mexicans, my co-nationals, that they should always remember that they live in a foreign nation, that they came by their own choice to the United States, and that they have no right to disturb the existing social conditions here; if luck is bad in one place, they should seek their fortune in another or return to their country."[92] In this editorial, then, a

Mexican official in his official capacity was negating Mexican belonging in the United States, regardless of birth or citizenship. In his view, the United States was a "foreign nation" not "their country." Thus, over the course of the 1920s, exiles' cultural nationalism grew increasingly intertwined with the new Mexican nationalism of the revolutionary state. Mexicans living abroad accepted the authority of the state to define belonging and culture.

By the late 1920s and the early 1930s, Mexican nationals had excluded bicultural Mexicans and US-born Mexicans from México de Afuera, or the strong sense of belonging formed through the shared experiences of destierro and a particular form of Afuerense nationalism with a prescriptive and conservative definition of Mexicanness and patriotism. Differentiation began to take place, not a division along the border—*este lado y el otro lado*—but a separation between authentic and imitated—mexicanos versus pochas/os. This divide caused a good deal of conflict. Concha Gutiérrez del Río, a Mexican migrant originally from Durango and living in El Paso, explained the relationship between pochas/os and "true" Mexicans: "It is impossible for the Mexicans and the Mexican-Americans to get along very well together here, because the latter are always speaking badly of Mexico."[93] Many times Mexican nationals lumped pochas/os and Anglo-Americans together in terms of culture and ignorance. One migrant remarked, "I don't even like to deal with those *bolillos* [white Americans] for the truth is that they don't like the Mexicans. Even the pochos don't like us."[94] Elías Garza, a resident of Dallas, Texas, originally from Cuernavaca, Morelos, explained the conflict between the Mexican nationals and pochas/os in simple terms: "the pochos don't like us."[95] Another Mexican migrant explained the tension between Mexican nationals and pochas/os in plain terms: "the Mexico-Texanos are *malos*."[96] Another migrant commented, "I haven't gotten mixed up with either the Americans or the pochos. I don't care what they think of us, for after all we don't like them either."[97]

An El Paso newspaper article criticized US-born Mexicans harshly: "Are they Americans? Are they Mexicans? Real Americans dislike them. Real Mexicans look upon them with fear. They are 'Texas Mexicans,' cursed for being half-Mexican and whose ambition is to be all American. They rebel against the seal of their race which nature put upon them."[98] C. R. Escudero described Afuerense disdain of US-born Mexicans in no uncertain terms. He called them "a race of white blackbirds or ugly ducklings without a race, name, or legacy." They were a group "that Anglos consider Mexican even though they are US citizens and Mexicans consider ugly apostates because they do not even know their own language."[99] Jorge Ainslie's character José, a pocho himself, expressed the feeling of Afuerense nationalists toward US-born Mexicans when he asked his pocha sister, "And what are you? A sad wannabe American who does not come close to being white."[100]

Whether they considered US-born Mexicans as cursed and deformed Mexicans, ugly white blackbirds, or sad wannabe Americans who were not even close to being white, Mexican nationals did not think highly of US-Mexicanness.

In the first three decades of the twentieth century, transnational ethnic Mexican communities in Texas tried to come to grips with the changes of ideas and identities that were occurring at local, regional, national, and global levels. Conversations reflected competing nineteenth-century regionalisms and notions of patriotism in the face of twentieth-century nationalisms and citizenship. US-born Mexicans and Mexican nationals grappled with the meaning of eroding regionalisms and growing nationalisms across the US Southwest and Mexican North. They participated in a growing global discourse of citizenship and contributed to a conversation that helped nationalize belonging in the early twentieth century.

The Mexicanist tradition of the late nineteenth and early twentieth centuries built unity among various groups as *mexicanos*, or *raza*. This tradition depended upon nineteenth-century liberal ideas that stressed a balance between the individual and collective, the local and the national. In the years surrounding the Mexican Revolution, the large influx of Mexican nationals into the United States undermined the Mexicanist tradition. At first, Mexican nationals used the concepts of patria and patriotism as a way to deal with exile and social, economic, and political transformations. Even though they were pushed out of their homes and homelands, they still represented the national essence in terms of thoughts, convictions, aspirations, and identity.

Because it was the people who embodied this essence, the patria could exist outside of a physical place. Nonetheless, their return to Mexico was paramount, and their pristine, unadulterated patriotism was just as important.

These ideas grew into another concept of Mexican political and cultural allegiance. Mexican nationals formed a nation outside of the nation-state—a México de Afuera. For Mexican nationals in the United States, exiles represented the future of Mexico. They needed to return home and, more importantly, remain Mexican. Mexicanos de Afuera created a new form of cultural nationalism that conceptualized Mexican belonging as located exclusively in Mexico. For them, there could not be a transnational, bicultural community that cooperated binationally. Instead, Mexicans needed to remain Mexican and return to Mexico. What it meant to be Mexican was defined conservatively: Mexicans spoke Spanish, ate Mexican foods, subscribed to specific gender roles, and retained their Mexican citizenship. To prove their Mexicanness was authentic, Mexican nationals turned US-Mexicanness into pochismo. This nationalism, formed outside of Mexico, helped to strengthen the modern Mexican nationalism that the Mexican state was forging in the 1920s and 1930s. A contradictory composite of prerevolutionary regionalisms and post-revolutionary nationalisms made meaning of Afuerense belonging in an increasingly internationalized borderland.

US-born Mexicans were pushed out of México de Afuera. Their cultural idiosyncrasies and syncretism made them suspect. To Mexican nationals, US-born Mexicans were not Mexican at all, but pochas and pochos. Afuerense thought left a lasting impression on US-born Mexicans' notions of belonging. Afuerense nationalism made them aware that they were not Mexican and neither were they American. They were not welcome either in the United States or in Mexico. Where then did US-born Mexicans belong? It would seem, as Gamio claimed, that they were a people without a home. But US-born Mexicans were already thinking about their position in the world. Two important strains of thought were already developing in the waning years of México de Afuera. One contradicted Afuerense nationalism by arguing that US-born Mexicans were citizens of the United States. As such, they needed to learn the language, laws, and culture of their new nation. In this view, however, ethnic Mexicans in the United States were still immigrants in a foreign nation. The other mindset imagined global belonging on the basis of working-class solidarity, not citizenship. As the borderlands grew increasingly internationalized, this philosophy refused to take sides; it chose people over borders.

CHAPTER 2

"Mendigos de nacionalidad y hombres sin patria"

MEXICAN AMERICANISM AND THE FORGING OF BELONGING NORTH OF THE BORDER, 1920–1954

In 1922, the Order of Sons of America (OSA), established in San Antonio, Texas, declared in its constitution, "It is our sincere opinion that the Order of Sons of America has emerged in the field of North American civilization as a path in the evolutionary processes in which we have come, unfolding our destiny as citizens of the United States of North America." Furthermore, "nearly a hundred years have passed since the time when our ancestors were the first laborers, half-civilized because of the environment in which they lived, to this day, today, in which we proclaim ourselves citizens: conscious of, in love with, and devoted to our native soil."[1] By 1934, University of California economist Paul S. Taylor reported that a growing number of US-born Mexicans had started calling themselves Mexican Americans: "The term Mexican-American is as yet little used. I have employed it here, however, to denote a small but significant group in south Texas, which, as its members have become conscious of their American citizenship, has assumed this name." He continued, "Mexican-American suggests national citizenship and a parallel with the amalgamating Irish-Americans, German-Americans, et al., rather than the State of birth of an alien group, as the term Texas-Mexican suggests. . . . But the term 'Mexican-American' conforms more closely to the ideals which the group holds for its people, and is used consciously by them."[2] Starting in Texas in the 1920s, developing strongly through the 1930s, and continuing through much of twentieth

"Mexican Girls, San Antonio, Tex.," April 1934.

Photograph by Alan Lomax. Library of Congress, Prints & Photographs Division, Lomax Collection (LC-DIG-ppmsc-00277)

century, the term "Mexican American" and its attendant ideas spread widely throughout the United States.

Mexican Americans deliberately emphasized citizenship for political and social reasons. Even though the Treaty of Guadalupe Hidalgo, signed in 1848, gave Mexicans then living in the United States citizenship, in the nineteenth century most of them had not given citizenship a great deal of thought. However, after Mexican nationals effectively expelled from México de Afuera ethnic Mexicans whom they perceived as too Americanized, and both the US and Mexican governments became intent on incorporating their borderlands more closely into the economic and political center, the importance of citizenship began to grow. By the 1920s it was the primary means of belonging, in both nations and globally.

Beginning in Texas, Mexican Americans attempted to fashion themselves into Americans and distinguish themselves from Mexican nationals. They stressed that they were US citizens and their belonging was rooted firmly in the United States. This was not a simple semantic change, but an important ideological shift, although it was not a neat metamorphosis or clean paradigmatic schism. Mexican Americanism did not just *acknowledge* citizenship, but rather *understood* it as the legitimate means of belonging. In order to conform to ideals of US citizenship, Mexican Americans participated in the racialized language of citizenship; embraced norms of American middle-class comportment; and engaged with popular ideas about progress, race, and evolution.

As the foundation of national belonging shifted between 1880 and 1920, citizenship came to define belonging, and the nation-state became the main arbiter of identity. Mexican Americanism prioritized citizenship over other modes of imagining. In a unique form of ethnic American nationalism, Mexican Americans viewed their failures at assimilation as flaws of their ethnic group, not flaws in the American system.[3] The importance of citizenship in Mexican Americanism displaced alternative understandings of the relationships between people of the world. Mexican Americanism focused its horizontal camaraderie among other citizens instead of on people who shared their own cultural, racial, and linguistic commonalities. Mexican Americanism encouraged US-born Mexicans to think about themselves as a small ethnic group in the United States.[4]

The ideology of Mexican Americanism did not *co-opt* the language of citizenship, but instead *cooperated* in its reproduction. As Mexican Americans understood citizenship, it had become the legitimate means of belonging in the United States and the world. Even though birthright citizenship conferred upon them the status of citizens, Anglo-Americans did not perceive them as social, political, or economic equals. Mexican Americans believed that emphasizing citizenship would be the best avenue to achieve this recognition.

US-born Mexicans, however, needed to be made into citizens—true and loyal—cast and formed by an American mold. As a uniquely positioned group, middle-class Mexican Americans needed to teach other US-born Mexicans how to behave like Americans in order to be recognized as citizens. Comportment, which had a long tradition in ethnic Mexican thought, as I illustrated in chapter 1, was certainly not new to ethnic Mexicans. But this group aligned themselves with a set of behaviors and beliefs that they perceived as modern and American.[5] Modernist ideas about evolution and the inevitable linearity of progress influenced Mexican Americanism. This belief in progress translated into hierarchical arrangements of races, ethnicities, and classes. Mexican Americans did not have a problem with dividing people into superior and inferior races, usually with African Americans at the bottom. However, they chafed at what they believed to be unfair generalizations about ethnic Mexicans in the United States that lumped them at the bottom with blacks. Social gradations and class differences needed to be acknowledged. Mexican Americans believed that they were the prime examples of their race and that it was their duty to uplift the masses. Their successes illustrated that they deserved to be held up as equal to Anglo-American citizens.

CHANGES IN THE LEGITIMATE MEANS OF BELONGING IN THE BORDERLANDS

Citizenship became increasingly important in the era of global migrations during the late nineteenth century. Prior to the explosion of the modern capitalist world system, national authorities had tried to keep subjects bound to the land, but that system became increasingly unsustainable. Whereas feudalism demanded immobile workers in order to reproduce itself, capitalism needed mobile workers in flux with the local, regional, national, and international labor markets. The newfound mobility of people during the nineteenth century threw off-balance the previous system's ability to regulate membership and the right to benefits of belonging.[6] The experience of being rooted in a specific place, voluntarily or involuntarily, for a long period allowed for "local" and "outsider" identities to be distinguished quite easily. The breakdown of this system forced national governments and local communities to redefine belonging.

With the rise of the nation-state in the nineteenth and twentieth centuries, "governments became increasingly oriented to making distinctions between their own citizens/subjects and others," explains historical sociologist John Torpey, and that distinction "could be made only on the basis of documents." The nation-state needed its people to have a new identity, one that was categorical and defined. So it issued them one and called them citizens.[7] Moreover, states needed to delimit their populations and assign them to a specific territory, in order to increase their control over individuals, land, taxation, conscription and, later in the twentieth century, the distribution of privilege and benefits. Legibility, or the ability of a state to "see" its human population, became crucial. The standardization of identity into citizenship was an important precursor to standardizing the administration of rights and obligations.[8] Citizenship increased in importance because it became a way of celebrating an imposed stationary existence as progress and belonging to the nation. This ideology suggests why a transnational community like ethnic Mexicans would be so vexing for the US state.

The two world wars had important consequences for how people imagined belonging. World War I put an end to the laissez-faire sentiment regarding the movement of peoples promoted by economic liberalism. The outbreak of war made the distinction between citizens who belonged and potentially dangerous interlopers important. The passport and other authoritative documents that officially conferred citizenship aided nation-states in figuring out whom the state could embrace and from whom it could demand services. Many governments reintroduced stiff passport regulations: France in 1912, Britain and Italy in 1914, Germany in 1916, and the United States in 1917. Mostly introduced as temporary wartime measures, they became permanent regulations in the interwar period. The demise of non-nation-state configurations (such as the Austro-Hungarian and Ottoman empires) and the massive flows of refugees after World War II further elevated the importance of citizenship and its attendant documents.[9] Without either a state or citizenship, refugees could make no claim to rights or access to national territory. By mid-century citizenship had become a form of access to rights, and consequently nation-states began to develop the bureaucratic systems necessary to issue, investigate, validate, and control identity.

Citizenship gained importance in the United States as well as internationally. In the United States, however, citizenship became racialized. This caused problems for many ethnic groups that called the United States home. Over a few decades, the state gained the power to regulate identity both within the nation and without. In 1856, Congress asserted its exclusive right to issue passports. By 1878, the US Supreme Court had ruled that sovereignty and territoriality were one, meaning the state had the right to control its borders.[10] A few years later, in 1882, Congress first used its power to restrict immigration by passing the Chinese Exclusion Act, which barred Chinese immigration for ten years and prohibited Chinese people already in the nation from becoming citizens. This was the first time in the nation's history that immigration was restricted on the basis of race and class. This act was historic because it marked a definite change in immigration policy for the nation. The United States became a "gate-keeping nation." Immigration law, through the "aliens" under its jurisdiction, defined the limits of who could become a citizen, both socially and spatially.[11] Immigration policy reflected the belief that the United States was a white nation, only white people were citizens, and only white people could belong.

"Aliens" were both territorial outsiders and racially different anti-citizens. Illegal aliens, as the new immigration laws outlined, were a caste "unambiguously situated outside the boundaries of formal membership and social legitimacy."[12] The connections between racialized migrants and ethnic groups in the United States created a caste of what Mae Ngai calls "alien citizens."[13] These were persons who were citizens by birth but were perceived as culturally foreign by the state and the white population. As Ngai argues immigration policy was one of the ways that race was made in the United States, and exclusion helped specify the meaning of American. In 1924, Congress passed the Johnson-Reed Act, a comprehensive immigration act that established numerical limits on immigration and created a global racial hierarchy that favored certain nationalities over others. More importantly, the act helped create the racial boundaries for citizenship in the twentieth century. The quota system that emerged after the passing of the act considered all Europeans, regardless of nationality, as white. Because officials assigned all Europeans whiteness, they became assimilable and ready citizens.[14] While these early immigration rules did not restrict ethnic Mexicans immediately, the white supremacy and racial thought that reinforced them did. Ethnic Mexicans across the nation were suspect citizens at best, to be kept at arm's length by the nation.[15]

By the 1920s the authority of the nation-state—predicated on complex bureaucratic structures and an elite core of civil servants trained to manipulate them—had replaced previous, spatially conceived notions of homeland and belonging that had shaped relationships between individuals and communities.[16] The nation-state now organized these relationships and the extent of state responsibility to human beings. In other words, citizenship, not a common humanity, became the limitation for moral, ethical, and political responsibilities. The state assigned identity to its subjects through documents. These documents had the international legal standing to make claims of belonging valid and recognized or unrecognizable and alien. Citizenship, in the form of documents that legally identified people, became the dominant mode of imagining across the globe and, importantly, to US-born Mexicans. Unfortunately, the state did not "see" their citizenship. For example, the 1930 census counted the community as "Mexicans." From the "synoptic view" of the state, there was no significant difference between Mexican nationals and US-born Mexicans.[17] Their status as citizens was not meaningful. This was troubling for the US-born Mexican community.

So entrenched was the notion of citizenship in the United States by 1958 that Supreme Court Chief Justice Earl Warren wrote in an opinion, "Citizenship is man's basic right for it is nothing less than the right to have rights. Remove this priceless possession and there remains a stateless person, disgraced and degraded in the eyes of his countrymen. He has no lawful claim to protection from any nation, and no nation may assert rights on his behalf."[18]

US-born Mexican belonging was unmoored at the beginning of the twentieth century. Mexican nationals had effectively cast them out of México de Afuera. The Mexican state disregarded their presence in the United States. Their fellow Anglo citizens refused to recognize them as equal citizens, socially or politically. And it seemed that the US state was blind to their presence as anything other than racialized or foreign workers. The development of Mexican Americanism must be understood in this context.

OUTSIDE OF MÉXICO DE AFUERA AND INSIDE THE UNITED STATES

In 1922 the OSA became the first major ethnic Mexican civic organization to make membership dependent on citizenship, although it was not the last. In the OSA book of rituals, under the section "Obligation," newly inducted members had to promise to "cultivate and highly develop our sense of Nationalism, American Citizenship and Love of Country."[19] In 1927, OSA members formed a new association called the Order of Knights of America (OKA).[20] They based their claim of belonging on citizenship. Describing themselves as having "healthy judgement," they communicated the goals of the group: "this group consists exclusively of individuals of Mexican origin, labors for the education of its members in respect to their rights and obligations as citizens of this country."[21] Another group that emerged in 1927 in South Texas was called the Latin American Citizens League. The organization's first objective was to "define with clarity and absolute and unequivocal precision our indisputable loyalty to the ideals, principles, and citizenship of the US." Under the league's code, members' first obligation was, "Respect your citizenship, preserve it; honor your country."[22] In

1929, the OSA, OKA, and Latin American Citizens League combined to form the League of United Latin American Citizens (LULAC), perhaps the most famous Mexican American civil rights organization. Its primary aim was to "develop within the members of our race the best, purest, and most perfect type of a true and loyal citizen of the United States of America."[23] In sum, by the end of the 1920s Mexican Americans did not just insist on their status as US citizens, but understood citizenship as the legitimate avenue through which to claim belonging.

The emphasis on citizenship was a significant rupture from the precedent of the late nineteenth and early twentieth centuries.[24] Just a decade earlier, *mutualistas* operated under different ideas and pursued different goals. The Orden Caballeros de Honor y los Talleres (Order of Knights of Honor), with twenty-four chapters across Texas in 1911, and the San Antonio chapter of the Alianza Hispano Americana (founded in Arizona in the 1880s), were two major ethnic Mexican organizations open to ethnic Mexicans regardless of citizenship. Moreover, their goals focused on mutual aid, such as workers' and burial insurance; brotherhood; and social life.[25] As I showed in chapter 1, the contentious battle over the definition of Mexicanness in the United States unmade the Mexicanist *mutualistas*. Mexican Americanism was a response to US-born Mexicans being denied Mexicanness and expelled from México de Afuera, along with the global changes in the legitimate means of belonging.

The debates surrounding belonging in Mexican American circles during the 1920s illustrate just how deeply their exclusion from México de Afuera resonated. For many Mexican American organizers and members, their community was indeed on the verge of becoming a people without a country. It was their responsibility to make sure Mexican Americans were recognized as citizens of one. As the 1922 OSA constitution stated, "until today, and never in the past, [have Mexican Americans] had a single well-defined idea of what they should try in their present position and their duties, rights, and prerogatives as citizens of the United States."[26] The organization's members believed they needed to consider themselves Americans and make themselves conscious of the political, moral, and social obligations that citizenship entailed. They needed to change their individual and collective ideas in order to place themselves on the same "social, moral, mental, economic, political, and industrial field" on which "normal Americans" lived.[27]

According to the OSA constitution, Mexican Americans could not "claim the blessings and happiness of our country" until they demonstrated Mexican Americans' loyalty to the nation. Consequently, they chose as their motto "por nuestra patria."[28] Well into the 1920s Mexican nationals were struggling with the shifting meaning of patria and nation. It is no surprise that US-born Mexicans were also thinking about the ramifications and transformations of nationhood. Mexican nationals dealing with the contradictions of exile explained patria as a place of birth or an ineffable national essence that they alone carried. The OSA's use of the term "patria," within the context of the constitution and the group's ideas, meant specifically the US nation-state. Their country, the place where they belonged, was the United States. The ideology of Mexican Americanism settled the issue of US-born Mexican belonging by rooting it in the United States.

In a group mailing in 1926, OSA president Andrés de Luna declared, "Once and for all we want to stop being beggars of a nationality, men without a country, an inconsistent and disoriented racial element, or pilgrims who across various generations live in a state of incomplete uncertainty when dealing with their interests regarding nation and citizenship."[29] Luna's message encapsulated most of the ideas regarding the ethnic Mexican community at the time. The Afuerense idea that US-born Mexicans were people without a country or place where they belonged was front and center. He accepted the Afuerense conclusion but not their solution. The answer was not for US-born Mexicans to become more "Mexican," return to Mexico, or become Mexican citizens. The answer was for US-born Mexicans to show their independence and strength, and claim belonging within the United States. The OSA declared a new epoch of US-born Mexican belonging and the end of an era of being beggars, pilgrims, or foreigners in their own country. OSA ideas promised them a new home and a new sense of certainty in their belonging.

In 1929, at the conference in Corpus Christi, Texas, where the OSA, the OKA, and the Latin American Citizens League consolidated into LULAC, participants produced some of the most definitive statements on Mexican Americanism and belonging. Representative José G. González said in his speech, "I see that we form a conglomerate without country, without prerogatives, and what is ever [*sic*] more sad, with very few hopes of obtaining a betterment of this deplorable condition of parias [*sic*]." But González concluded that "perhaps this union [LULAC] will serve to give a country to our children, who otherwise each time they thought of us would say: They lived parias, and they left us this sad inheritance."[30]

Other LULAC members echoed the sentiment that US-born Mexican belonging was unmoored. In April 1929, one member wrote in *El Paladín* that "our children [are] the vestiges of a great disinherited family and tomorrow, if our apathy permits, they will be begging for a country and even for homes."[31] Another member commented on the sad fate of being a person without a country: "the only recourse for him is to bow his head and go out of that place and sob out his shame and sadness on finding himself turned into a new Wandering Jew, condemned to travel, a stranger among strangers, and a stranger even in his own land."[32] The answer that Mexican Americanism provided was "to seek for ourselves a definite nationality and a country of our own which we are to serve."[33]

Taking a swipe at Afuerense ideas, one LULAC member complained, "If other races acted like us, this nation would be a conglomeration of countries outside of their countries: Germany outside Germany, England outside England, Switzerland outside Switzerland, etc., etc., [succeeding] no more or less than we are in forming an actual México de Afuera."[34] Instead of attempting to form a nation outside a nation, the solution was to abandon those ideas entirely. "So long as we do not elevate ourselves to the level of citizens, we will be nothing more than a conquered people," explained another member.[35] US-born Mexican belonging would not be found in some transnational diaspora. Their homes, their lives, their futures were American.

Mexican Americans needed to become Americans inside and out. No longer could they be anything "de Afuera." In a radio address at the end of the 1930s, LULAC addressed the issue of belonging yet again: "In this small piece of land in the border states of the United States the tricolor flag, the glorious country of our ancestors, does not extend to cover us." Consequently, it was necessary to "ask for a country within one's own country."[36] For this reason, another member explained, "We fought the battle to make the league purely an American institution and to exclude all foreigners."[37] In 1929, in a dramatic break from precedent among ethnic Mexican organizations, LULAC excluded Mexican nationals from membership.

Mexican Americans hoped that if they rooted their belonging in the United States and focused on citizenship, they would be fully accepted into the nation. Once the shared bonds of citizenship were made clear, Anglo-Americans would accept them. "We will demonstrate that we actually have a country" wrote one Mexican American, "and we love her and we want to strengthen her, and in that way we can erase the strong barriers that separate us from our co-nationals, the Anglo-Americans."[38] Citizenship was made concrete by the state, and Mexican Americanism, as a set of ideas and an identity, rested its legitimacy on the increasingly powerful reach of the state apparatus. If they were citizens, they could not be expelled from their communities, deported, or discriminated against. But by basing their belonging on a racially prescriptive and conservative citizenship, Mexican Americans did not enlarge the definition of US citizenship. Instead, they placed their claims of belonging on a concept that was under state control. "Citizenship" was also a term that was becoming increasingly exclusive because of the racial limitations associated with the social imaginary that made up citizenship.

Only by appealing to the state for identity and access could ethnic Mexicans claim a sense of place in the United States. As one historian described it, Mexican Americanism was a "politics of supplication."[39] It was a set of beliefs that reified the state and reinforced US-born Mexicans' dependence on modernist, state-centered notions of belonging.[40] The historian John Chávez argues that US-born Mexicans' view of the Southwest marked a definite ideological break in the way they perceived their location socially and spatially. Mexican Americanism saw the region as part of the "'American Southwest,' an integral part of a country whose language and customs were Anglo, a region that was only theirs insofar as they were true U.S. citizens."[41]

BEHAVING AND BECOMING MIDDLE CLASS: CLASS, COMPORTMENT, AND MODERNITY

Having staked their claims to citizenship, Mexican Americans had to create ways of making them stick. They did not challenge the race- and class-tinged standard that underwrote citizenship because they based their belonging on those circumscribed notions of citizenship. Mexican Americanism was ideologically sympathetic to much of the modernist thinking that informed racial and class exclusion in the twentieth century. Only after becoming modern could US-born Mexicans progress and become Mexican Americans. Once Mexican Americans behaved like Americans, they could become Americans. Mexican Americans spent the better part of the twentieth century trying to do this.

Mexican Americanism was a set of ideas of middling and middle classes that desired to shift the community's national consciousness northward.[42] Mexican Americanism derived its elitism from the composition of Mexican American civic organizations. By the early 1930s, the demographic trends of Mexican Americanism were already evident. Oliver Douglas Weeks surveyed the various LULAC councils regarding their social contours. All fourteen members of the Encino, Texas, council owned property, and seven were large landowners. The Falfurrias council was even larger, with sixty-five members. Of these members, 75 percent were property owners, 25 percent were businessmen, and 20 percent were merchants. The San Antonio council was the most affluent of those surveyed by Weeks. In San Antonio, 95 percent of the sixty members owned property. There were three lawyers, a journalist, and multiple businessmen. The prevailing types of businesses were furniture stores, car repair garages, drugstores, grocery stores, and funeral parlors.[43]

The middle class continued to be important in Mexican Americanism throughout the decade. The *First Year Book of the Latin American Population of Texas* (1939) served as a directory that highlighted key members and ideas with which they wanted Mexican Americanism to be associated. The short biographical section of the publication featured fifty important Mexican Americans, including LULAC luminaries J. T. Canales, Alonso S. Perales, Carlos Castañeda, Gus García, and

Manuel C. González, along with eighteen storekeepers, seven lawyers, two journalists, two pharmacists, two doctors, two managers, two engineers, a public accountant, and a bookkeeper, among others. The yearbook described these businesspeople as quintessentially modern and featured thirty-six Mexican American–run businesses, including nineteen in the food industry (from grocery stores to restaurants), three publishing houses, and two gas stations.[44] Demonstrating business acumen was incredibly important because, as a feature story on a businesswomen explained, running a business "constitutes a demonstration that intelligence and skill are not the exclusive patrimony of certain ethnic groups."[45]

Capitalism, as portrayed in the yearbook, was not necessarily a malevolent force. Instead, the problem was that the free enterprise system was not free and open to Mexican Americans. Yet only through capitalist competition could Mexican Americans best their Anglo-American counterparts and raise up their community.[46] According to Mexican Americanism, economic advancement correlated with social and moral development. Those who succeeded in business were those with the best character. Mexican Americans found it difficult to point to the structural failings of the American capitalist system, which depended on an exploitative labor system buttressed by a system of white supremacy. American capitalism was critiqued, not condemned. It could be reformed without the need for revolution. The US-born Mexican community played a role in their own exclusion too.

Middling and middle-class advocates often placed the onus of racial discrimination on the shoulders of lower-class US-born Mexicans.[47] These middle-class leaders often held the same pejorative views as Anglos in regard to the poor members of their community. It was their duty as superior examples of their race to uplift the less fortunate. The idea of uplift appeared early on in Mexican Americanism. The OSA constitution stated that the organization was created to "better the moral, social, and intellectual condition" of the US-born Mexican community, and that "The Order of Sons of America has been created with the fixed purpose of changing the course of events, fighting the negligence and slowness of the citizens of Mexican or Spanish racial origin of this country" in adopting American values and citizenship.[48]

In 1927, the OKA had a similar project of uplift. In the second issue of the *OKA News* the group expressed its goal as "before all else the moral and material elevation of our group who only need reasonable preparation to be able to occupy their positions in the course of modern civilization." In the same issue, the organization emphasized that racial uplift was necessary for a "social and moral refinement" that would lead to community "progress."[49] The following month, in the third issue of the *OKA News* member Mauro Machado declared that the goal of the OKA was "to elevate our brothers to bring about greater progress and general advancement."[50]

The first president of LULAC, Ben Garza, and prominent founding member Alonso S. Perales expressed similar views. In 1928 Perales, stationed at the diplomatic post in Managua, wrote to Garza in San Antonio. He described Nicaraguans disparagingly but stated sadly that US-born Mexicans were not much more advanced:

> I belong to the Mexican-American component element of our nation, and as a racial entity we Mexican-Americans have accomplished nothing that we can point to with pride. Were I to criticize Nicaraguans for their filthy and backward towns and cities, they would in all probability retort: 'How about your Mexican villages (otherwise known as Mejiquitos) in San Antonio, Houston, Dallas, and other Texas cities and Towns? . . . Now, then, the question is: What are we Mexican-Americans going to do about the matter? Are we going to continue in our backward state of the past, or [are] we going to get out of the rut, forge ahead and keep abreast of the harddriving [*sic*] Anglo-Saxon? There is the big problem before us, my friend, and one that we Mexican-Americans must solve if we have any sense of pride at all. Hence the need for a strong, powerful organization composed of and led by intelligent, energetic, progressive, honest and unselfish Mexican-Americans.[51]

By the time the OSA, the OKA, and the Latin American Citizens League merged into LULAC, the emphasis on uplift and middle-class social and moral preeminence was a central tenet of Mexican Americanism. At the 1929 Corpus Christi conference where LULAC was formed, J. T. Canales exclaimed in his speech that LULAC needed to "educate our people, hygienize [*sic*] it so that necessity will not make it necessary that they live in houses with roofs of thatch, have ideas and practices admitted of not spending their money in games."[52] J. Luz Saenz declared that LULAC "fight[s] to elevate the good man of our race."[53] Also in 1929, Perales wrote that LULAC "proposes to promote the intellectual, economic, political, and social evolution of the American citizens of Latin origin in order that they be cultured elements, conscious, useful, and insuperable."[54]

In 1931, LULAC president M. C. González wrote that "the League is trying to play the role, metaphorically, of a minister of the gospel trying to save souls by preaching and doing church work, and showing the way to the path of righteousness." By comparing their work to that of a preacher and their role to that of the church, González revealed the attitude that his fellow ethnics were poor uneducated souls. It was the poor who needed saving, but not from capitalist expansion, Anglo racism, or other structural problems. Instead, they needed saving from themselves. González went on to explain that if "a member is well educated and intelligent, the work of the League as to him is rather slight, whereas, in the instance of the common laborer, the work to be done is very great, as in that instance we must seek to better his social position [and] his economic situation." The goal of LULAC was to teach the common person "to comport himself as a gentleman . . . [to] learn to economize, in order that he may better his economic situation . . . [and] improve intellectually."[55]

Comportment became one of many important factors in race uplift. US-born Mexicans needed to be taught not only how to be true and loyal citizens, but also how to be civil. For example, according to the OSA ritual, OSA members would present an initiate by vowing to the president that the new member was "worthy." In return, the inductee had to "promise to so conduct yourself at all times as not to bring reproach upon this Order . . . promise to elevate your caracter [*sic*] by careful study of the noble and lofty ideals of this Organization. . . . And lastly, will you lend us your co-operation to the end that we may cultivate and highly develop our sense of Nationalism, American Citizenship and Love of Country?"[56] Behaving in a socially acceptable manner was part of being a citizen. The sixth principle of the OSA was to "recognize as an obligation of the contract with our nation, with ourselves, and with our north-American civilization, to evolve and establish in our home the principle that we should adopt in its totality the living conditions of the American people."[57] At the Corpus Christi convention that inaugurated LULAC, J. T. Canales opened his speech with, "There were taken the first steps of our moral and economic emancipation, as is attested by the fact that many members of the Order bettered themselves civically but materially as well."[58] For Canales and other subscribers to Mexican Americanism, there was a deep connection among comportment, class, citizenship, and social worth. If Mexican Americans could only get US-born Mexicans to *behave* like members of the middle class, then the avenues that allowed them to *become* middle-class would open.

While organizations like the OSA, OKA, and LULAC denied membership to women, they still recruited women and mothers for the task of teaching proper comportment to children. LULAC began women's auxiliaries in 1932. Texas women organized some of the strongest chapters in the nation. From 1933, when LULAC established the official position of "ladies organizer general," to 1940, Mexican American women from Texas held that position.[59] Some women, including Esther N. Machuca and Alice Dickerson Montemayor, pressured LULAC to recognize women. Machuca founded the women's chapter of LULAC in 1934 and Montemayor founded the Laredo chapter in 1936.[60] Although some ladies auxiliary chapters engaged in politics, in general most focused on charity activities.[61] They were hesitant to step too far out of the bounds of the domestic sphere. Both Mexican American civic groups and the US government promoted the idea that the careful management of the home was an important service to the nation.[62] For the most part, women and men supported the social norm that the role of women was to be good mothers who kept their homes clean, their children happy, and their husbands satisfied.[63] Thereby, sons and husbands were enabled to serve the nation militarily, materially, or civically. Yet, although not explicitly feminist organizations, Ladies LULAC provided an avenue for women to gain experience in organizing and politics and certainly promoted the idea of uplift.[64]

Mexican Americans were not alone in their emphasis on uplift and comportment. Other racial and ethnic groups in other parts of the nation adhered to this belief system. Class differentiation was a way to escape the weight of racism while not overtly undermining the race-based science of the time. In the US South, Midwest, and Northeast, black Americans and Jewish Americans underwent similar ideological transitions. They often promoted class distinctions in an effort to gain acceptance from the majority. Upper-class ethnics often resisted segregation for a section of their community, mainly themselves, but did not challenge the underlying ideologies of racism. If they failed to distinguish themselves, the better classes, from their lower-class compatriots, the larger white mainstream would continue to see their communities as a uniformly lower-class mass.[65] As historian Willard B. Gatewood has explained, "like other Americans, [Black Americans] assumed that proper conduct, manners, and other evidence of good breeding were indicative of one's character. But unlike whites, they believed that the genteel performance would in fact promote racial progress." Black elites, whom Gatewood calls "aristocrats of color," were persuaded that crude and improper behavior in public places was one of the major reasons why whites saw them as inherently inferior. For this reason, they encouraged their community to comport itself according to mainstream norms.[66] Respectability politics and behaviors often led minority leaders and their organizations to adopt an assimilationist agenda.

Similarly, organizations like the Jewish Educational Alliance and the African-American Urban League in New York mirrored the same goals and language as the Order of Sons of America, the Knights of America, the Mexican American Movement in Los Angeles, and LULAC. These groups, in trying to uplift the masses of their ethnic community, imposed ideas that reinforced cultural (but not racial) inferiority. In trying to make their community acceptable to Anglo-American culture, these intellectuals and reformers emphasized their commitment to capitalism and the existing political economy. Their "approach not only assumed the need for elite stewardship over each group; it led . . . organizations to try to separate the deserving from the undeserving poor. Groups like these would call for imparting proper values to some and containing those who threatened each group's progress."[67]

Uplift promoted a class hierarchy that gave Mexican Americanism a markedly assimilationist bent. At the top were the aspirational middling and professional middle-class Mexican Americans, and at the bottom were the poor helpless masses. Those at the top had adopted manners and mannerisms of the mainstream; they were mature and modern. At the bottom were "wayward workers" who willingly wasted their time, money, and efforts. Through this lens middle-class Mexican Americans saw such differentiation as a natural outgrowth of improper comportment rather than unfair capitalist forces. Indeed, capitalism had enabled many Mexican Americans to achieve their elevated social position as proprietors of a grocery store, garage, or law firm. They believed that they were responsible for teaching their poorer community how to behave middle class, even if they could not become middle class. The ideas of uplift held that the mass of ethnic Mexicans needed to be taught how to comport themselves correctly.

RACE, EVOLUTION, AND MEXICAN AMERICAN PROGRESS

Adherents of Mexican Americanism, or "Latin Americanism" as some called it, believed that the ethnic Mexican population in the United States could be made progressively more modern.[68] For many early twentieth-century reformers and intellectuals, evolution and progress were synonymous and interchangeable.[69] Not all views of social evolution countenanced the notion that racial groups like ethnic Mexicans and African Americans could progress to the level of white civilization. Indeed, evolutionary thought helped reinforce white supremacy. Civilization was a racialized concept that could mark stages in human progress and could also serve as a hierarchy that naturalized white supremacy through the observation that only whites had achieved the status of civilized people.[70]

Nonetheless, Mexican Americans used a more progressive version of evolution and racial progress to encourage change. But their at times quasi-Lamarckian outlook was not always so benign since it allowed for the creation of hierarchies of civilization. Mexican Americans were certain that as long as they hitched themselves to evolution it would carry them forward. One journalist echoed this sentiment as early as 1919, when he wrote "the races do not move backwards, on the contrary they are advancing incessantly."[71] Mexican Americanism held firmly to the belief in the positive possibilities of modernity and evolution. This produced an interesting ethnic version of social Darwinism that combined the biological with the social.

An example appears in the OSA constitution, which stated the organization's social advancement goals in evolutionary terms: "we want ample and complete opportunity . . . for our social, economic, and political evolution. We will adapt ourselves to the phenomenon of evolution, step by step progressing, step by step learning to be prosperous . . . step by step emerging from the uncertainty of the past." The twelfth principle of the OSA was that "through the means of moral and mental cultivation of our racial element, we can put ourselves on the path of progress to the substantially beneficial enlargement of society and the civilization of our beloved [United States]." "We are resolved to continue advancing in our march of progress" they explained, "with our eyes fixed on the horizon of our future. . . . We trust even more in the eloquent teaching of evolution."[72]

This racial evolutionism carried over into LULAC. In 1931, one journalist called LULAC a revolution, but not a violent one like the Mexican and Russian revolutions. It was "an ascendant movement of progress that happens subtly behind all obstructions . . . no one can hold the revolution back in its incessant march forward."[73] The foreword of the OKA constitution was adapted into the LULAC constitution when the three organizations merged. According to the resulting text, "backward races" and "enlightened races" could "in this age of civilization . . . tread hand in hand."[74] LULAC's code read to "trust in the work of human progress, slow and sure, unmistakable and firm."[75] In *El Paladín* Saenz argued that "in order to be in better condition to claim our rights and fulfill our duties it is necessary to assimilate all the favorable part[s] [of Anglo-American civilization] within our ability that we find in the new civilization in which we shall have to live," adding, "Upon the ruins of our past there is to be founded a new solidification of a new Mexico-American generation."[76]

This emphasis on biocultural evolution fostered the creation of social hierarchies because it posited a chronology of civilization in which different races occupied different spots on a developmental timeline. Many Mexican Americans believed in this hierarchy of civilization, which led them to think about race in ways that paralleled and supported popular evolutionist thought. As far as their stage in the evolutionary process, Mexican Americans believed they were somewhere in the middle: "In the Latin fief is found the roots of our genealogical tree, and we have its blood, its language, and what is even more important, its costumes [*sic*] and its feelings which are the things in brief which always establish the difference between the various races," reasoned one Mexican American.[77] Another explained, "The Anglo Saxon is positivist and materialist because he is from that philosophical school, we are romantics and dreamers because we are from a philosophy that has its roots in a different school. . . . It is not possible for the Indo-Americans to be like the Anglo Saxons, [Native Americans] are not like us either. . . . Our essence appears to the Anglo Saxon as being unprepared, a failure to see certain aspects as utilitarian and practical." The author then argued the two races were mutually unrecognizable because their ways of thinking and acting appeared alien and extreme to the other.[78]

Based on their beliefs in the hierarchical organization and immutable and inherent characteristics of race, Mexican Americans concluded that they were members of the white race. Whether they adopted this stance to gain the "wages of whiteness" is controversial.[79] It is however clear that by the 1930s the whiteness of ethnic Mexicans was a popular idea in Mexican Americanism.

Historians of race have demonstrated that whiteness is a social, intellectual, and legal concept.[80] Cracks and cleavages exist within whiteness, and certain groups have been able to exploit them at different points in history. Not all whites, in other words, are equally white.[81] The period of mass migration from 1840 to 1924 fractured whiteness, while the introduction of scientific and evolutionary thought changed the epistemological foundations of race. The ranking of physical difference gained a new and powerful authority: "Science provided an alternative vocabulary to the polarities [of difference]" argues historian

Matthew Frye Jacobson, "a vocabulary keyed to physicality and 'nature' rather than to belief, yet marking peoples nonetheless as possessing an inherent degree of righteousness, now refigured as innate capacity."[82] In 1924, the Johnson-Reed Act made whiteness the central characteristic of US citizenship, while marking the rest of the world as not white and hence unfit for the American body politic.[83] Whiteness was again opened for Europeans but closed for many others. All these developments left ethnic Mexicans in the Southwest in an interesting position. While the Johnson-Reed Act would eventually reconsolidate whiteness, vestiges of "variegated whiteness" still existed in the 1930s and 1940s.[84] Mexican Americans tried to exploit these openings. They needed the status of whiteness because from 1790 until 1952 being white was a precondition for citizenship.[85]

Consequently, an early goal of Mexican American activists was to establish their whiteness. As early as 1922, the OSA made this very clear in article II, section 1a of its constitution, which stated that "our race . . . should be considered, as it is, the white race."[86] Mexican Americans chafed at the negation of their whiteness. The author of a 1932 article in *LULAC News* exclaimed heatedly, "Conditions have reached a point where your neighbors say, 'a white man and a Mexican!' Yet in your veins races the hot blood of the adventurous Castilian nobleman, the whitest blood in the world." Later, he tempered his statement with the addendum that the "blood of the cultured Aztecs" too ran in the veins of Mexican Americans.[87]

In 1936 Gregory R. Salinas, secretary of LULAC Council 16, wrote to Louis Wilmot, president of LULAC Council No. 1, complaining that local black musicians were having "illicit relations" with "ignorant and ill-informed Mexican girls." According to Salinas, black musicians were playing at public dances and other LULAC functions, and they and the young women were getting along a little too nicely. Angrily, Salinas exclaimed that "every member of LULAC should resent this shameful and dangerous situation, and should exert himself to the limit to put an end to it . . . let us tell these negroes that we are not going to permit our manhood and womanhood to mingle with them on an equal social basis."[88]

In the 1939 Corpus Christi city directory ethnic Mexicans were classified separately as either "Mexican" or "English-Speaking Mexican." (The other groups were "American" and "Colored.")[89] This distinction between Mexican Americans and whites irritated the members of LULAC. The secretary of Council 1, Robert Meza, wrote to Jeff Bell, the manager of the Corpus Christi Chamber of Commerce, complaining that "the fact of the matter is that the scheme is nothing more than an unparalleled singularity purporting to discriminate between the Mexicans themselves and other members of the white race when in truth and in fact we are not only a part and parcel but as well the sum and substance of the white race." For Meza there were many groups within the white race, with Mexicans being one of them. He reiterated that "to reduce the entire group of all peoples of separate and distinct nationalities who are members of the white race to the same classification and to the exclusion of the Mexicans themselves who are also members of the same race is the object of our strenuous objection."[90]

LULAC did not object that the term "American," which was used in the city directory to delineate whites and exclude black Americans. The equation of American with whiteness did not bother them at all, they simply wanted to be included in the normative whiteness of "American." Meza offered his proposal: "All that we now require is that all names of Spanish origin or extraction be classified integrally the same as any other names pertaining to the white race, without any deviation whatsoever therefrom."[91]

In the same year, former LULAC president Manuel C. González wrote an article titled "No Segregation!" in English and a parallel not identical version "Iguales, no segregados!" (Same, Not Segregated) in Spanish. In it he insisted that Mexican Americans were white: "the Supreme Court of the United States has ruled as a matter of law, that the so called 'Mexican people' are a part of the White Race. A careful ethnological study conclusively proves the soundness of that legal conclusion." For this reason, he persisted, "it is to be regretted that Latin American Citizens are segregated in some of the public schools in Texas and their facilities are inferior, in some instances, even to the colored school."[92] González was angered that white Mexican Americans attended worse schools than black Americans did. Clearly, he believed whiteness privileged Mexican Americans to receive first-class citizenship. It did not matter to him that citizenship was racialized, only that Mexican Americans were not recognized as white.

The 1940s proved to be an important decade for ethnic Europeans in the United States in terms of claiming whiteness. Whereas the Johnson-Reed Act had reconsolidated whiteness through immigration restrictions, World War II had also done much to ameliorate divisions among ethnic Euro-Americans. The fact that racial thinking in the United States paralleled that of Nazi Germany embarrassed the nation.[93] Nazi scientific racism pushed the discussion in the United States regarding differences among people of European descent toward ideas of cultural difference, or ethnicity.[94] State-sponsored propaganda visually reordered the American nation by promoting a whitened image of those who belonged. Wartime posters, movies, and photographs all projected the central image of whiteness along with the racial hierarchical structures associated with white supremacy.[95] Irish Americans, Italian Americans, Polish Americans, and Jewish Americans, among many others, were portrayed in film and print media free of ethnic European caricature. In the absence of marked ethnic depictions, Euro-Americans participated in whiteness through images that mirrored their racial complexion. Although such ethnic European representation was intended to portray the United States as tolerant of diversity and to promote commitment to the war effort, working-class ethnic Europeans used the wartime propagandic imagery of whiteness in order to consolidate their own whiteness and national belonging. The historian Gary Gerstle explains that "for ethnic [European] workers the war was the historic moment when they felt fully accepted as American."[96] Through working in factories, purchasing war bonds, becoming naturalized citizens, and performing other rituals of citizenship, ethnic Europeans managed to participate in Americanness. Even though ethnic Europeans became accepted, however, the race line separating black from white was still drawn starkly.

Among Mexican Americans, the strategy of claiming whiteness was uneven at best and often backfired. The contradictory results of claiming whiteness emerged in the cases leading up to the Supreme Court ruling in *Hernandez v. Texas* (1954). Mexican American activists and LULAC lawyers during the postwar period emphasized the "other white" legal strategy. That is, Mexican Americans did not protest segregation in its totality, but only their segregation based on their status as a white group.[97]

In the context of jury selection, the emphasis placed on ethnic Mexican whiteness worked to their disadvantage. For decades not a single US-born Mexican sat on a jury in Jackson County or many other counties in Texas. LULAC lawyers attempted to appeal convictions on the basis that ethnic Mexican defendants were not judged by a jury of their peers, as the juries were all Anglo-American. In cases in 1946 and 1951, judges dismissed this argument, reasoning that the juries were white and so too were ethnic Mexicans. Legally, then, there was no discrimination because defendants and jurors were of the same race—even as the bathrooms outside the courtroom were segregated. As the opinion in *Salazar v. State* (1946) stated: "the Mexican people are of the same race as the grand jurors. We see no question presented for our discussion under the Fourteenth Amendment to the Constitution of the United States . . . dealing with discrimination against race."[98] The right to sit on a jury was no trivial matter for US-born Mexicans in the mid-twentieth century. Jury duty was tantamount to achieving equal status with Anglos because it dismantled the idea that whites were the only ones suitable to render judgment on others.[99]

In 1954 LULAC lawyers successfully argued for protection under the Fourteenth Amendment as a separate racial group. After the ruling in the *Hernandez* case, however, some members of the US-born Mexican community believed the decision eroded their claims of whiteness. Nonetheless, Mexican American organizations like LULAC continued their quest for an untenable recognition of whiteness through the 1960s. The hope of attaining recognition as white never ended for some, but the 1960s saw the rise of a new ideology that rejected the previous generation's infatuation with whiteness.

The first half of the twentieth century saw the rise of a group of US-born Mexicans who did not simply acknowledge their citizenship but understood citizenship in complex ways. Citizenship had become the legitimate means of belonging between the late nineteenth and early twentieth centuries. This meant that the means of belonging was controlled by the state and was increasingly exclusive based on race and class. Nonetheless, Mexican Americans, as they began to call themselves, emphasized their belonging on the grounds of citizenship. While they made ardent exclamations of "por nuestra patria," they had learned a harsh lesson in the 1930s that they could easily be repatriated. Their patriotism was boastful and boisterous because their belonging based on citizenship was so tentative. This approach to belonging was a gamble because, as historical legal scholar Ian Haney López has shown, citizenship as a political status could easily be taken away, and had been from many groups in the past.[100]

Mexican Americanism was a set of ideas that rooted US-born Mexicans' belonging in the United States through citizenship. Mexican Americanism emerged at a time when the changing power of the state demanded a different kind of loyalty. It was not just a moment when Mexican boys went to war and were killed, but part of a global shift towards a nation-state-based system where identities were regulated, authorized, and issued. In response, Mexican Americans crafted an imagined authorized community that emphasized their position as members of a nation-state system.

Mexican Americans formed their ideology in conversation with ideas circulating in the United States. They did not co-opt the coercive charges of citizenship but reproduced them. Mexican Americans battled segregation and discrimination on grounds that they were white US citizens. They did not attack the underlying arguments and racial ideologies that upheld Jim Crow in the United States; instead they found ways to make themselves part of the group that was not discriminated against. Making claims of whiteness, they avoided challenging white supremacy. Becoming middle class, they refused to question the morality of capitalism. Becoming modern, they chose not to question scientific racism and eugenicist thinking.

It would be impossible, and nearly foolhardy, to argue that citizenship did not provide US-born Mexicans with political and material benefits. Being recognized as citizens gave them power to access a legal system that offered avenues of protection and redress. As citizens,

US-born Mexicans could claim inclusion into an important imagined community. However, the turn toward an emphasis on citizenship did indeed limit the intellectual and ideological possibilities of other forms of connection among people of the world. In the process of becoming Americans, Mexican Americans reinforced national borders and drew lines in the sand within their imagined community.

CHAPTER 3

"Entre las masas mexicanas"

BELONGING, LABOR INTERNATIONALISM, AND THE ETHNIC MEXICAN LEFT, 1910–1942

In October 1910, *La Crónica*, a newspaper in Laredo, Texas, reported, "In the state of Texas there have never been Mexican tramps, not even among the most indigent. It does not matter the age, social condition, or level of education: the Mexican always works to earn the bread he eats." The article went on to describe Mexican workers as the best available, adding "the fact that he is a good worker is demonstrated by the fact that his work is preferred on the railroad tracks, in the coal mines, on the agricultural farms, and on the range as cowboys."[1] As the article made clear, Mexican labor was widely sought after. Labor in general was a contentious issue in the United States during this period. Mexican labor, in particular, was complex because it intersected with concepts of race, nation, and belonging.

In a period when citizenship was gaining acceptance as the legitimate means of belonging across the globe and Mexican nationals and US-born Mexicans were beginning to articulate new visions of belonging that conformed with that reality, the labor movement was at the forefront of challenging the idea that citizenship limited individuals' responsibility to one another and to citizens of other countries. The ideology of Mexican Americanism promoted citizenship as the primary lens through which to view belonging. Citizens owed each other certain responsibilities and were owed certain privileges from the state. They performed their citizenship through spectacles and proclamations of national pride. Mexican Americans carefully distinguished themselves from poor Mexican nationals. Similarly, the Mexican nationalism of the early decades of the twentieth century articulated a conservative

Mexican pecan shellers at work in a small, nonunion plant, San Antonio, Texas, March 1939. Photograph by Russell Lee.
Library of Congress, Prints & Photographs Division, Farm Security Administration Office of War Information Photograph Collection (LC-USF34-032601-D).

Mexicanness which expelled US-born Mexicans. US-born Mexicans were insufficiently Mexican to belong to the imagined community of México de Afuera.

More radical ethnic Mexican labor organizations, influenced by labor internationalism and worker solidarity, advocated that all ethnic Mexicans were part of the same class of underpaid, alienated, and exploited casual workers, irrespective of citizenship. Thereby they redrew the boundaries of belonging and replaced the enclosures of citizenship. Instead of a world of nation-states and citizens, they imagined a world of united workers. Radical labor organizations denounced US racism for these reasons and offered all ethnic Mexicans, regardless of citizenship or gender, a place in their organizations. Although many labor and leftist organizations fell short of their interracial promises, some did open up spaces for interracial and international cooperation.

ıportantly, they created a consciousness that emphasized class over tizenship and race, motivating many ethnic Mexican workers to challenge limiting forms of nationalism, citizenship, and the nation-state.

THE CHANGING ECONOMY

Between 1900 and 1930, the Southwest, especially Texas, underwent a dramatic economic shift that upended previous race relations and imposed new racial hierarchies, placing ethnic Mexicans in new economic, social, and racial positions. The historical sociologist David Montejano describes this new economic order as a transformation from the previous ranch system toward the modern farm society. This transition was characterized by the decline of the Mexican ranchero elite and small Anglo tenant farmers, an increase in industrial jobs, and the rise of large-scale Anglo-American agribusiness, or commercialized farming, served by casual, alienated, migrant ethnic Mexican laborers.[2] By 1910 most ethnic Mexicans had lost their economic status while increased migration from Mexico was swelling the number of available laborers. In the first half of the twentieth century, the future was bleak and times were hard for many U.S-born Mexicans and Mexican nationals in Texas.

Between 1911 and 1920 the average daily wage of ethnic Mexican ranch and farm laborers in Texas (a large segment of the ethnic Mexican population) was 75 cents, or less than ten dollars a day when adjusted for inlation.[3] Ethnic Mexicans composed 70 to 90 percent of the railroad workers in the Southwest,[4] with those in Texas earning an average daily wage of $1.25.[5] In a 1926 survey in San Antonio, Texas, of 1,296 ethnic Mexican male heads of households, 47.7 percent were common laborers while only 3.2 percent were professional workers. Of the common laborers, 50.1 percent were Mexican nationals and 33.5 percent were US-born Mexicans. In El Paso, ethnic Mexicans in nearly every occupation earned less than their Anglo counterparts. Whereas the average weekly wage of ethnic Mexicans was $8.69, the figure for Anglo-American workers was $18.56.[6] This dual wage market was by no means a new creation, but one with a long history tied to nineteenth-century colonialism.[7]

dual wage market

By the eve of the Great Depression, the transformation to a scientifically managed, modern, agricultural mode of production had been established and the US Southwest was producing 40 percent of the country's fruits and vegetables. Texas maintained the largest reservoir of cheap labor in the country, and agricultural production was the biggest industry; nearly half of that production was cotton.[8] The Great Depression only exacerbated the poor working and living conditions for ethnic Mexicans, and their circumstances continued to deteriorate through the decade. Ethnic Mexicans increasingly served as casual, alienated labor in a lean production model. In 1936, more than 12,000 ethnic Mexican men, women, and children labored in the seasonal pecan-shelling industry in San Antonio, where wages averaged only five cents per hour. The annual income for the average-sized family of 4.6 persons was only $251. The weekly income of pecan workers, who worked an average of fifty-one hours a week, was $2.73, much lower than the average income of agricultural laborers, which was $3.50 a week. Nearly a quarter of those who worked in the pecan-shelling industry also worked as agricultural laborers in Texas or other states at some point during the year.[9]

By 1937, nearly 85 percent of the state's migratory workers were ethnic Mexicans.[10] Most worked in the fields of South, Central, and West Texas, picking cotton. Texas was home to the largest cotton migration in the Southwest, with ethnic Mexicans traveling from Brownsville to Amarillo annually, a nearly 1,600-mile roundtrip. Harvest season began in July and ended in November or December, lasting six to ten weeks in each area. The largest cotton district was around the Dallas–Fort Worth area. At the highpoint of cotton production, ethnic Mexican migratory cotton pickers harvested 1,130,713 bales of cotton in the High Plains area alone.[11] In 1938, most ethnic Mexican cotton pickers were paid between 40 and 50 cents per 100 pounds. To put this wage in perspective, an able-bodied worker could pick 150 pounds per day.[12] Even though workers could outpace a mechanized cotton gin, they could not earn more than a dollar a day.[13] The economic outlook for ethnic Mexican laborers in Texas was bleak. In one instance, growers shot holes in Mexican workers' truck tires to prevent them from leaving the state in search of better wages.[14] In sum, ethnic Mexicans found themselves at the bottom of a stratified labor market.

THE WHITE LEFT

As white laborers lost their economic foothold, their whiteness came into question.. More affluent whites viewed the failure of white tenants to achieve landownership or economic success as reflecting a deficiency in their moral character and racial pedigree. In other words, the fault lay squarely on the shoulders of the white tenants and their work ethic, not on the changing economies of scale that made ever larger farms more profitable and productive. Industrial workers and white tenant farmers alike were becoming alienated from the means of production—they only had their own labor to sell. The ladder that led to the idyllic life of the Jeffersonian yeoman had broken.[21]

Many poor white farmers chose to organize to resist their exploitation. Disparaged as "white trash" and economically dislodged, white tenants and sharecroppers turned to organized labor and socialism. Labor organizations blossomed across Texas. The American Federation of Labor (AFL), the Socialist Party of America (SPA), and the Communist Party USA (CPUSA) all recruited from the ranks of angry white industrial and agricultural workers. Oklahoma, Texas, Louisiana, and Arkansas provided fertile ground for SPA recruiters, becoming one of the regions with the strongest support for the party.[22] In Texas, the SPA was strongest in the cotton belt of East Texas and in the newer cotton counties north of Abilene and around Lubbock. Across Texas in 1910, the SPA vote increased to 11,000, up from 1,841 votes in 1900 and 8,000 in 1904.[23] In the 1912 and 1914 elections, the Texas Socialist Party replaced the Republican Party as the second largest party in the state.[24] In addition, *The Rebel*, published in Texas, was the third largest Socialist weekly in the United States.[25] Socialists denounced high rents, absentee landowners, and the moneyed interests.[26] As the years wore on, many white tenants became both increasingly radical in their politics and reactionary in their racism. They believed that reformism would not solve their problems and could not end the oppression of monopoly capitalism.[27] Rather than being attracted to international solidarity shared as part of a global proletariat, many white workers joined unions to regain their manliness and status as primary breadwinners and white workers—which many believed entitled them to better and fairer treatment.[28]

Although many radical leftist organizations paid lip service to the concept of a united working class, race undoubtedly tainted class consciousness. Race shaped the ways in which many white workers and farmers thought about class.[29] Many white tenant farmers and workers blamed African Americans and ethnic Mexicans for their precarious economic position.[30] In their view blacks and Mexicans stole their jobs because they worked for less money. Both the SPA and the AFL kept blacks and ethnic Mexicans at arm's length. The AFL rarely challenged Jim Crow within or outside the workplace.[31] Indeed, many in the AFL, which represented mainly skilled white workers, believed that Mexicans and blacks would eventually out-compete them for jobs.[32] Some SPA organizers distanced themselves from workers of color because they feared the kinds of assumptions the larger white working class might make about Socialists that "mixed" with communities of color. In fact, the Democratic Party tried to win votes away from the SPA by hinting that Socialists were race mixers.[33] One SPA organizer tried to turn the table on this characterization with an alternative description of the political parties in Texas: "The Republicans, like [Theodore] Roosevelt, eat with the negro; the Socialist will work with the negro and the Democrats mix with the negro."[34] In addition, the rampant use of the word "nigger" by many leftist groups showed "the desire to signal that one accepted Black participation but did not necessarily question white supremacy outside the union."[35] The limits on white radicalism was a problem of its longer intellectual heritage, one that mixed Christian and Jeffersonian thought with a moderated Marxist analysis to demand more independently owned white farms rather than a proletarian revolution.[36]

The AFL also had problems creating a united working class across racial lines. In many AFL locals, black and white workers competed in segregated outfits. Many white workers refused to work with black workers, even if they were in the same union. Along the Texas coast, the International Longshoremen's Association (ILA) had separate black and white locals. Frequently, the black and white locals had disagreements, with each claiming that the other had undermined their wage or their contract.[37] Dual wage systems often operated in industries with segregated locals. Although the ILA had passed a resolution at its 1914 convention that encouraged greater interaction between white and black locals, hoping to build solidarity among all workers, the resolution was not heeded.[38] Throughout the early twentieth century, black and white locals each continued to complain bitterly about the unfair practices the other used to take work away from them. The racial politics of the working class was exacerbated by employers that imported Mexican labor to break strikes. As early as 1915, both black and white ILA locals complained about Mexican labor, complaints that would continue for decades, still being raised at the 1935 ILA convention.[39]

It seemed that the racial and class solidarity of labor and the left existed only in speeches and theory. Organizations like the AFL would briefly mention racial equality as a component of working-class solidarity, but continued to maintain segregated locals and often refused to organize ethnic Mexican and black workers. Although the CPUSA and SPA spoke more adamantly about racial equality and a radical economic vision, many white rank-and-file members merely hoped to use the leftist parties to regain their lost economic positions that were rooted in racial privilege. Nonetheless, ethnic Mexicans found some room for participation in labor organizations and leftist politics, infusing certain locals and parties with more radical ideas. Some ethnic Mexicans would find sympathetic Anglo-American organizers to aid them or would find more progressive parties to join. Often, these sympathetic parties overlooked citizenship even though citizenship had become the legitimate means of belonging.

THE ETHNIC MEXICAN LEFT

The changing economic order, deteriorating living conditions, racist attitudes, and exclusion from unions influenced ethnic Mexican thinking in the United States. Ethnic Mexican workers were not passive in the face of the larger social changes that caused them to be dehumanized and mistreated as workers and human beings. Many Mexicans, regardless of nationality, organized to protect themselves. Whereas race served to splinter white-black cooperation, race helped create class

Relief Line in the Mexican section of San Antonio, Texas, March 1939. Photograph by Russell Lee.

Library of Congress, Prints & Photographs Division, Farm Security Administration Office of War Information Photograph Collection (LC-USF34-032666-D).

consciousness among many working-class ethnic Mexicans, who were often more radical than their white or black counterparts, being influenced by transnational ideas coming from the Mexican Revolution.[40]

The strongest connection between ethnic Mexicans in the United States and Mexican radicalism was the exiled Partido Liberal Mexicano (PLM, Mexican Liberal Party), headed by two brothers, Ricardo and Enrique Flores Magón, who arrived in San Antonio in 1904. At that time the PLM had more than forty local groups spread across the United States and Mexico, with several thousand supporters in the United States, at the beginning of the twentieth century.[41] Initially, the party was reformist in bent, aimed at ending the dictatorship of Porfirio Díaz but it quickly moved towards anarcho-syndicalism.[42] As the party radicalized, Texas became the largest base for PLM activities, with more than fifty chapters sprouting up in that state alone between

1911 and 1917. In San Antonio, the largest ethnic Mexican barrio in the country in 1908, military intelligence officers estimated that the PLM had more than one thousand supporters.[43] The party's organ, *Regeneración*, was incredibly influential across the Southwest, and especially in Texas. By 1915 nearly half of its subscribers lived in Texas, twice as many as in Mexico and California combined.[44] *Regeneración* was only one of thirty-nine PLM papers circulating in Texas between 1907 and 1913. Women PLM members Andrea and Teresa Villarreal, from San Antonio, founded *El Obrero* in 1909 and the first socialist-feminist paper, *La mujer moderna*, in 1915, while Blanca Moncaleano founded *La Pluma Roja* in 1913.[45] These women combined Marxist critiques of capitalism with feminist critiques about gendered wage structures and sexism. The context of revolution in Mexico and dramatic changes in the United States led working-class and left-leaning ethnic Mexican women to articulate a "revolutionary idealism" that described social and gender equity as the objective of the true revolution.[46]

These existing ideas drew ethnic Mexicans towards the more radical labor organizations, such as the SPA and the Renter's Union (founded in 1911). Having witnessed the excesses of extractive capitalism in Mexico, they saw that American-style reform fell short in ameliorating the excesses of capitalism.[47] Many ethnic Mexican Socialist locals in Texas evolved from PLM clubs, and many PLM members went on to become very successful organizers of other leftist organizations.[48] One of the most efficient organizers of the Land League, José Angel Hernández, was the president of a local PLM club before he joined the SPA.[49] The Renter's Union, whose objective was to end "landlordism" in Texas, hired Antonio Valdez in 1910 to organize Spanish-speaking chapters.[50] Valdez, a US-born Mexican, had developed his labor consciousness earlier as a PLM member. Part of the reason the PLM and its newspaper were influential in the Mexican communities of Texas was because readers hoped that the Mexican Revolution could resolve the issue of land and then could inspire redistribution, if not revolution, in the United States. As PLM leaders became increasingly mired in the troubles of radical exiles and neutrality laws, and as conditions worsened, ethnic Mexicans chose to engage with many leftist organizations in Texas.[51]

Mexicans joined nearly twenty industrial unions affiliated with the Texas Socialist Party, representing farm renters, farm laborers, and urban workers. In 1915 around one thousand ethnic Mexicans were members of Socialist unions in Texas.[52] The New Braunfels and Seguin locals were the largest in the state, but other locals existed in Gentress, Mario, Clear Springs, Devine, Whitsett, Campbellton, Mathis, Tilden, Rockdale, Nordheim, Runge, Helena, Yorktown, Charco, Cuero, Thomaston, Belmont, and San Antonio, as well as in Travis County.[53] There were also close relationships between the PLM and the SPA in California, especially in Los Angeles.[54]

Similarly, the CPUSA set about recruiting ethnic Mexican workers. The party had strongholds in cities like San Antonio, where it helped the working-class ethnic Mexican population address police violence, worker relief, and discrimination.[55] Famed tejana organizer Emma Tenayuca was a Communist Party member who helped lead other ethnic Mexican women pecan shellers on strike. Her husband, Homer Brooks, was also a Communist Party member. The International Workers of the World (IWW, or Wobblies) was also successful in recruiting ethnic Mexican workers. In fact, one of the founders of the IWW was a Texas-born Afro-Latina named Lucy Gonzalez Parsons. The IWW printed several Spanish-language papers in Texas, including *El Proletario* (The Proletariat) and *Trabajadoras y Trabajadores de El Paso* (Women Workers and Men Workers of El Paso), and as many as two hundred Mexican smelter works were affiliated with the IWW in El Paso by 1913.[56]

In this context, ethnic Mexicans had a myriad of ideas and organizations from which to choose. Some, such as early LULAC member Clemente Idar, were drawn to the reformist tendencies of the AFL, while others were attracted to the radical possibilities offered by the PLM, SPA, and CPUSA. The more radical leftist organizations promoted racial equality and labor internationalism, but they often did not deliver. Nonetheless, labor internationalism and its encompassing vision of the relationship among people of the world competed with concepts of citizenship and race that were increasingly important in ethnic Mexican thought. Class consciousness and labor internationalism intersected with citizenship to produce conceptions of belonging that differed from both Mexican nationalism and Mexican Americanism. Labor internationalism emphasized class over citizenship to create very different possibilities for the world than increasingly narrow nationalisms did—nationalisms that would soon lead to world wars.

RACE, CITIZENSHIP, AND LABOR INTERNATIONALISM

The historian Mario T. García has posited that most ethnic Mexicans were drawn to labor organizing and leftist politics for pragmatic reasons. They were not necessarily interested in the rhetoric of revolution, but hoped for the possibility of reform. Even García, however, is quick to acknowledge that labor had a powerful draw due to its encompassing vision of the world and social relations. In contrast to LULAC and other groups that used citizenship as a divisive criterion to restrict membership, labor organizations saw ethnic Mexicans as part of an interconnected global working class that transcended citizenship.[57] Yet, while many white labor organizations spoke at length about interracial cooperation and international solidarity, few actually lived up to their lofty ambitions, and some were downright antagonistic toward interracial cooperation. Some groups in Texas did build an ideological framework based on labor internationalism and interracial cooperation to overcome the conceptual boundaries of citizenship. These groups experienced mixed success.

Whereas the AFL did not go out of its way to recruit ethnic Mexican workers, its more progressive counterpart, the Congress of Industrial Organizations (CIO), focused on organizing craft unions, did try to organize unskilled workers. The United Cannery, Agricultural, Packing, and Allied Workers of America (UCAPAWA), an affiliate union of the CIO, went out of its way to organize ethnic Mexican workers, recruiting a surprising number of women across the Southwest from California to Texas. UCAPAWA was a remarkably democratic organization that encouraged people of color and women to participate in empowering the working class.[58] One of the founding members was the Guatemalan-born immigrant activist Luisa Moreno, who would eventually become the vice president of UCAPAWA.[59]

The union had an odd beginning within the AFL. In 1936, a small group of organizers tried to persuade the AFL to form an agricultural union, but the executive board ignored them.[60] After being spurned, the organizers decided to create their own union, so UCAPAWA held its first national convention in Denver, Colorado, July 9–12, 1937. The union did not envision itself as an isolated alliance of poor cotton and fruit pickers, but as the fulcrum between the agricultural and industrial segments of the overall labor movement. In his keynote address, the chairman Donald Henderson addressed worker solidarity, exclaiming, "We [agricultural workers] are in a very peculiar position. . . . We are the laboring population in the countryside. We are the beginnings of the labor movement in agriculture. We are part of the labor movement. . . . We are bound up with the fortunes, the hopes, and the fears of the million or so farmers. We are the link between the great industrial movement and the millions of toiling farmers in the United States."[61] UCAPAWA believed that agricultural workers would serve an intermediary role as the connective tissue uniting casual industrial workers with alienated farmers. The union members' idealistic goal was to be a united force that closed the chasms in the ranks of labor—urban versus rural, industrial versus agricultural, white versus black, white versus Mexican, man versus woman, or national versus international.

UCAPAWA emphasized the multiracial composition of labor, as represented physically by the many ethnic delegates present and the resolutions passed at the convention. Among many Spanish-surnamed delegates were four from California, thirteen from Colorado, two from Wyoming, four from Nebraska, and three (out of four) from Texas.[62] Filipino and African American delegates were present as well. The "Resolution on Racial Discrimination," passed at the first convention, mixed equal parts of worker solidarity, interracial cooperation, and labor internationalism, as follows:

> Whereas: Race discrimination and national hatred are superimposed curses of humanity designed to separate the peoples of the world, and thus subject them to continuous exploitation and subjugation by the employers; and

> Whereas: The pitting of one nationality against the other to prevent unity and solidarity among workers particularly in the agricultural industry, inducing one group to scab against the other, has proven a great obstruction and barrier to a genuine organized labor movement; and
>
> Whereas: Progressive labor and social legislation . . . has been retarded due to the unpardonable practice of race discrimination within and outside the unions; be it therefore. . . .
>
> Resolved: That we exert all our forces to fight for the rights of all minority peoples in extending any and all articles of legislation, Federal and State; and that this convention commit itself to uphold the fundamental principle of NO DISCRIMINATION, toward the foreign born and other minorities regardless of nationality, color, creed or political belief; be it further
>
> Resolved: That we go on record condemning the reactionary practice by relief authorities [of] discriminating against foreign-born and other minorities; be it further
>
> Resolved: That we assert our condemnation of the policies of many A.F. of L. leaders against nationalities as a blot on organized labor; be if further
>
> Resolved: That we go on record fighting for the extension of franchise to all American citizens, particularly the Negro people, and to all peoples not yet extended such a right.[63]

This resolution connected issues of citizenship, race, and labor, railing against the limiting of rights based on citizenship. The logic of the resolution asserted that all people should be afforded rights, not because of their citizenship, but because of their status as workers. Other resolutions agreed on at the convention addressed civil liberties and lynching. The "Resolution on Lynching" supported anti-lynching legislation. It denounced lynching as "a brutal means of coercion directed against the Negro people . . . who strive for an improved social order . . . [and] the act of lynching by vigilante mobs destroys the fundamental rights of trial by jury as guaranteed by the United States Constitution."[64]

Labor internationalism was implicit in the many resolutions on race and in discussions on citizenship, as well as in the debates surrounding war. In the "Resolution on World Peace," UCAPAWA opposed war on the basis that it was a construct of the international bourgeoisie aimed at dividing the working class through the mystification of nationalism. The resolution stated that "loving peoples of all nations are so bound together by economic and social ties that the threat of war to one nation is a threat of war to all."[65] Moreover, war was an extension of colonial conquests, of attempts by the international bourgeoisie to exploit workers. The union urged the government to pursue the path of peace.

UCAPAWA promoted interracial cooperation, worker solidarity, and labor internationalism not only on the national level, but also on the local level. One example occurred in San Antonio, home to the nation's pecan-shelling industry, employing nearly 12,000 workers—most of them ethnic Mexicans. A small local union of pecan shellers began there in 1933. In 1937, a UCAPAWA representative visited San Antonio for the purpose of affiliating with the CIO, and the local union rebranded itself the Texas Pecan Workers Union, Local #172. On January 31, 1938, the Southern Pecan Shelling Company, the largest in the city, announced a wage cut from six or seven cents per pound to five or six cents. This announcement caused a spontaneous walkout. The workers organized quickly, with more than six thousand applying for union membership and nearly three thousand paying dues during the strike period. Authorities responded swiftly in support of the factory owners. On February 7, 1938, the police rounded up three hundred picketers from around the shelling plants, and more than one thousand other picketers were arrested on trumped-up charges of blocking sidewalks, disturbing the peace, or congregating in unlawful assemblies. A week later, 52 police officers and 125 firemen were sent to break the strike. The police chief branded the strikers communists, exclaiming, "I did not interfere with the strike. I interfered with a revolution." On March 8, 1938, the workers agreed to return to work, pending a meeting with an arbitration board.[66]

During the strike, the Pecan Workers Union showed surprising awareness of the transnational and interconnected nature of labor. Not only did the members organize both Mexican nationals and US-born

Mexicans, they issued resolutions against the war brewing in Europe. The union declared, "Finance Capital and the monopoly enterests [*sic*] of our own nation are also plotting and hoping to drag our nation in the war in order to enable them to deprive the American people of their democratic rights, and to increase their already swollen profits from the sale of war supplies, profiteering and enslavement of the American Worker." The critique continued "by the participation of our nation in this war it would be the workers who would be herded to the slaughter, to again shed their blood and die upon the battlefields of foreign soil. It would be the families of working people who would be the victims of profiteering, destitution, and misery. . . . Regardless of which side wins in such a war as this the workers can only lose."[67] Similar critiques of war emerged in another Pecan Workers Union bulletin that argued the war was a product of the international bourgeoisie, who aimed to extract more profit by fomenting conflict while murdering more workers. The bulletin concluded, "Our greatest bulwark for democracy, for peace, and for a maintenance of our living standards is a stronger and more powerful Labor movement. Our unions are our only defense against the profiteers. We cannot be satisfied to stand still, we must go forward."[68]

Other UCAPAWA locals promoted labor internationalism. Weslaco Local No. 223 and Donna Local No. 180 also encouraged workers to look past citizenship. In a joint letter the ethnic Mexican presidents of both locals articulated the goal of uniting workers and protecting them from exploitation, regardless of their citizenship. They pledged to organize all workers, regardless of age, sex, nationality, or race.[69]

Both the CPUSA and the SPA also participated in organizing the Pecan Shellers Strike. An important organizer during the strike was George P. Lambert, an SPA member.[70] However, because San Antonio had fewer SPA than CPUSA members, the CPUSA played a very important role in the Pecan Shellers Strike and in the Southwest more broadly.[71] The party's antiracist positions and willingness to support all workers helped win ethnic Mexican workers to its cause. The Communist Party in Texas was indeed multiracial. In 1938, the party nominated tejana Emma Tenayuca as its candidate for US Congress, white CPUSA organizer Homer Brooks for governor, and black civil rights activist Cecil B. Robinet (from Houston) as lieutenant governor.[72]

LULAC members in San Antonio opposed the Communist Party of Texas, organizing poorly attended anti-communist counterrallies. They failed to recognize that ethnic Mexican Communists were challenging not only Jim Crow laws, but also the very basis of citizenship undergirding Mexican Americanism. As a teen in 1932 Tenayuca herself had joined a LULAC women's auxiliary, but she ultimately left the organization because of its emphasis on citizenship and Americanization.[73] The Texas Communist Party offered her a global ideological alternative not defined by gender or citizenship, and she ran with it.

During the 1938 Pecan Shellers Strike Tenayuca and Homer Brooks, cowrote an essay, "The Mexican Question in the Southwest," that outlined an alternative vision of belonging. It departed dramatically from the Mexican nationalism of the early twentieth century and from Mexican Americanism. The essay's focus on class and the capitalist world system elevated the expansive vision of labor internationalism above the narrower debates centered on homeland politics. Tenayuca and Brooks argued that Mexican nationals and US-born Mexicans were part of the same class of "superexploited wage workers" in the Southwest. Specifically, "The Spanish-speaking population of the Southwest, both the American-born and the foreign-born, are one people. The Mexican population of the Southwest is closely bound together by historical, political and cultural ties." All workers, regardless of citizenship should be afforded dignity and respect, but especially ethnic Mexicans because "their historical rights in this territory [are] unchallengeable."[74] This short essay undermined the previous claims of belonging rooted in class, citizenship, and Mexican nationalism. Labor internationalism, worker solidarity, and interracial cooperation promoted by labor offered a vision that could move past the ideological and political limitations of the nation-state. In place of narrow ethnic Mexican nationalism that separated US-born Mexicans and Mexican nationals in the borderlands into two different nation-states were ideas of a global proletariat with common causes that connected them to people worldwide.[75]

The International Ladies Garment Workers Union (ILGWU) approached the shellers' strike differently than other labor organizations did. Although the union organized ethnic Mexican women, the leaders of the ILGWU in San Antonio were middle-class Anglo women. Nearly

90 percent of workers in the pecan-shelling industry were ethnic Mexican women, and some leaders of the ILGWU treated them with condescension and racism. Educational Director Rebecca Taylor was disliked by many of the ethnic Mexican women.[76] Taylor was a well-educated Anglo woman who was born in Mexico to a landed family that lost its properties in the Mexican Revolution. She explained to one interviewer that while she sympathized with moderate labor organizations in the United States, she thought that the labor movement in Mexico was "fanatical."[77] Taylor was charged with the responsibilities of educating the women in English, dancing, swimming, and dramatics, but not in organizing or labor politics.[78] Her educational agenda resembled an assimilationist curriculum more than labor activism. She also expressed negative stereotypes of Mexican workers—namely, that they were lethargic, passive, and lacked ambition.[79] Labor internationalism and interracial cooperation in the labor movement was uneven, even in places like San Antonio. This only highlights the foresight of UCAPAWA and CPUSA in offering visions of the world independent of racism, nationalism, and the concept of citizenship.

The San Antonio Pecan Shellers Strike was not the only case where labor internationalism played a substantive role in organizing. In April 1935, three thousand onion pickers, led by Juan Peña and José Jacobs, went on strike in Laredo. Peña, a Works Progress Administration (WPA) employee, and Jacobs, a self-employed photographer, both had histories with labor organizations. This strike was important because it marked a shift in the ethnic Mexican labor movement. Both US-born Mexican and Mexican nationals in Laredo turned to labor organizations in Mexico for guidance and assistance.[80] The recently formed Confederación de Trabajadores Mexicanos (CTM) aided the workers in Laredo. Although local authorities called in the Texas Rangers and the strikers failed to win concessions from the growers, the strike forged transnational connections based on class and labor internationalism.[81]

A similar case of transnational cooperation between labor organizations in Mexico and ethnic Mexican labor organizations occurred in El Paso. From 1939 through 1943, smelter workers in El Paso organized to protest the dual wage system, discrimination, price gouging at the company store, and unfair firing practices at Phelps Dodge and the

American Smelting and Refining Company (ASARCO).[82] These workers organized into a local of the International Mine, Mill and Smelter Workers Union (Mine-Mill). Mine-Mill contacted the CTM in Juárez for help with its organizing efforts. Both the CTM and the Mexican consul in El Paso aided the Mine-Mill workers, trying to protect them from redbaiting by the local sheriff.[83] Despite red scare tactics and deportations, the Mine-Mill workers persevered until 1946, when they won considerable gains from ASARCO and Phelps Dodge.

Another organization that foregrounded ethnic Mexicans' experiences at the intersections of race and class was El Congreso del Pueblo de Habla Española. UCAPAWA vice president Luisa Moreno founded El Congreso in April 1939. It operated within the left-liberal alliance of New Deal Popular Front politics, which aimed to address labor exploitation and racial discrimination. With nearly 30 percent women members, it took a strong stance against sexism. Moreno and Congreso Secretary Josefina Fierro had both been involved in leftist politics in Latin America and bohemian movements in Mexico and the United States. They saw the transnational connections of power in social structures, whether structures of capitalism or sexism. This transnational perspective and the fact that its leaders were immigrant women gave El Congreso an expansive view of the responsibilities and connections of the people of the world. It made ideological sense that El Congreso protested police brutality, redlining, and segregation; demanded integrated and multicultural education; and pushed for labor rights. El Congreso had chapters in Phoenix, El Paso, San Antonio, Brownsville, and even Kansas City, but its strongest base of support was in California, particularly Los Angeles.[84]

Although radical ideas circulating in labor and leftist organizations helped some US-born Mexicans and Mexican nationals to see themselves as part of one global proletariat regardless of citizenship, the political power of citizenship as the legitimate means of belonging was difficult to overcome. The predominantly Anglo-American International Association of Oil Field, Gas Well and Refinery Workers of America, Local #37, in Fort Worth, Texas, accused ethnic Mexicans of lowering wages and flooding the labor market. In response it resolved "that all Mexicans . . . shall carry at all times on their persons their registration papers and shall present them to duly accredited officers of the law for inspections, and where found working anywhere except on the farms and ranches, shall be immediately deported."[85] And 1938, the year when ethnic Mexican pecan shellers were fighting exploitation, was the same year when the government demanded that all WPA workers have citizenship papers. In consequence, only 702 unemployed pecan workers were certified by the WPA to work in 1,800 available positions the organization created for work relief. In addition, old-age assistance, unemployment insurance, and workers' compensation had citizenship requirements. To receive unemployment payments, workers had to have been employed by the same employer for twenty weeks out of the year. Due to the seasonal and casual nature of ethnic Mexican employment, most failed to reach this prerequisite. Of the two thousand unemployment compensation claims filed by pecan shellers in San Antonio in 1938, about 40 percent were rejected.[86]

The children of Mexican nationals tried to help their parents gain access to some benefits. The Socialist organizer George Lambert started a petition that was signed by US-born children of Mexican parents, asking that relief benefits cover their parents. His words in a letter to the Pecan Workers Union were prescient: "This is going to be a long drawn out fight for justice from the foreign born residents of the United States and their children, and one of the most important fights we can carry on at present."[87]

THE END OF REFORM AND THE DECLINE OF THE ETHNIC MEXICAN LEFT

The Great Depression set the context for changes in ethnic Mexican politics and culture, but New Deal policies also affected the ethnic Mexican community. The most substantial national attempts at reform occurred between 1932 and 1937, when a flurry of approaches were enacted to deal with the crisis of the Depression. With the New Deal, President Franklin D. Roosevelt tried to right some of the failing and fallen pillars of the American economy.

When policy changes did not effect economic recovery as soon as expected, government attention turned to work relief and workers' protections. The Public Works Administration and the WPA were designed to offer temporary work relief, providing Americans with enough money to maintain morale without supplanting private employers. The Civilian Conservation Corps offered young men paid positions improving the nation's national parks and public lands. Workers also gained important protections. The National Labor Relations Act and the Fair Labor Standards Act gave workers the right to organize, established the process for collective bargaining, set a minimum wage and forty-hour workweek, and banned child labor from interstate commerce. All of these reforms combined were supposed to address the shortcomings of capitalism in the previous era and establish a fairer system.

Still, the New Deal failed to address underlying realities of racism in the nation and the economy. Agricultural and domestic workers were omitted from the benefits of social security and the protections provided by the new labor laws.[88] Without government mandates for minimum wages, safe working conditions, limitations on child labor, and eight-hour workdays, many US-born Mexican workers in the Midwest and Mexican workers in the Southwest continued to labor under similar conditions from the pre-1929 era well into the 1960s.[89] Cannery workers and fruit packers suffered from similar exclusions until 1935, when the National Labor Relations Board distinguished between field workers and processing workers.[90]

Agricultural consolidation continued and, in many cases, was accelerated by the Agricultural Adjustment Act. The historian Neil Foley argues that the AAA actually helped end the nation's Jeffersonian infatuation with the farm as a bedrock of American character and values.[91] After the 1930s, the small farm was no longer seen as a venerable social institution. The small size of farms and their economic decline were reinterpreted as evidence of their failure to achieve efficiencies of scale. Agricultural industrialization created factories in the field that were subject to the dictates of economic efficiency and scientific management. The decline of the farm in the national imaginary was intensified by the increased presence of ethnic Mexican workers, who were already perceived as inferior and foreign. The independent farm was replaced by the industrialized one, the family replaced by the corporation, and the white farmer by the Mexican worker. Much of this was overlooked during the early recovery years as Americans moved to cities seeking high-paying factory jobs. The agricultural consolidation fostered by the AAA left ethnic Mexican workers—citizen and immigrant alike—socially marginalized and exploitable. Through either deliberate omission or obliviousness, US-born Mexicans were excluded from some of the key protections of the era.

Importantly, the New Deal entrenched citizenship as a tool of discipline in the United States. With the growth of the welfare state in the 1930s, citizenship became the determining factor in who could access benefits. For noncitizens who had been in the nation for decades and for communities of color who because of their perceived foreignness were already suspect, documenting their citizenship to obtain protection and benefits was difficult. From 1929 through 1942, deportation and repatriation campaigns swept up US-born Mexicans regardless of their US citizenship.[92] Throughout the New Deal, US-born Mexicans were denied relief because officials believed they were immigrants.

The historian Justin Chacón described the New Deal as "an illusion for [ethnic] Mexican workers." White bureaucrats from the city level to the federal government often sought to deny New Deal benefits to US-born Mexicans, despite their citizenship. The policies of exclusion targeted this population with precision. In Texas, local officials prevented US-born Mexicans from receiving relief to force them into low-paying agricultural work. In many places in the Southwest, New Deal relief required proving yearlong residency, which was difficult for the large migratory populations of ethnic Mexicans who worked in agriculture. In California, state senator Ralph E. Swing sponsored a bill to deny relief funds to anybody who could not document their status or prove their citizenship. It passed both houses, but pressure from the Congreso del Pueblo de Habla Española caused the governor to veto the bill.[93] Because of these issues, there was an uptick in naturalizations among Mexican nationals in California.[94] Some US-born Mexicans in the Midwest were able to benefit from the worker protections offered through the New Deal when they joined unions in midwestern factories.[95] But for most, the New Deal offered very little and, in some cases, worsened their economic and social position. After nearly four decades, it seemed that revolution, radicalism, and reform could not address the economic transformations faced by ethnic Mexicans. The problems of the New Deal laid a troubling foundation for mid-twentieth-century statist liberalism with regard to race. Consequently, such liberalism exhibited a racial blindness, at times intentional, other times unintentional, that patched over its shortcomings with cultural deficiency theories. It papered over its racist outcomes with its color-blind intent.

Thus, for many ethnic Mexicans across the nation, the New Deal did little to change their working conditions or economic positions. Writer and scholar Américo Paredes wrote about this feeling in his novel *George Washington Gómez: A Mexicotexan Novel*:

> The Mexican laborer, who had subsisted on tortillas most of his life, wondered how people who could afford biscuits and bacon could be poor. He heard how people in the big cities were lining up to receive free soup and bread because of the Depression, and he would joke with his friends, 'I wish what they call the Depression would come down here so we could get some of that.' And in due time the Depression came. La Chilla, Mexicans called it. The Squeal. Or perhaps a euphemism for that most useful of Mexican expressions: La Chingada. . . . La Chilla.[96]

The historian Alan Brinkley has argued that 1937 marked a profound shift in liberal reform in the United States; namely, "the end of reform."[97] After the 1936 election, the 1937 recession, and the coming of World War II, liberals dropped their most biting critiques that industrial capitalism was deeply flawed and that its basic structures needed to be remade. The American economy's ability to convert itself into the "arsenal of democracy" relegitimized capitalism for many Americans. Near full employment, better wages, and feelings of patriotism did not hurt the cause either. Between 1937 and 1942, liberalism switched its focus from the structures that perpetuated economic inequality to economic growth as a form of social progress. This version of liberalism did not require a robust state that dramatically regulated private corporations to achieve its economic goals, but instead a government that promoted economic growth and consumption through federal taxation and spending. After nearly a half century of economic disruption, liberal reformers made peace with capitalism in the 1940s, conceding that its productive power was a greater asset than its structural flaws.

This shift in the focus of reform occurred in ethnic Mexican politics too, to the detriment of the ethnic Mexican left. The most radical critiques of capitalism were silenced by the 1940s. For many reasons, membership in the CPUSA, the SPA, and the IWW all declined across the Southwest. The Congreso disbanded in 1943. Even the AFL and CIO merged in 1955. Mexican labor activism, based on a global borderless proletariat, declined in the face of Mexican Americanism. The radical labor internationalism of the ethnic Mexican left, which refused to concede that the nation-state was the primary organizational unit of human relationships, faced the challenge that New Deal relief and social safety nets were based on the nation-state. Refusing to acknowledge citizenship as the legitimate means of belonging became increasingly difficult as citizenship became the prerequisite to access the protections of the social safety net. Even the Mexican state, which had been a model for some US activists, turned away from its reform model after Lázaro Cárdenas's presidency ended in 1940. Mexican policy turned to a growth model. In the post–World War II years, economic growth gave birth to the "Mexican Miracle."[98]

Labor played an incredibly important role in politicizing ethnic Mexicans. Through labor internationalism, interracial cooperation, and worker solidarity, ethnic Mexicans came to see themselves not as Mexicans or Mexican Americans but as part of the global proletariat. They were workers playing a small part in the larger battle against capital. International solidarity and belief in the interconnectedness of the global proletariat was perhaps an entirely too romantic idea. Few organizations lived up to those ideals. After the superpatriotism during two world wars and the rise of McCarthyism and anticommunism, labor in the United States retreated into a nationally focused consortium of the AFL-CIO that focused on protecting wages, not trying to bring about a revolution between the proletariat and bourgeoisie. Mainstream labor succumbed to the allure of citizenship, both to protect unions from accusations of communism and as a tool to demand rights from the state. For some ethnic Mexicans, however, the idea of being connected to the greater world through relationships based on something larger than an identity issued by a state was too seductive to be ignored. This ideal would continue to influence activist organizations in the 1950s and 1960s, even though the left-liberal alliance had unraveled and would never regain the influence it had in the 1930s.[99]

Labor internationalism helped grow the imaginative dimensions of some US-born Mexicans. They were able to envision themselves as something other than wandering pilgrims in search of a home. Labor radicalism helped elevate them above the raging homeland politics of the twentieth century. They belonged not in the United States or Mexico, but with the working people of the world. The need to root one's belonging in a nation-state was a less pressing concern in the ideology of labor internationalism. The driving forces that affected individual workers' lives were not limited to local civic politics, but extended to the capitalist world system and the global machinations of capital. Labor internationalism injected an important idea into US-born Mexicans' beliefs about belonging. Whereas Mexican Americanism used class and citizenship to create divisions, the radical ideas of labor, and the class consciousness it inspired, served to unite the ethnic Mexican working class beyond citizenship in a specific nation-state.

CHAPTER 4

"They continue to be regarded as 'Mexicans'"

MIDCENTURY MEXICAN AMERICAN LIBERATION THROUGH LIBERALISM, 1930s–1970s

In mid-December 1968, the US Commission on Civil Rights held a hearing at Our Lady of the Lake University in San Antonio, Texas. After nearly four decades of liberal policies, four years of Great Society funding, and four years of the War on Poverty, one would expect the hearings to have been a forum announcing the success of policies aimed at eliminating poverty and minimizing discrimination. They were not. The data presented to the committee painted a grim picture of the ethnic Mexican population in Texas and the nation, most of whom were US citizens.

The hearings began with bleak testimony from Domingo N. Reyes, a social science analyst for the US Commission on Civil Rights. He testified that Mexican Americans had been bypassed in the prosperity of the postwar American economy and were not extended the protections of the American welfare state. The US-born Mexican population in Texas was overwhelmingly urban, young, undereducated, and poor. Nationally, 80 percent of US-born Mexicans lived in urban areas. Texas mirrored this trend. More than 60 percent of US-born Mexican lived in towns with population over 10,000 people, and one-third of US-born Mexicans resided in San Antonio, El Paso, or Houston. Their median age was eighteen years, compared to twenty-seven and twenty-four years of age for Anglo-Americans and African Americans, respectively. The average ethnic Mexican fourteen-year-old had completed 6.2 years of education, compared to 10.7 years for white Americans and 8.7 years for African Americans. Nearly 40 percent of adult US-born Mexicans in Texas had

Tenement houses on the west side of San Antonio, Texas, 1960s.
Photograph by John Poindexter. University of Texas San Antonio Special Collections (082-0550).

completed fewer than four years of education. Nearly 80 percent of the US-born Mexican population between the ages of twenty and forty-nine had never completed the twelfth grade. The median family income for US-born Mexicans in 1960 was only $1,536 (less than $13,500 in 2020 when adjusted for inflation), which was 57 percent of whites' median income. In San Antonio, only 60 percent of US-born Mexicans lived in housing designated as "sound" in the 1960 US census.[1]

The wages and living conditions of the US-born Mexican population in Texas had not changed significantly between the 1930s and 1960s. A 1938 study of ethnic Mexicans in Crystal City found the average annual family income was $561, which was almost two times higher than the income of their peers in San Antonio.[2] Adjusted for inflation, the 1938 family income in Crystal City would equate to $1,161 in 1960 dollars, nearly identical to the median income of US-born Mexicans in that year.[3] Because of poor housing and a lack of running water, between 1936 and 1938, in counties with an ethnic Mexican population of more

This image of homes in San Antonio, Texas, shows ethnic Mexican living conditions in March 1939.
Photograph by Russell Lee. Library of Congress, Prints & Photographs Division, Farm Security Administration Office of War Information Photograph Collection (LC-DIG-fsa-8a25702).

than 20 percent, children under two years of age were more than eight times more likely to die from diarrhea than in the remainder of the state, and as the concentration of ethnic Mexicans increased, so did that rate. In 1944, the tuberculosis rate among US-born Mexicans was nearly seven times higher than that among Anglo-Americans, at 209 per 100,000 compared to 31 per 100,000. Not surprisingly, the death rate among US-born Mexicans was seven times that of Anglos.[4]

Such findings challenged the US-born Mexican population to explain why poverty, disease, and exploitation persisted nearly unchanged between the 1930s and 1960s. Young US-born Mexican activists would begin to criticize US political and economic structures. But many Mexican Americans who came of age in the mid-twentieth century could not reject the collection of ideas, policies, and solutions that explained inequality and discrimination through modernization theory. For them, and the larger domestic social science field, American history, American principles, American liberalism, and American capitalism provided a road map for social equality through economic growth at home and abroad.

In the postwar decades leading up to the Chicana/o Movement, American liberalism and global liberation shared an intellectual space. In Mexican American liberalism the ideas of belonging rooted in citizenship that had emerged in the 1920s and 1930s matured and established themselves in postwar American politics, with implications for both domestic and foreign policy. As the language of self-determination spread globally over the course of the twentieth century, local geographic and political translations transformed its meanings, but those meanings were still bound to the liberal grammar of the American-led liberal international order, which was directly connected to American statist liberalism at home. American liberalism shaped the arc, narrative, tools, endpoint, and understanding of social change and how to achieve it. The United States was the model, the archetype, and proof of its success, and Mexican Americans needed to mold themselves into participants in that story and the positive social transformations of American liberalism.

THE WILSONIAN MOMENT AND THE AMERICAN CENTURY

After World War II the United States would spearhead the creation of a new liberal international order that promised an end to the colonial order that unfairly extracted resources and imposed markets on colonies while oppressing colonial subjects. Political sovereignty and individual autonomy were universal desires of humankind, American leaders asserted. The foundations of this liberal international order were laid after World War I, during what the historian Erez Manela has labeled the "Wilsonian moment." For a brief instant President Woodrow Wilson became a global icon associated with a new vision of the world as an international society based on self-determination.[5] What was important about the American challenge to the international status quo was that it coopted the language of anticolonial activism, which had been closely associated with communist and Bolshevik movements, and tied it to an American grammar, effectively changing the meanings, purposes, and outcomes of the words. For many at the time, "independence," "liberation," and "social change," meant violence. In particular, Bolsheviks used the term "self-determination" in the context of a violent revolutionary overthrow of colonial rule. When Wilson began to articulate his understanding of self-determination after 1918, it meant popular sovereignty, or democracy.[6] The transformation of the global order would involve European countries voluntarily relinquishing their colonies, an end to war, democratic elections, free trade, and an international order composed of sovereign, equal nation-states represented in a global body. These changes were important in beginning a "movement away from empire and toward the self-determining nation-state as the organizing principle of governance in the non-European world."[7]

The language promulgated on the world stage influenced both American ideas about social change and colonies struggling for colonial liberation. The universal language and promises of American-style self-determination cast the United States as a supporter of global change and made its history an example to follow. The United States was a model for the future, and other countries could model its past. For colonial subjects, the universal language assured them that they should indeed be included in the promises of the new international order, that they were right to demand inclusion and that they had every right to equal status.

The concepts of self-determination; independence; liberation; and a fair, equal international order based on mutual respect among sovereign independent nation-states would be revived during and after World War II. In the late 1930s, US and Latin American bureaucrats explored possible experiments with international development financing that would become influential in the eventual 1944 Bretton Woods agreement.[8] Concerned about the possibility of war in the Western Hemisphere, in 1933 the United States initiated the Good Neighbor Policy, aimed at building unity across the Americas. The program had various cultural, economic, and even domestic components, but many Latin American nations particularly welcomed US abandonment of the "dollar diplomacy" of the late nineteenth and early twentieth centuries and adoption of an international model of the reformed capitalism of the New Deal. In 1939, as part of the Good Neighbor Policy, the

United States planned a new lending program that would be different from the extractive investment and banking practices of the previous era. In marking this shift, the assistant secretary of state for Latin American affairs declared that "economic imperialism is dead as the brontosaur." The Inter-American Bank was intended to pioneer a new model of international lending that would provide poorer nations with the credit and capital they needed to develop mature industrial economies and infrastructures, without foreign control or manipulation.[9] The bank was never established, but the planning for it was influential in the later creation of the World Bank and International Monetary Fund.

The 1941 Atlantic Charter, signed by the United States and Great Britain, revealed the level to which colonial independence and free trade were mutually reinforcing even before the end of the war. The charter promised "the enjoyment by all States, great or small, victor or vanquished, of access, on equal terms, to the trade and to the raw materials of the world which are needed for their economic prosperity."[10] The United Nations was built on the principle that the independence, integrity, and sovereignty of each nation-state, whether large or small, had to be recognized in the world in order to avoid another global war. To end imperialism and the messy alliances that had plunged the world into war, the world would be organized into independent states. To end genocide, each state would protect the rights of citizens. To avoid world war, nation-states would practice free but fair trade. At the core of all these ideas was the centrality of the independent nation-state. It secured and made possible all necessary rights.[11]

These principles are reflected in article 1 of the Charter of the United Nations, signed in 1945. It reads, "The Purposes of the United Nations are to develop friendly relations among nations based on respect for the principle of equal rights and self-determination of peoples, and to take other appropriate measures to strengthen universal peace."[12] The charter of the Organization of American States, adopted in 1948, more emphatically emphasize the sovereignty of the nation-state and its connection to self-determination. Article 9 reads,

> The political existence of the State is independent of recognition by other States. Even before being recognized, the State has the

right to defend its integrity and independence, to provide for its preservation and prosperity, and consequently to organize itself as it sees fit, to legislate concerning its interests, to administer its services, and to determine the jurisdiction and competence of its courts. The exercise of these rights is limited only by the exercise of the rights of other States in accordance with international law.[13]

This emphasis on national sovereignty and self-determination as democratic practices co-opted a worldwide radical language of the early twentieth century and fused it to a mid-twentieth-century liberal American grammar. The implication was that other nations could follow the American past into a brighter future, led by Americans of course. Political and human evolution had culminated in the American model. If other nations wanted to evolve through the stages of growth required to achieve modernity, American liberalism was the way to achieve it.

Americans' certainty in their models and solutions to social problems like inequality, poverty, and discrimination took shape in modernization theory. After World War II, the US government believed it was responsible for leading the world toward peace and prosperity. Many politicians, policy makers, academics, and others believed that the United States had managed something other countries, peoples, and ideologies had failed to do: create long-lasting positive social change, without violent conflict or communism. The United States had achieved this change through liberal democratic reform of capitalism and other countries could replicate this model to achieve similar outcomes. New Deal bureaucracies like the WPA, Public Works Administration, and others could be scaled up to international bureaucracies like the International Monetary Fund or the World Bank.

Modernization theory, which was the driving ideology of both US foreign policy and much of US social science, rested upon some crucial assumptions. The first was that all human beings had similar desires, wants, and needs, which could be expressed as universal truths. Others included that there was a sharp distinction between "traditional" and "modern" societies; that social, political, and economic changes were interconnected; that progress toward modern societies was linear and unidirectional; and that interaction with developed nations could catalyze progress in un- and underdeveloped nations.[14] Crucial was the presumption of American superiority—in cultural if not necessarily racial terms. As the best example of a nation-state that had achieved economic, social, and political modernity, the United States sat at the apex of universal development; evolution; and social, political, and economic organization. Most importantly, it had achieved that status without turning to communism, violence, or Marxism.

Modernization theory envisioned development as a universal process that progressed along the same linear path for all nations, and that foreign aid could stimulate exogenously. Theorists like Walt Rostow, in his *Stages of Economic Growth: A Non-Communist Manifesto* (1960), offered an alternative model to Marx's dialectic and model of inevitable conflict. Rostow argued that nations and cultures passed through uniform stages from "traditional societies" to an "age of high mass consumption."[15] The postwar United States was the ostensible example proving the validity of modernization theory and its models of linear development. Of course, the persistence of discrimination and economic inequality among communities of color in the United States, including the ethnic Mexican community, tarnished the image of the United States as a global model. Nonetheless, Mexican Americans, like many educated people, believed in these ideas and ideologies. Modernization theory rested on the epistemological authority of a "science of society" and Mexican Americans worked to make themselves part of it.[16]

INTEGRATING MEXICAN AMERICANS INTO AMERICAN HISTORICAL MODELS

Modernization theory was in many ways a theory of history that affected both the present and the future. The right history could provide a blueprint for nations to alter their future for the better. The paramount model was the American past, and the American Revolution in particular. The American Revolution could not be portrayed as radical, because radicalism was communistic. Instead, the Revolution needed to be liberal, legal, rational, and orderly. It could not be a class-based conflict, as Progressive historians of the early twentieth century had asserted. Instead, it was presented as stable and ordered because the United States lacked the history of class conflict and division that existed in Europe.

In 1959, John Higham critiqued the emerging historiographical school on the Revolution as "consensus history." Consensus historians explained the Revolutionary era as one where rational people created a stable rational order through legal means that protected individual and property rights. Historians like Richard Hofstadter, Daniel J. Boorstin, Louis Hartz, and David Potter gave modernization theorists the necessary evidence of a universal continuum of sociopolitical development embodied in the US past. Using their historical interpretations of the American Revolution, historians, social scientists, and policy makers believed that twentieth century colonies need not turn to Marx or violence but could follow the American model, which was Lockean and legal. As historian Nils Gilman explains, "the consensus historians view of American society and history as an unchanging story of conservative liberalism provided the basic vision for modernization theorists of what a healthy modern polity should look like."[17]

If American history provided the model for development, then Mexican Americans needed to make themselves part of that past, even though their material reality of poverty and discrimination in many ways challenged the central conceit of modernization theory. Throughout the mid-twentieth century Mexican Americans continued to seek a way to include themselves in modernization. Though Mexican Americans did not play a part in the American Revolution or in the civilizing mission of Manifest Destiny, they wrote themselves into the historical narrative through the Spanish Conquest, the Texas Revolution, and specific folk heroes.

In a time when the United States was modeled as the apex of human development, Mexican Americans wanted to be included in that narrative. They knew that the prominent parables of the nation's past excluded them. In order to secure their belonging they needed to add themselves to the central stories that the nation told about itself, but preferably without challenging the basic plot of US history.[18] In that context, in 1931 LULAC President M. C. González urged his peers to learn the history of the United States: "I would say that if you want to be a one hundred percent American citizen you must first learn the history of the United States, the meaning of the American Flag, understand the Federal Constitution and have a sufficient background of English History to really appreciate the sacrifices of our fore-fathers who gave to this blessed land of freedom."[19] González's emphasis on history was not accidental. The ideology of Mexican Americanism aimed to cement US-born Mexican belonging in the United States through a specific understanding of citizenship.

Early on, Mexican Americans tried to reproduce American nationalism. One Mexican American wrote, "I know the history of our Country and its glory for which I am ready to sacrifice my existence." He emphasized the sacrifice of US-born Mexican soldiers who died in US wars: "their departed spirits mingle now beyond, together with those of Washington, Lincoln, and Thomas Jefferson in the camp of ETERNAL REST."[20] Yet it was difficult for Mexican Americans to sustain this narrative. The OSA's official hymn was "America."[21] But there was dissonance in singing of the "land of pilgrim's pride" which most certainly did not include Tejanos or Hispanos.

For this reason, Mexican Americans quickly adapted the story of Spanish colonization of the Southwest as a partner to the French and British colonization of the East. Mexican Americans often reminded Anglo-American audiences, with direct intent, that the Spanish were also white. Through the Spanish presence, Mexican Americans were able to participate in the civilizing and Christianizing mission of the United States—the benign colonization that led to American expansion. Ethnic Mexicans were neither brutes nor barbarous Indians but white Europeans whose lineage made them fit for citizenship and gave them a parallel narrative of belonging to the nation.

The story of Spanish colonization and Texan independence proved incredibly useful because the story paralleled the developments of the American Revolution. Texans often used both myths interchangeably, a fact that Mexican Americans used to their advantage, as this 1931 newspaper article makes clear:

> We have been taught from the very wee years of our existence the true meaning of what the stars and stripes stand for; what

> price our forefathers paid for Texas Independence, and that includes Don Lorenzo de Zavala, Garzas, Gonzalezes, Ruizes, Garcias and Navarros etc. and many others of Mexican and Spanish extraction. They did their part besides those most renowned heroes of Alamo, Goliad, and San Jacinto whom we all know made it possible that Texas might also be embraced by that benign tree of liberty "the Constitution of the United States of America."[22]

In 1936, as Texas celebrated the centennial of its independence, Rubén Rendon Lozano, a San Antonio lawyer and the chairman of LULAC's state education committee, published *Viva Tejas: The Story of the Mexican-Born Patriots of the Republic of Texas.*[23] Lozano was very much part of the Mexican American attempt to add US-born Mexicans to the story that the nation told of itself, without altering too many of its themes. Lozano emphasized that the Texas Revolution was a joint effort of Anglos and Mexicans. He pointed out that Mexican Americans were still fighting for liberty and quintessentially American ideals. Throughout the work he drew explicit parallels between Texas and the United States, referring to Texan settlers, both Mexican and Anglo, as "citizens" whose "hearts were trembling for liberty" and calling the battle of Gonzalez the "Lexington of Texas."[24] A few pages later, he made explicit connections between the events in 1836 and the American Revolution: "exactly sixty-one years after the Battle of Lexington, Houston crossed the Buffalo Bayou."[25] Lozano concludes *Viva Tejas* with a revealing statement: "may the progress made in these one hundred years of Texas freedom carry us even farther in the direction of Americanizing this native population. . . . Today, on the hundredth anniversary of the events which created history, the descendants of those patriots whether Mexican-Texan or American-Texan, share equally the glory of a resplendent ancestry."[26]

This strategy of establishing belonging through reimagining the history of Mexican Americans in the American nation continued. LULAC member J. C. Machuca wrote in a 1938 letter, "we are *not* United States citizens by conquest. Our forebears fought for the independence of Texas, and most of us were born in this country subsequent to the time

Texas was admitted to Union."[27] In another letter, he elaborated his understanding of US-born Mexicans' role in Texas history:

> Texas was not conquered. There is abundant proof that Texas won its independence from Mexico and it existed as an independent republic for over a decade, before it became a state of the Union. In fighting for its independence many Texas patriots of Mexican extraction participated actively in the Military campaigns. Such Texas patriots as Lorenzo de Zavala, Colonel Juan N. Seguin, Jose Antonio Navarro, Placido Benavides, and a host of others rendered valiant services for the independence of Texas.[28]

The historian Carlos E. Castañeda contributed to this historiographical project with his 1939 article "The Contribution of the Mexican to the Development of Texas." In it, he maintained that "there is no other racial group in the cosmopolitan population of the state of Texas that has contributed more to its history, its material and cultural development, than the Mexican." Adding that "it is necessary to remember that as inevitable conflict with Mexico became clear, many of the Mexicans in Texas not only believed the new colonists were right but they made [independence] their own cause," Castañeda concluded by vociferously reminding his readers that three Tejanos signed the Texas Declaration of Independence.[29]

In the 1940s, many leading Mexican Americans were able to use the rhetoric and ideas of the Good Neighbor Policy for their own purposes, domesticating this international program aimed at hemispheric unity in order to protect Mexican-American civil rights.[30] For them, the Good Neighbor Policy and the subsequent Texas Good Neighbor Commission (created in 1943) offered a way to achieve a "double victory" during World War II; namely, victory abroad and equality at home.[31] The treatment of ethnic Mexicans in Texas became the proving ground of US "neighborliness."[32] Undergirding the Good Neighbor Policy was the concept of Pan-Americanism, that all people of the Americas shared similar values, traits, and identities. George I. Sánchez, a University of Texas professor and New Deal–era bureaucrat, contributed to the development of Pan-Americanism by authoring the Inter-American textbook series aimed at intercultural education for Macmillan Publishing Company. At a time when most textbooks about and popular depictions of ethnic Mexicans were derogatory at best and discriminatory at worst, Sánchez's series described ethnic Mexican and Latin American culture in a positive light and as a corollary to American culture. Ethnic Mexican culture in the United States, especially, showed the compatibility and connection of US and Latin American cultures.[33]

Sánchez's contemporary and fellow University of Texas professor Carlos Castañeda also used Pan-Americanism as a discursive avenue to include Mexican Americans in greater American narratives. Castañeda built on the influential American historian Frederick Jackson Turner's idea that the frontier was the defining feature of American history and culture, as adapted by Herbert Eugene Bolton, who focused on the Spanish movement northward into what is now the US Southwest. For Bolton and Castañeda, the Spanish represented a similar civilizing force to American westward expansion. Civilization did not move only from east to west but also from south to north. As historian Natalie Mendoza explains of Castañeda, his "Boltonian interpretation of Latin American and US history . . . ultimately shaped the way he and other Mexican Americans imagined their sense of place as *Americans* in not just the US Southwest, but the western hemisphere."[34] The frontier was essential for Turner's and Bolton's understanding of progress. In fact, progress was metonymic with frontier, since the frontier was the very site where progress was made. Its adaptation and adoption by Mexican Americans like Castañeda and others was crucial in creating a hemispheric frontier where progress was made. Frontier was both a process and a place that centered Latin Americans, and especially Mexican Americans. They were not inferior; in the past, they had been civilizing agents and in the present they were civilized Americans.

The 1950s saw the publication of titles that connected the Mexican American ideological project of inclusion in the nation's history to similar strains in the consensus historiography. *Juan N. Cortina, Bandit or Patriot?* (1951), by former LULAC president and early proponent of Mexican Americanism J. T. Canales showed the maturation of Mexican Americanism and its project of writing ethnic Mexican contributions into US history. This short work made important revisions to the story of the popular nineteenth-century mexicano folk hero Juan N. Cortina, who shot an Anglo marshal in South Texas then occupied the city of Brownsville in protest against the treatment of Mexicans.[35] He was regarded as a bandit by most Anglos and as a hero by many ethnic Mexicans in Texas. In Canales's retelling, however, Cortina was not a bandit but a *citizen*, inspired by patriotism not violence. He rewrote the story of Cortina, removing him from both the Anglo story of banditry and violence and the mexicano story of folk heroism and anticolonial struggle and placing him within the boundaries of an emergent bourgeois Mexican American worldview.

In Canales's version, Cortina was an esteemed and honorable member of an elite Spanish hacendado family. Part of the reason that Cortina was reviled was that he had failed. Canales explained that "whether a man is called a 'bandit' or a 'hero' often depends just upon one word—SUCCESS; for very often a successful bandit turns out to be a real hero and a true patriot, such as our Washington."[36] Furthermore, Canales argued that Cortina never stole from anybody; he was only defending the rights of the people.[37] If cattle rustling occurred, it was only by a few unsavory individuals but definitely not Cortina. The idea that Mexican Americans were not conquered people, but a partner in the conquering, made it into his story. The Treaty of Guadalupe Hidalgo, which ended the Mexican-American War, was not a theft of Mexican lands but a document that established Mexican American citizenship. Because of this, Canales reasoned that Cortina was a US citizen who fought injustice. "There is no record that any of the Cavazos or Cortina ever formally repudiated their American citizenship; but there is abundant proof that they considered themselves American citizens and acted as such," he wrote.[38] The comparison to Washington was salient in Canales's rendition of Cortina's story. Cortina was not a racialized Mexican bandit, but a recognizably American citizen and patriot.

A similar example occurred at the July 1951 state convention of Latin American Leaders Creating a Texas Pro Human Relations Fund in Corpus Christi. The famed lawyer Gus C. García opened his keynote address with the question, "Just who are we and what are we doing in this State of Texas?" His answer, "We, the so-called Latin Americans, or Mexican-Americans, or Texas-Mexicans—take our choice as to terms because it really does not matter—I say we are here now because we were here first. . . . We are descendants in some instances of pioneers who helped forge a civilization two centuries ago."[39]

These historical interventions were part of a Mexican American intellectual project aimed at rewriting US-born Mexican contributions into to the main narratives of the nation. Mexican Americans did not want to upend the dominant historical narratives of the nation, but only to include themselves in the established plots. In terms of Texas history, Mexicans were not present at Valley Forge, Lexington, or Concord, but they were present at the Alamo and San Jacinto. They may not have ridden with Washington, but they did fight with Houston. These efforts in the Texas Revolution were just as important as participation in the American Revolution. Both were important developments in leading the United States to its position as world leader and global model.

Over the postwar years, Mexican Americanism matured and expanded beyond Texas. It was no longer an ideology with a limited geographic impact. Organizations that subscribed to it were spreading across the nation. LULAC had eighty chapters in Texas, New Mexico, Arizona, California, and Kansas by 1941.[40] The American GI Forum, an organization of Mexican American veterans formed in 1948, had chapters nationwide by 1958.[41]

In 1959, José Antonio Villarreal reintroduced and reinterpreted an insult that had been hurled at US-born Mexicans just decades before. His novel *Pocho*, distributed nationwide, was in conversation with the ideological developments in ethnic Mexican thought over the first half of the century. In the 1920s and 1930s, Mexican nationals had labeled US-born Mexicans "pochas/os," signifying effeminate cowards without a country (see chapter 1). *Pocho* revised and dramatically reordered that narrative.

The novel begins with the protagonist's father, Juan Rubio, leaving Mexico because the virtues and principles of the Mexican Revolution have been compromised. Mexican government officials are thieves who have made themselves rich by preying upon the poor. In *Pocho* the idea that only dishonored and emasculated Mexicans stay in the United States is overturned—quite the opposite, only true and honorable men leave Mexico for the United States. Juan Rubio is described as the zenith of manliness. Just before he shoots a light-skinned member of the elite for calling him a peon, Juan Rubio declares "the peon has larger balls than the city-bred gachupin."[42] The theme of US-Mexican masculinity permeates the book. Richard, the protagonist, enforces traditional gender roles in the family when his sisters refuse to keep up with the housework.[43]

In titling his novel *Pocho,* Villarreal demonstrated the confidence of late Mexican Americanism. Richard is unbothered by being called "pocho" because he sees himself as thoroughly American. Whereas his father, Juan, remembers Mexico nostalgically and wishes to return, Richard understands that he does not belong in Mexico. His place is in the United States. Hinting at key ideas of Mexican Americanism, Richard's primary concern is his individuality not his community. Indeed, he sees his community as a burden. "It bothered him that they [white liberals] should always try to find things in his life that could make him a martyr of some sort, and it pained him when they insisted he dedicate his life to the Mexican cause, because it was the same old story, and he was quite sure he did not really believe there was a Mexican cause—at least not in the world with which he was familiar," Richard explained.[44] The novel ends with Richard joining the US Navy to fight in World War II. Villarreal's emphasis on American citizenship, belonging in the United States, and assertion of Mexican American authenticity and virility illustrates that Mexican Americanism had solidified in the 1950s.

Mexican Americanism was clearly on the rise outside of Texas as well. In 1965, the major California Mexican American organizations (Mexican American Political Association, LULAC, the Community Service Organization, and the GI Forum) wrote a joint resolution to President Johnson asking for aid. Written in the language pioneered in Texas, it followed the ideological contours of Mexican Americanism: "Over 150 years ago, Spanish-speaking Mexican-Americans stopped the Russian colonial advance and conquest from Siberia and Alaska, and preserved the Western portion of the United States for our country, which at that time consisted of thirteen colonies struggling for their existence, into which nation we and our predecessors became incorporated as loyal citizens and trustworthy participants in its democratic forms of government."[45] According to this logic, US-born Mexicans were loyal citizens even before there was a nation, and they had resisted territorial incursions into the United States by the forerunners of the communist USSR. They had been fighting communism on American soil since at least the Spanish colonial period. While their logic was flawed, their ideology was clear.

Instead of writing a new narrative of the nation, Mexican Americanism made US-born Mexicans minor addenda to a teleology that reproduced American exceptionalism. They added to the idea that the history of the United States was not premised on the exploitation of an underclass or a rapacious capitalism that led to conflict, but was a God-inspired, under-analyzed teleology of success in which ethnic Mexicans took part. They made themselves part of American history, now they had to be part of the social models and the prosperity it produced. Mexican Americans believed that progress, development, and modernization would come to them through participating in American liberalism

MEXICAN AMERICAN LIBERATION THROUGH LIBERALISM

The international system that held up the United States as a global model for development and progress used American domestic policies and politics as evidence of its success. Since they had achieved modernization, peace, and prosperity at home, American policies could do the same abroad. During the postwar years a liberal consensus emerged in American politics. This consensus centered on government regulation of corporations, high tax rates, social safety nets (such as social security, public housing, and the GI Bill), commitment to public education, and commitment to defeating communism at home and abroad. The world needed to unite against the chaos wrought by two world wars and industrialization, but not through the proletarian revolution Karl Marx had envisaged in the mid-nineteenth century. Instead, the sociopolitical institution that would unite diverse political goals and social desires was the nation-state. The liberal state was the institution that could and would counter the influence and power of corporations and protect citizens from the economic insecurity endemic to capitalism. The liberal state could provide this kind of economic protection through social programs, paid for by taxes during periods of economic growth and deficit spending during moments of recession. Workers of the world did not need to unite, citizens of individual nation-states did. Regular people found the means to counter the disrupting and devastating effects of capitalism in Keynes, not Marx. Cooperation, not conflict, would win the day.

Mexican Americans believed that American liberalism would also improve their community's material condition and social status if they followed the developmental steps of growth within the nation. Once Mexican Americans educated and modernized themselves, then they would attain American prosperity. As Gus García explained, "The problem of Anglo-Latin relations in Texas can be reduced to its lowest denominator—if at all—on the basis of better educational and job opportunities for the minority—and of a more understanding and less unbending attitude on the part of the majority."[46]

Both Mexican American and Anglo-American liberals believed this. The former executive secretary of the Good Neighbor Commission of Texas, Pauline R. Kibbe, wrote in 1946 that although "our people of Mexican descent have generally adopted many of the dietary habits of the Anglo Americans," they still remained poor and in poor health.[47] This fact was especially troubling because Mexican Americans were, after all, Americans. "They know no other country, want no other country; yet they continue to be regarded as 'Mexicans' and considered as foreigners."[48] And while she was certain that the postwar American economy and liberal state could bring prosperity to Mexican Americans, they would need to move away from their traditional culture toward modern American culture. Discrimination and exploitation, she explained,

> could not prevail were it not rooted in the shortcomings of the Latin Americans: their exaggerated individualism and consequent lack of interest in cooperation toward a given goal; the personal, and frequently petty, jealousies and animosities which separate them and prevent their working together for the

> common good; even the desire and willingness on the part of some to curry favor with the political "powers that be" at the expense of the best interests of their own group. . . . Unity of purpose and a determination to subjugate personal considerations to loftier ends must be developed by Latin American leaders and political aspirants before the group as a whole can hope to secure adequate representation in city, county, state, and school government.[49]

For Kibbe and many others, a modern, educated, and developed leadership class was needed to push the Mexican American community along the stages of development.

In the 1940s and 1950s, a wave of Mexican American politicians won election across the United States. Raymond Telles was elected as El Paso County clerk in 1948 and then as El Paso mayor in 1957, the first Mexican American to be elected mayor of a major US city.[50] In 1953, Henry B. González won election to the San Antonio city council, the first Mexican American to do so in the modern period.[51] In 1956, González was elected to the Texas state senate, again the first Mexican American to accomplish this, and in 1961 he was elected to the US House of Representatives. Albert A. Peña Jr. was elected Bexar County clerk in 1956 and would hold that seat for sixteen years. These political victories epitomized the political aspirations of Mexican Americans.[52] They had achieved acceptance and had won election to political office because they were college educated, many were lawyers, and all were professionals. They had followed the stages of development, discarded the traditional, and moved toward the modern. They had earned belonging and prosperity by becoming true and loyal Americans

These Mexican American liberals limited their critiques of American institutions, which they believed were fundamentally sound. Liberal programs did need to be expanded, but the economic structures of the nation were working and it was Mexican Americans themselves who, in many ways, were preventing their own prosperity. These rather mild criticisms of American policies were limited by the Cold War context in the 1950s. During these years, domestic policies and civil rights problems could have international repercussions because of the perception that the United States was the prototype for how modern nation-states behaved.[53]

The political career of Albert A. Peña Jr. in San Antonio illustrates the development of this tension in Mexican American liberalism from the 1950s into the early 1960s. In 1956, Peña was elected Bexar County commissioner, with responsibility for hiring and directing funding for roads, bridges, and parks. Yet Mexican Americans across San Antonio would call Peña regularly to complain about police brutality, discrimination, crime, and poverty. He tried to do his best through hiring more Mexican Americans on road crews and hiring the first African American employees in the Bexar County government.[54] Eventually, Peña would begin using his position to sway popular opinion through regular columns in area newspapers, arguing for integration, liberal policies, and inclusion.

In 1960, Peña traveled to Los Angeles to attend the Democratic National Convention as the leader and sole voting US-born Mexican member of the Texas delegation. Using his power as the head of the powerful Texas delegation, Peña was able to ensure that a civil rights platform was adopted by the national convention.[55] Unfortunately, the liberal civil rights platform largely ignored the issues of the ethnic Mexican community in the United States. Coming out of the convention, Mexican American Democrats across the nation began to organize in support of Democratic presidential candidate John F. Kennedy. In Texas, Peña, Héctor P. García, and Henry B. González were the leaders of so-called Viva Kennedy clubs. The Viva Kennedy clubs were important in turning out Mexican American voters, which helped the Kennedy-Johnson ticket win Texas and the presidency. The Viva Kennedy clubs built upon the membership of organizations like LULAC and the GI Forum, the latter of which supported the clubs because of Héctor P. García's central role in them. The Viva Kennedy clubs were short-lived, only lasting three months before the election.[56] In the process, Peña and Mexican American liberals learned that just because political promises were made, that did not mean they would be fulfilled. They received few of the political spoils they had helped others earn.

Although frustrated, Peña continued to believe in the promises of liberalism. He defended civil rights through anticommunism. In a letter asking a movie theater manager to integrate his theater, he wrote "you cannot preach democracy to the world if you do not practice it at home."[57] In response to being ignored politically by the Kennedy administration, Peña and others created a new organization, the Political Association of Spanish Speaking Organizations (PASO) in 1962. PASO represented a significant political development, as its goal was the election of Mexican American candidates, but it continued speaking the language of mainstream liberalism.[58] In his address to the Texas state PASO convention, Peña declared that the organization should "play the role of the conscience of the Liberal movement [and] the Democratic Party." He explained that his belief in liberalism was based "on a simple but eternal credo that all men are born in the image of God; and that all men are endowed by their Creator with certain inalienable rights." He added that "in the liberal Democratic Party of Franklin D. Roosevelt, Harry Truman, and John F. Kennedy," liberalism promised a job, decent wages, an education, a moderate workday, the availability of quality medical care to all, and decent housing. Because these benefits of a healthy and equitable democracy were not available to all, "we have failed as a liberal movement."[59]

An important event that pushed Peña to the left of mainstream liberalism occurred at the 1962 conference of the Equal Employment Opportunity Commission in Washington, DC. Peña and a handful of other Mexican American politicians who attended the conference quickly discovered that the US-born Mexican community was being overlooked, in large part because American liberalism understood race relations in terms of black and white.[60] When Peña approached the commission about the problems facing the ethnic Mexican community in Texas and the Southwest, the members of the commission were unaware of the issues and unenthusiastic about offering solutions. They told Peña that Mexicans did not "raise hell enough" to get noticed."[61] Frustrated, he returned to San Antonio and spoke at LULAC Council No. 2, demanding that they march, protest, and demonstrate. The members of LULAC were unmoved, and Peña's calls for more militant protest "went over like a dull thud."[62]

In September 1962, Peña went to the state Democratic convention in El Paso. The Texas Democratic Party, in particular, had no interest in a civil rights platform or social reform aimed at the ethnic Mexican community. In fact, the conservative Democrats leading the state party opposed such measures.[63] Peña left the convention frustrated and angry.

Through PASO, he went looking for a project and found the small Texas town of Crystal City (Cristal in Spanish) as a potential case study to demonstrate the electoral power of the US-born Mexican community.[64] Peña was going to test the promises of self-determination in the United States through electoral politics in 1963.

Crystal City was a small spinach-growing town in the Winter Garden of Texas, just southwest of San Antonio. Ethnic Mexicans composed 80 percent of the population.[65] Mexican-origin voters outnumbered Anglo voters by nearly two to one. PASO was invited to join a struggle led by the local Teamsters union aimed at electing an all-US-born Mexican slate to the city council. The Teamsters had already organized but wanted PASO to give them a more legitimate cover to organize under.[66] The campaign was staffed by Teamsters but run by PASO. The campaign succeeded, and in 1963 Crystal City elected an all US-Mexican city council, after the Teamsters and PASO purchased 1,129 poll taxes while Anglos purchased only 542.[67]

This marked a different strategy for PASO and a significant break with liberalism and Mexican Americanism. Instead of organizing the relatively affluent Mexican American middle class, the coalition targeted the working class. Martin García, the PASO district director sent from San Antonio to organize the efforts in Crystal City, explained, "We cultivate the lower class. The middle-class Latin American doesn't have many grievances. There are few new frontiers for him."[68] Instead of using euphemistic terms like "Mexican-American" and "Spanish-American," the coalition used "mexicanos" in its mailings to build community support.[69] Middle-class Mexican Americans were divided over the victory. They had spent years working to be accepted by whites as benign, fellow middle-class citizens. The political takeover by five politically inexperienced and uneducated candidates threatened their accommodationist perspective and politics.[70]

LULAC and even more so the GI Forum disapproved of PASO's Crystal City strategy. GI Forum head Héctor García adamantly opposed the involvement of the Teamsters union.[71] The GI Forum believed PASO should not be involved in issues like those in Crystal City, considering the campaign too radical, too distant from the liberal center. The Texas Rangers had called the organizers in Crystal City "communists" and the veterans group did not want to be involved with communists. The GI Forum felt that PASO "had no business interfering with the city over there."[72] This opposition would cause a growing schism in PASO.

At the GI Forum convention that year in Corpus Christi, the conservative contingent was unhappy with Peña's leadership of PASO, but he was scheduled to give the opening address. Unsure of the reception he would receive, Peña delivered his speech anyway. If García and others were looking for an apology, they did not receive one. He was adamant: "I do not apologize for Crystal City. I do not apologize for Crystal City . . . and we need more Crystal Cities. This is what PASO is all about. If it isn't, then we don't deserve to be here."[73] Later he wrote to Héctor García that PASO was part of a "more militant posture of our people in the last few years. No one can deny that there is a revolution stirring in our people in Texas."[74]

Crystal City represented the apex of PASO. Although the organization would continue under the leadership of Peña, its broad liberal coalition had dissolved. Mexican American liberals refused to adopt a more confrontational approach—revealing the cracks and contradictions in the movement that Peña and his allies had already recognized in the early 1960s. By 1964, it was clear that Peña was moving in a direction that was politically and ideologically different from mainstream liberalism and Mexican Americanism. It was not deferential or accommodating to Anglo liberals or politicians. In a speech to the McAllen chapter of PASO that year, Peña contemplated US-born Mexican political and cultural autonomy: "I say to one and all that in PASO we have no political bosses, no political machines, no tio Tomases [Uncle Toms], and we are not for sale. No somos vendidos."[75]

Peña broke from liberal and Mexican American explanations of cultural deficiency as the origins of economic subordination. The relegation of the ethnic Mexican community to the bottom of the socioeconomic ladder was not due to some inherent flaw in US-Mexican culture but was a product of racial discrimination. He argued that "discrimination, indifference, and poverty have combined to give the Mexican-American minority the highest illiteracy rate of any ethnic or racial group in the United States."[76] In a 1965 article, he connected racism and poverty similarly: "In San Antonio poverty is color. It's also language. The color is Black and the language is Spanish. If anyone doubts this all they have to do is visit the poverty areas in San Antonio."[77]

By 1966, Peña was pushing further away from middle-class Mexican Americanism. In a speech to PASO, he ridiculed middle-class Mexican Americans who thought demonstrations were beneath them. "The Tio Tomases said, 'March? Demonstrate? Why, that's below our dignity.' Where is your dignity if you live in poverty, if you have a high illiteracy rate, if you receive lower wages than your Anglo counterpart, and if you suffer job discrimination." Peña announced that the new role of PASO was not to elect middle-class liberals but to organize the community in "the militant protest of injustice. . . . To organize the unorganized into a more militant posture. This is the role of PASO. To push into a more militant posture the Tio Tomases—whether he wear khakis or a Brooks Brothers suit."[78]

THE LIMITS OF LIBERATION THROUGH LIBERALISM

Peña began his political career as a mainstream liberal, but by 1966 he was testing American liberalism's promise of delivering the revolution, self-determination, and community liberation it was purported to produce on a global stage. Because few in the United States believed that the election of an entirely US-born Mexican city council could ever happen, many believed a "revolution" was indeed occurring in South Texas. Unfortunately, two years later all of "Los Cinco," as they were called, were voted out of office after failing to make substantive changes in the city.[79] It was a stinging defeat as things went back to the way they used to be in Cristal.

The election of Los Cinco was not the beginning of the Chicano Movement but the beginning of the end of Mexican Americanism, which proved unable to win a victory against an entrenched and racialized system of exclusion and discrimination. Many of the hopes of Mexican Americanism—belief in electoral politics, gradual change, accommodationist policies—were tested in Cristal, but there was still no appreciable change after two years. This failure would leave a lasting impact.

In 1968, a graduate student from Crystal City named José Ángel Gutiérrez completed his master's thesis in political science at St. Mary's University in San Antonio. Gutiérrez had been present in Cristal during the election of Los Cinco five years earlier and had participated in organizing as a young teenager. His master's thesis, titled "La Raza and Revolution," laid out his theoretical understanding of social change and was influenced by what he witnessed as well as extensive reading. An important activist in the burgeoning Chicana/o Movement, he cofounded the Mexican American Youth Organization (MAYO) and the Raza Unida Party, a Chicana/o political third party. He stated that "the empirical conditions for revolution have been found to exist in the four counties in South Texas . . . as the rest of the evidence in this thesis indicates, the Mexican American will revolt."[80]

Although Gutiérrez used the increasingly radical anticolonial rhetoric emerging from third world nationalists, his language was still bound by the liberal grammar of the prevailing social sciences of his time. When he spoke of revolution, he meant large-scale social change. When he wrote about violence in the revolution, he referred to direct actions, protests, and picketing. When discussing class conflict as the defining feature of human history, he cited Plato not Marx. And, in a rebuke of Louis Hartz, he argued that Locke established the "right to rebel" and the "moral obligation to revolt" if political systems in general and in the United States in particular failed to rest on the consent of the governed.[81] He reasoned that South Texas was more like the third world than the rest of the United States, comparing it to Latin America under a stable dictatorship.[82] The goal of Mexican-origin activism then, the final act of liberation that would achieve self-determination, was not a violent war but the creation of a third party composed exclusively of Mexican Americans in South Texas counties where they had sufficient demographic numbers to take control of political offices and systems. They would then enact a "radical redistribution of political power to include Mexican-Americans" in order to "promote the interest of Mexican Americans only."[83] Importantly, Gutiérrez's desire was not a redistribution of wealth along Marxist lines, but instead a redistribution of political power. He was testing the limits of electoral politics to achieve Mexican American self-determination, pushing liberalism to the edge in order to achieve liberation.

Gutiérrez's thesis and the 1968 Civil Rights Commission report showed that domestic and international developmentalist models were being tested. Whereas Gutiérrez tried to include ethnic Mexicans within social science models, sociologist David Montejano claimed social science explanations modeled on developmentalist explanations were incapable of explaining the politicization of US-born Mexicans that was occurring in Texas and the Southwest. As a Yale University graduate student in the 1970s, Montejano had been trained in the various ideas of Edward Banfield, Leo Lowenthal, Eric Hobsbawm, and Antonio Gramsci. Although diverse, these theorists shared an idea that lower-class youth—the lumpen—could not arrive at a political consciousness because they were impossibly underdeveloped or unalterably arrested. Initially Montejano tried to use Hobsbawm's idea of "primitive rebels" to explain US-born Mexican youth and their politicization. Eventually, however, he concluded that "literature of all political persuasions saw lower-class culture, and particular male culture, as violent-prone, pleasure-seeking, and authoritarian: to be eradicated, according to one side; to be dismissed, according to the other."[84]

Consequently, Montejano decided to study the Brown Berets in San Antonio's Southside and across Texas. Founded in Los Angeles in 1967, the Brown Berets quickly spread across the working-class barrios of the Southwest. As a sociologist, Montejano wanted to understand how "batos locos" (literally, "crazy guys," figuratively "street youth") became political activists. He had imagined these two groups as opposite poles of political development—on one end was "being loco" and on the other was "being political."[85] The more he studied the Brown Berets, the clearer it became that the prevailing social scientific theories which offered neat linear developments failed to explain the group. Given that the "science of society" failed to explain the persistence of ethnic Mexican poverty and racial discrimination, he abandoned his dissertation to develop a new explanatory model.[86] He instead turned to historical sociology to explain the cause of a "segregated social-political order."[87] After more research and the emergence of world-systems theory, he offered his initial explanation: "For the development of labor-repressive agriculture in Texas in the twentieth century cannot be seen as some 'anomalous' capitalist transformation; rather it must be seen as the type of development made possible by racial domination in the internal peripheries of a 'core state.'"[88] Montejano concluded that ethnic Mexicans in the United States were not culturally deficient or developmentally arrested. Instead, their poverty and racial discrimination were central features of American capitalism and culture. US-born Mexicans were not aberrant or culpable for their "underdevelopment"; capitalist development and maturation was to blame.

Modernization theory was being tested on both domestic and international levels, and it quickly collapsed by the mid-1970s. The earliest promising efforts of the developmental model never came to fruition. For example, the Inter-American Bank, intended to provide for the "economic liberation of Latin America," died in committee without ever coming before the US Senate for a vote.[89] By 1943, the Good Neighbor Policy had given way to a binational labor agreement between the United States and Mexico (the Bracero Program) and to a focus on discrimination against ethnic Mexicans in the Southwest (the Texas Good Neighbor Commission).[90] After the meetings at Bretton Woods, Latin American nations started to lose confidence in the possibility of a reformed liberal international order in which capitalism would allow poor nations to develop mature and equitable economies. Modernization theory was increasingly criticized by both left and right.

Across the third world anticolonial nationalists began to reject the imposed stages of development, the cultural conditions necessary for those stages, and the economic policies of the United States. In place of individually contained nation-states bound to achieve economic and cultural uniformity, they saw nations interconnected in a single economic world system that created different deeply unequal outcomes for individual nations.[91] As Immanuel Wallerstein, one of the leading theorists of world-systems theory, remembered it, social scientists did not begin challenging the assumption that the next stage of development could be reached out of some ideological or dogmatic belief, but because their own experiences in the late 1960s showed that the distance between rich and poor nations and groups was increasing.[92] In place of a set of independent but essentially similar nation-states in a linear movement toward development, they turned to an understanding of the world as an integrated whole operating within an integral economic system.

In *The Development of Underdevelopment* (1967), the economist Andre Gunder Frank introduced dependency theory, which postulated that underdevelopment was a result not of traditional cultural stagnation, but of first world economic development.[93] Many Latin American intellectuals turned toward this theory, which broke the historical teleology of development. A combination of dependency theory; English translations of works by third world anticolonial writers like Frantz Fanon, Aimé Césaire, and Albert Memmi; the Vietnam War; and the failure of American-style liberalism at home and abroad broke the prevailing "science of society" and shattered belief in the inherent cultural superiority of American models.

Whereas in the 1950s and early 1960s, third world countries had used American theoretical models to diagnose their shortcomings, by the late 1960s and 1970s Chicana/o academics and activists were using third world theoretical models to diagnose American shortcomings. US Chicanas and Chicanos rejected the prevailing cultural deficiency theories that blamed the Mexican American community itself for poverty and discrimination. The problem was not that Mexican Americans lacked the cultural, economic, and political preconditions for prosperity, but rather that they were a colonized people. US institutions were not liberal, they were colonial. Racial subordination and capitalist extraction were their primary function. Chicanas and Chicanos represented an internal colony, a colony inside the United States.[94]

In viewing their people as colonized, Chicanas and Chicanos were influenced by Latin American intellectuals and liberation movements. The term "internal colony" was coined by the Mexican social scientist Pablo González Casanova, who used it in reference to indigenous people in Mexico. Chicanas/os applied it to describe their subordinate status within their own homeland, which had been absorbed into a nation-state.[95] Chicanas and Chicanos were, as sociologist Tomás Almaguer explained, "indigenous people of what is today the Southwestern states" and "the United States wasted little time in adding Mexican land, raw materials, and labor to its growing empire. Within several decades Anglo domination and Mexican subjugation had become a complete and irreversible reality in the Southwest."[96]

This younger, more theoretically radical group of academics and activists challenged the Mexican American conceptualization of belonging to the United States, as well as its prevailing belief in citizenship and liberalism. Instead, armed with internal colonial and dependency theories, they imagined a Chicano nation, Aztlán. Aztlán was an amorphous concept. Some imagined it as a colonized territory that would eventually gain liberation and become an independent nation-state, providing Chicanas and Chicanos equal footing, sovereignty, and recognition in the international order. Some believed such a nation-state would prove that US-born Mexicans were capable of attaining political development. But for others, Aztlán was not an actual independent nation-state but a mythical Chicana/o homeland that offered an alternative discursive space and history to reject the racialized and exclusive foundations of US citizenship and the US nation-state.

Chicanas' and Chicanos' rejection of central Mexican American ideological tenets angered their liberal elders. LULAC member Jacob Rodríguez wrote in a lengthy screed,

> the younger generation doesn't know any better. It still has a lot to learn. . . . Our youngsters' lack of living, practical experience and comprehension is impelling them to "identify" with something and—unfortunately for them and all the rest of us—they don't even know what with or why. All they feel is that this word is a call to rebellion. . . . Imagine burning your own Flag for something like that, and hoisting a foreign, alien, flag in its place! Only the years will teach them better![97]

The venerable liberal congressman from San Antonio Henry B. González tried to undermine the budding Chicano Movement.[98] He berated Chicano Movement leaders, ideas, and organizations, in 1969 even calling the youth "new racists." Refusing to acknowledge any fault in American liberalism or modernization theory, he proclaimed adamantly, "I cannot accept the argument that this is an evil country or that our system does not work. . . . I cannot find evidence that there is any country in the world that matches the progress of this one."[99] He would continue staunchly defending Mexican Americanism and attacking the younger activists for their lack of patriotism and their portrayal of the US-born Mexican community as an internal colony.

To understand Mexican American liberalism and liberationist Chicana/o nationalisms at midcentury, it is necessary to understand the shared intellectual space of liberalism and liberation in the twentieth century. Chicano liberation used anticolonial language that was given meaning but also constrained by a liberal grammar. At the end of World War I President Woodrow Wilson co-opted the term "self-determination" from Bolshevism and communism. Instead of a revolutionary self-determination that required violence and bloodshed, Wilson sought to offer peaceful American self-determination—using it as synonym for the long-held liberal idea that the consent of the governed is the legitimate derivation of authority in society. This peace-based self-determination would unfold as a measured, gradual process of reform leading to democratic participation, representative government, and liberal democratic nation-states. Of course, the hopes of the "Wilsonian moment" were not fulfilled, but they were long-lasting.

The framework of twentieth-century decolonization and liberation outlined by Wilson was developed more fully in the post–World War II years by Franklin D. Roosevelt and the many international institutions founded after the war. In the postwar era development was not understood in strictly economic terms but was also concerned with global social development and the pressing question of what kind of place the world should be. Emerging as a superpower after World War II, the United States promoted the Wilsonian vision of a world composed of liberal democracies, nation-states, and free trade. More importantly, US leaders believed with conviction and certainty that they had a portable, reproducible, one-size-fits-all plan for modernization and development. Modernization theory at midcentury promoted a "global modernity" that looked, felt, and thought much like the United States and reinforced the United States' central role in the world.[100] Modernization theory universalized the American model, providing a non-communist and non-revolutionary alternative to achieve social change and self-determination. In his intellectual history of modernization theory, the historian Nils Gilman explains that "by defining a singular path of progressive change, the concept of modernization simplified the complicated world-historical problems of decolonization and industrialization, helping to guide American economic aid and military intervention in postcolonial regions."[101] In the new American-led liberal international order, nations would reach liberation through liberal state machinations. Revolutionary social, economic, and political changes did not require attendant revolutions. Instead, international experts and bureaucracies could bring about those changes by following American leadership and American models.

If American institutions were the best-suited institutions in the world to bring economic growth, social stability, and resolution of social conflict, then it was no wonder that Mexican American liberals supported American institutions and Chicana/o activists eventually targeted their criticisms on them. What appeared in mid-century Chicana/o declarations for liberation and self-determination was a palimpsest, still bearing visible traces of the liberal roots of liberation but also hints of altogether new postmodern conceptualizations of nation and world. Mexican Americans and Chicanas and Chicanos were not simplistic in their understandings of global ideas, but articulately and fluently conversant in the prevailing discourses. Mexican American liberals continued to believe in the ameliorative power of the federal government and the importance of limiting inter-group conflict within the nation.[102] Most Chicanas and Chicanos did not actually desire violent revolution or the physical creation of Aztlán as an independent nation, but they recognized that nation-states were the political organizational units that commanded authority and respect on an international level. They understood the developmental models and used them for their benefit.

CHAPTER 5

"The pang of mendicant yesterdays"

RETHINKING BELONGING THROUGH CHICANA/O CULTURAL NATIONALISMS, 1967–1979

In the 1960s, some U.S.-born youth of Mexican descent started to call themselves Chicanas and Chicanos. While pushing for equality, civil rights, and political power, they also began to craft their own understanding of themselves and the world. They broke with many of the central premises and promises Mexican Americanism in a movement for global social justice. Through multiple cultural nationalisms, Chicanas and Chicanos reimagined themselves as belonging to Aztlán. The amorphous concept of Aztlán attracted a wide array of artists and activists across the political spectrum because it could stand in for an independent state, independence from the state, or a philosophical state of independence.

El Movimiento, as participants often called the Chicano Movement, was a social campaign that headed in multiple directions, reflecting the goals of the activists. Community centers, migrant rights, equal rights, higher education, bilingual education, third world liberation, and gender equality were among the many issues of the Chicano Movement. Even "brown capitalism," or community control of economic resources as a way out of colonial control, had many proponents. Chicanos and Chicanas founded community development corporations in a modest effort to help ethnic Mexicans accumulate capital in the form of housing.[1] There were ardent Marxists who scoffed at the idea of cooperation with the capitalist world system that threatened the global proletariat. This movement encompassed an explosion of complex and conflicting ideas that some scholars have labeled Chicanismo. The Chicano Movement as a single noun belies the complicated intellectual and ideological milieu. There was not one Chicanismo, but many Chicanismos, or cultural nationalisms, that reflected the multitude of ways in which these young activists understood the multiple problems and positions of their community.

BREAKING FROM MEXICAN AMERICANISM

Chicana/o activists criticized the limited imagination of Mexican Americanism. As activist, author, and administrator Abelardo Delgado explained, "Middle class Anglos are ready to invite to their party the educated, professional Chicano who trims his mustache and practices dropping his accent but the man having picked onions for the last twelve hours smells too bad and remains outside." Delgado called Mexican Americans "agringadas and vendidos" who were willing to leave behind members of the Mexican-origin community for their individual gain.[2] Ricardo Sánchez, another Chicano author, activist, and administrator, described the growing distance between Mexican Americanism and the many Chicanismos: "Middle-class mentalities and escuardas-de-a-madre (square, non-bato loco, clean-cut types) . . . [are] the new elitists. It appears that being Chicano has become a lucrative credential—especially if one has the other loftier credentials also. And some Americans of Spanish surname (A.S.S.) do in fact have all kinds of credentials."[3] Sánchez deliberately used the acronym ASS to describe Mexican Americans who decades earlier had started to use terms like "Latin American" and "American of Spanish surname" to distance themselves from the derogatory connotations of "Mexican." For Sánchez and many other Chicanas and Chicanos, Mexican Americanism was an ideology that invested U.S.-born Mexicans in a racialized and exclusionary sociopolitical system. Middle-class Mexican Americans were benefiting from a system that reproduced the subordination of their people.

In an article in the first issue of the San Antonio–based Chicana/o literary journal *Caracol*, Armando Cavada explained that there were difficulties in recruiting from the middle class. He emphasized that Mexican Americans were not really part of the middle class; they were "not the real professionals like doctors and lawyers, but bakery owners, construction workers, electricians, plumbers." Nonetheless, these middling U.S.-born Mexicans were problematic in that "their joining . . . may subvert the Movement, after a fashion, because the ideas and principles that activists have now don't coincide with middle class values."[4] As long as they were focused on electoral politics and becoming middle class, Mexican Americans could not push for the necessary types of change.

Conventional politics were in the realm of Anglo-American control and co-optation. Most Mexican American politicians, Chicanas and Chicanos believed, were puppets controlled by, or often even handpicked by Anglo power holders. In order to get re-elected, those politicians had to concede issues and stances that would help the U.S.-born Mexican community. In a 1973 article entitled "The Dilemma of the Assimilated Mexican" the author (identified only as "Z") criticized San Antonio mayoral candidate Roy Barrera as an Anglo-picked sellout: "Roy Barrera faced the Dilemma of the Assimilated Mexican [on election] night. Roy Barrera was offered to the Mexican people as a candidate who 'touched all segments of the community,' and possessed a 'broad based appeal,' which meant he was supposed to be better than nothing. The people chose nothing."[5] The author understood that the community could decode the messages that Anglos used to disguise politicians who were too invested in the system to advocate for US-born Mexican interests. José Ángel Gutiérrez described a "Mexican-American *politico*" as someone who is "middle aged, Catholic, married to a Mexican-American, a veteran, and from the middle class. He has a high school education and generally does not join the local [Chicano] community organization. When he does seek membership into such groups, he picks the LULACs, the G.I. Forum or Ciudadanos Unidos. This public figure does not believe in protests, marches or demonstrations."[6] The poet and activist Angela de Hoyos described Mexican American politicians in her poem "The Missing Ingredient" as

(lost in a ticker-tape mountain
of mundane ideas:
love-thine-enemy policies
hypocritical handshakes
social-science amenities

and e pluribus unum)
a formula infallible for painless living.[7]

Even established politicians were considered to be complicit. Henry B. González, one of the most prominent successes of Mexican Americanism, was revered by many in the community. In the 1950s he had led fights against segregation and discrimination. By the late 1960s and 1970s, however, he had set aside his status as a civil rights crusader and was openly attacking the Chicano Movement, trying to destroy it.[8] Many Chicana/o activists saw "Henry B." as the epitome of the Mexican American politician, complacent in his political position and unwilling to challenge or confront the problems of socioeconomic inequality. One activist under the pseudonym "la mano negra de Aztlán" (the black hand of Aztlán) wrote a poem entitled "un canto de amor para henry b." (a love song for henry b.) accusing him of having sold out:

has muerto
henry b.
has muerto
and i shed no tears
for your dying.

you are dead
henry b.
you are dead
por ver traicionado
a tu Raza

eras mi hermano
henry b.
but pieces of copper
made a judas of you.

You were my brother
henry b.
you were my brother
pero prefieres "atole"
a ser hombre honrado.

dormirás con gusanos
henry b.
dormirás con gusanos
in the muck and the slime of
white green exploitation.

sleep with the worms
henry b.
sleep with the worms
mientras la Raza levanta
"su casa en el sol"

has muerto
henry b.
has muerto
and i shed no tears by
your grave.

you are dead
henry b.
you are dead
por ver tracionado
a tu Raza.

but
i love you
henry b.
i love you.

porque en tu falsedad
has dado valor
a mi Raza, Aztlan.[9]

Just as Henry B. was dead to Chicana/o activists so too were accommodationist and traditional political methods of resistance. Henry B.'s unwillingness to fight for equality in any forum other than mainstream electoral politics showed the limits of Mexican Americanism.

Chicana/o criticisms of this ideology pointed at the complacency of Mexican Americans. The older generation of leaders was no longer trying to fight for equality but merely trying to find a place in the establishment. Mexican Americans were too invested in becoming middle class, which entailed conceding to an unfair, unequal, and exploitative capitalist system. When Mexican Americans became comfortable in their new middling and middle-class lifestyles, they stopped trying to help anybody else. Rene Abelardo González wrote in the Texas journal *Tejidos*:

> How do you explain to someone that there are older Mexican Americans and other persons who have "made it," that tell you that you are "lucky"; lucky because "you've got a chance to get more education than your parents"; lucky because "you won't have to suffer like your parents or grandparents did"; Puro Pedo (that means "Bullshit" to us, the "culturally deprived"); lucky because now you're going to be made into a gringo; lucky because you've got a better chance to get indoctrinated into the gringo ways; lucky because now Mexican Americans can suffer spiritually, culturally, and mentally.[10]

Chicanas and Chicanos chafed at the condescension of Mexican Americans who told them they should be thankful for all the previous generation had accomplished. They saw too many problems with society to be complacent with those accomplishments.

The Chicana/o denunciations of Mexican Americans were not the cleavages of a mere generational divide, but rather an ideological one. The unfulfilled promises of liberalism and Mexican Americanism pushed Chicanas and Chicanos to find new ways to understand inequality.[11] Angela de Hoyos highlighted the limitations of this ideology in her protests. As Mexican Americans and white liberals proclaimed segregation and inequality to be nonexistent, she uncovered the hypocrisy of liberalism by describing its shortcomings:

> No, you will never understand
> —you in your comfortable recliner,
> watching "cops and robbers"
> on your color TV—
> why the teen-age Chicano
> who shines your shoes

at the Hilton entrance
has not yet learned
to pronounce
the King's English correctly.

But on the other hand
since his problems
do not concern you
—and he shines your shoes very well—
why should you worry
over a simple, soft-spoken
gracias, mees-ter . . . ![12]

In another poem she went further in describing the situation:

On an empty stomach,
with the pang of mendicant yesterdays,
I greet my reflection
in the dark mirror of dusk.
What do the entrails know
about the necessity of being white
—the advisability of mail-order parents?
Or this wearing in mock defiance
the thin rag of ethnic pride,
saying to the shivering flesh and grumbling belly:
Patience, O companions of my dignity?
Perhaps someday I shall accustom myself
to this: my hand held out
in eternal supplication, being content
with the left-overs of a greedy establishment.
Or—who knows?—perhaps tomorrow
I shall burst these shackles
and rising to my natural full height
fling the final parting laugh
O gluttonous omnipotent alien white world.[13]

De Hoyos and many other Chicana/o activists rejected the politics of supplication in Mexican Americanism. They despised those who held out their hands to "a greedy establishment." Chicanas and Chicanos were beginning to see themselves as something more than US citizens, ethnic Mexicans, or a binational proletariat. They were part of a growing national and global movement against inequality and injustice. Some were beginning to see themselves as part of not "America" but the third world, connected to other people of color.

In Texas the rethinking of relationships among people of the world developed over a few years. As Chicanas and Chicanos began recognizing their position in the region and nation, they became increasingly aware of their position in the world as well.[14] They began to build upon strong localisms as the base for larger nationalisms and transnationalisms. In Texas, the consciousness of being a Chicana or Chicano occurred in different ways, but many found inspiration in school walkouts. For years ethnic Mexicans had been segregated into "Mexican schools" or Spanish-speaking classes, regardless of their English proficiency. Even in integrated schools, ethnic Mexicans were still separated. By the late 1960s, they were growing tired of being ignored and mistreated. Across the nation, they walked out of schools.

WALKOUTS AND BOYCOTTS: CONNECTING THE LOCAL TO THE GLOBAL

In March 1968, Chicana/no students in Los Angeles walked out of their high schools in a protest known as the East LA Blowouts. The subsequent widespread publicity encouraged and inspired other Chicana/o students across the country to protest against unequal treatment.[15]

Within a month after students walked out in Los Angeles, Chicana/o students in Texas began to protest their mistreatment. On April 9, 1968, seven hundred students at Lanier High School in San Antonio walked out. On May 16, 1968, students from Edgewood High School in San Antonio followed suit. In November 1968, Chicana/o students walked out of Edcouch-Elsa High School in the small South Texas town of Edcouch, followed in the spring of 1969 by students at Kingsville High School, also in South Texas. Students at all these schools presented similar demands, including that students, not faculty, select the candidates for student council; that students not be punished without due process; that teachers not curse at or hit students; that the cafeteria serve better food at affordable prices; that students not be punished for speaking Spanish; that Mexican American studies be introduced into the curriculum; that school administrators address the difficulties of migrant worker education; and, in sum, "that the blatant discrimination against the Mexican American student in this school stop immediately. We demand Justice."[16]

In October 1969, three hundred Chicana/o students walked out of Abilene High, Franklin Junior High, and Mann Junior High Schools in Abilene, Texas. Led by a sixteen-year-old Chicana named Gloria Bryand, the students were protesting an incident in which a teacher reportedly called Spanish a monkey language. Students left with yells of "Chicano Power" and "Viva la Raza!" Bryand had heard of Corky González and the Crusade for Justice, so she knew a larger student movement was occurring across the nation. Unfortunately, the Abilene walkouts did not bring change. When the students returned to class, their absences were not excused. Consequently, many failed their classes and a few dropped out of school.[17]

The most famous of the Texas Chicana/o student walkouts occurred in December 1969, in the same town where "Los Cinco" were elected, Crystal City. After the failure of the Mexican American city council, the town had returned to its previous system of discrimination. José Ángel Gutiérrez, a Cristal native who had worked with "Los Cinco" as a teen and was one of the founders of MAYO, returned to help organize the school walkout. By the time he returned to his hometown, he had organized walkouts in the Texas towns of Plainview, Lubbock, San Antonio, Kingsville, Uvalde, Hondo, Edcouch-Elsa, Alice, El Paso, Del Rio, San Marcos, and Houston. MAYO was an "organization of organizers" who would go out to communities to help activists achieve their goals. In Cristal schools, Chicana/o students were banned from speaking Spanish, or competing for homecoming king or queen; the cheerleading squad; or most handsome, most beautiful, or most popular elections.[18] The demands of Crystal City students were remarkably similar to those of the East Los Angeles and San Antonio students who had walked out a year earlier. After a protracted walkout and weeks of deliberation, the school district finally agreed to the students' demands in January 1970. It was a major win for MAYO and the Chicano Movement in Texas.

In the context of the war in Vietnam, the violence perpetrated against communities of color, and the efforts of the Federal Bureau of Investigation to infiltrate the growing civil rights movement, the students' demands might be viewed as trivial. On the other hand, the students were beginning to recognize their mistreatment in schools as part of a larger pattern of discrimination in society at large. Their unequal education translated into unequal treatment when they left school. Through the regional and national walkouts, they were learning that what had once appeared to be their unique and quotidian problems were actually larger patterns of exclusion.

Leaders like Severita Lara in Crystal City and Gloria Bryand in Abilene learned that whether they could join the cheerleading squad or be elected homecoming queen were not simply teenage problems but one of many reflections of how society undervalued and excluded the Chicana/o community. As they learned that what they had perceived to be local problems were actually national, Chicana/o students became more confrontational in their protests.

The walkouts broke the bonds between the Mexican American and Chicana/o generations because each generation explained inequality differently.[19] Chicanas and Chicanos reasoned that setting an objective of assimilating and becoming middle class only perpetuated the structural inequalities and subordination ethnic Mexicans faced within American society. Abelardo Delgado expressed this growing sense of awareness in a poem:

> we are coming in if the world will receive us
> as humans and not as pinto bean amoebas.[20]

Chicana/o localisms grew into larger regionalisms through multiple issues beyond the school walkouts. In Texas, United Farm Workers Union boycotts, which had started in California in 1965 under the leadership of César Chávez, influenced many Chicana/o activists. Although Chávez distanced himself from the Chicano Movement, many activists felt the union's refusal to accept unfair treatment from white landowners was part of a larger struggle and resonated with their efforts.[21]

Chicana/o activists used the image of Chávez and the farmworker boycotts as powerful symbols of resistance.[22]

Texas Chicana/o activists began to understand that local problems attached to a global system of oppression required more sympathy than anger. The ideologies of Texas Chicanismos had love and empathy at their center. Abelardo Delgado wrote in 1969,

say huelga [strike] with love
for the unborn chicanitos
put the salt of your tears into it.
don't be one more estúpido
thinking huelga only means strike,
shout it any way you like
say huelga over and over
like an ave maria.[23]

Many besides Delgado understood that *huelga* had meanings beyond "strike." Texas Chicano representative Joe J. Bernal expressed this clearly in his 1973 article "Boycott Si—Lettuce No":

To boycott then, is to be free of oppressors,
To boycott, too, is to recognize we do not live by prayer alone,
To boycott is to recognize that some people carry justice,
 charity, and love in their pocket books,
To boycott is to use my personal commitment to help others
 who haven't been able to make out as well as I,
To boycott is to show my independence,
To boycott is to be a complete human being.[24]

By the late 1960s and early 1970s Texas Chicanas and Chicanos were clearly aware they were more than an isolated community in South or West Texas. They were seeing issues rooted in their locales being replicated in national patterns. They were realizing that they were part of a larger movement. The Chicano Movement had spread across the nation, and Chicanas and Chicanos were developing a new way of understanding ethnic Mexican belonging and the relationships among people of the world. No longer could the limited constraints of the language of citizenship suffice for the kind of world they envisioned.

Chicana/o activists no longer wanted to lend coherence to the national narrative; they wanted to explode it and construct a more just world. For Chicanas and Chicanos in Texas and across the nation, the concept of Aztlán provided a discursive space upon which to map contesting notions of belonging, citizenship, and gender roles.

AZTLÁN, INDIGENEITY, AND AN INDEPENDENT STATE

Chicanas and Chicanos rediscovered the concept of Aztlán during the Chicano Movement and adapted it for their ends.[25] Aztlán, the mythical Aztec homeland, was an important concept because it postulated Chicana/o ancestors had migrated from the Southwest before settling in Tenochtitlan, meaning they were not immigrants, recent arrivals, or foreigners. Instead, they were indigenous to the land. The Southwest was their rightful homeland. Aztlán offered them an alternative spatial conceptualization that allowed them to deconstruct notions of citizenship and belonging.

The event that popularized the concept of Aztlán was the 1969 National Chicano Youth Liberation Conference in Denver, Colorado, hosted by Rodolfo "Corky" González's Crusade for Justice. From March 27 to 31, more than one thousand Chicanas and Chicanos from all over the country met to discuss common issues.[26] Perhaps the most important product of this national meeting was the Plan Espiritual de Aztlán (the Spiritual Plan of Aztlán). The manifesto read in part:

> Aztlán belongs to those who plant the seeds, water the fields, and gather the crops, and not the foreign Europeans. We do not recognize capricious frontiers on the bronze continent. . . . With our heart in our hands and our hands in the soil, we declare the independence of our mestizo nation. We are a bronze people with a bronze culture. Before the world, before all of North America, before all our brothers in the bronze continent, we are a nation, we are a union of free pueblos, we are AZTLÁN.[27]

As the text suggests, Aztlán had become a Chicana/o homeland, a space where notions of belonging could be envisioned outside of the

US nation-state. Not inherently separatist, Aztlán allowed Chicanas and Chicanos to imagine themselves as a community with the agency to make the world a more just and equal place—a place where those "who plant the seeds, water the fields, and gather the crops" were given a fair chance.[28]

In Texas, the concept of Aztlán continued to gain popularity as Chicanas and Chicanos in Dallas, Austin, Houston, San Antonio, El Paso, and the Valley all began to use it. There was a widespread understanding that Aztlán could be used as an organizing concept that would motivate people to join the Chicano Movement.[29]

The concept of Aztlán also encouraged Chicana/o activists to consider their indigenous roots more seriously. If they were Natives, they no longer needed to be "true and loyal citizens" because they belonged before the creation of the US nation-state. If Chicanas and Chicanos were indigenous, they were also part of the long history of colonial displacement and war with the United States. Activist and musician Juan Tejeda believed that Aztlán was one of the most important ideas to come out of the Chicano Movement because "the concept of Aztlán became a unifying cry that we are one nation and took us back to our birthright as American Indians. [Aztlán] connected us to our land and our American Indian spirituality."[30]

The Texas Chicana/o journal *Caracol* tried to connect the indigenous nation of Aztlán and the indigenous notions that it encompassed through a trilingual poetry contest in 1977. The editors of *Caracol* encouraged Chicana/o authors to use a mixture of Spanish, English, and Nahuatl in their poetry. The trilingual poetry collection was published as *Nahualliandoing: Español/Nahuatl/English.* Editor Cecilio García-Camarillo explained in the introduction that some people thought the contest was a gimmick but it was not: "I guess many of us are finding out that Nahuatl is a language that we know unconsciously with our Indian blood. It is a contemporary, flexible language. . . . Chicano acceptance of Nahuatl es dirección positiva. It's a good way to pegarle de aquellas a algo más íntimo, más netamente Chicano." In addition to the poetry contest, beginning with volume 2, issue 2 of *Caracol* (October 1975), the editors began using Mayan numbers next to the Arabic numbers as a way of "getting to the root de las cosas."[31] The editors hoped eventually to do away with the Arabic numbers, but this never happened.

Aztlán was important among the many Chicanismos emerging in Texas. As activist and author Carmen Tafolla explained, Aztlán countered a myopic view of belonging: "Aztlán was a one-word reminder that we were where we come from, that we weren't foreigners here, that we have every bit as much of a right to be here. . . . It was the right for people on this continent to have access to our homelands." Moreover, Aztlán "expressed an awareness of the cycles of oppression and the cycles of conquest."[32] In sum, Aztlán was an expansive concept that had many nuanced facets and provided a means to imagine an alternative nation.

BARRIO CULTURAL NATIONALISM AND INDEPENDENCE FROM THE STATE

Barrio cultural nationalism was a collection of ideas that explained Chicana/o subordination through the primary lens of the ethnic enclave of the neighborhood. Most but not all of its subscribers were working class. Barrio cultural nationalism could be at times sexist, masculinist, reactionary, and insular because it focused on the barrio as a protective community that needed to close itself off from the influence of "gringo" society. Some barrio cultural nationalists did connect the barrio with the third world but others did not. This ideology rejected assimilation and middle-class values, instead looking for solutions within the community. If gangs were a problem, reformed gang youth who had developed a Chicana/o consciousness could offer the answer. Barrio cultural nationalists often came into conflict with university-educated and other activists.

San Antonio was one place where gang violence was a problem in the barrios, with outbreaks of violence occurring in 1956, 1958, 1960, 1962, 1963, and 1966. Many of the gang fights over territory were actually motivated by the scarcity of resources within underserved and underemployed neighborhoods.[33] Rival youths disliked each other and sought revenge. But as Chicano Movement ideas entered the barrio, many street youth (or "batos locos" as they called themselves), realized that their problems were not intrinsic to their barrio. Poverty was a condition imposed by the outside "gringo" society, and Chicanas and Chicanos fighting and hurting each other did not help fix that problem.[34] In addition, the concept of Aztlán as a unified Chicana/o nation overrode the territorial boundaries of gangs. One youth described the spatial reorientation that barrio cultural nationalism evoked in San Antonio: "But what has happened now is that everyone sees only one big barrio. Now we can go to the South Side without having to be on alert and they can come over here. Just because you're in a bubble doesn't mean that you can't get to know guys from another bubble."[35] In barrios throughout Texas barrio cultural nationalism erased neighborhood borders using the concept of Aztlán.

The reframing of the barrio as a site of resistance and independence from the white-dominated state was central to barrio cultural nationalism. The wrongs against the barrio featured prominently in Chicana/o thought. In his poem "Bits and Pieces," Rudy Ortiz gave an extreme portrayal of the conditions in the barrio as outright murder and state violence:

> Bits and pieces de un hombre
> Bits and pieces of a Chicano Soul
> Rejected by an alien, Invader-Culture
> Not accepted by my very one. [. . .]
> Bits and pieces de un hombre
> Bits and pieces of a Chicano Soul
> Nacido en Sur Tejas
> Creados in los housing projects
> "Los corts" de los barrios de San Anto
> Chuco—Bato—Con Safos
> Me crie con el filero en la pansa
> and the zip-gun pointed at my head
> Los batos de los Altos, de la Dot
> del Ghost Town
> Camaradas de mi juventud—
> Bato Loco—
> Batas que se dejan

Solo yo vivo ahora—solano
Mis carnales—muertos
Enterrados—en la pinta [. . .]
Bits and pieces of broken children
in juvenile
the police stations
in prowl cars smeared with Chicano blood
in anglo school halls and classrooms
in the cubicles at Soughton; Gatesville
on the streets of the barrios
Bits and pieces of a culture
a history a heritage a people
Me.
DAMN![36]

The gang divisions of the Chicano community, enumerated in the names of various Texas barrios, had reduced Chicanos to "bits and pieces" of men and communities, torn apart by police surveillance and violence.

Another activist, Raúl Salinas, wrote about Chicano drug addicts in Austin barrios in "El Tecato." Anglos dehumanized addicts and viewed them as a problem endemic to the barrio. Yet Salinas and other barrio cultural nationalists were sympathetic, portraying drug addicts as human beings often victimized by the ebbs and flows of a casual labor market:

He turned the page of life
each day
in the hours of ham n' eggs.
Performing sacred rituals,
ministering to his body's needs

The Morning Fix:
(particular fuel for most particular machine)
the off to hustle up the milk and
bread.
the fix that 7 children would require
And when sandman's gifts were
rubbed from hungry progeny's eyes, that

> scourge
> that social leper beamed with pride,
> because he knew he could (in spite of
> sickness)
> well provide.
>
> Narcotics officers don't think so, nor
> do i feel they cared.
> And so one night they stalked their
> prey;
> a sick, addicted, father-brother-son
> who recognized his children's need for
> food & nourishment
> while no one recognized his need for drugs or treatment.
>
> So the predators gunned him down
> in the manner of that social madness
> that runs rampant across the land,
> dressing itself in the finery and
> raiments
> of
> JUSTIFIABLE HOMICIDE!!![37]

Salinas identified addiction as a real disease but also as a buffer against the exploitative and dehumanizing aspects of colonial capitalism within the barrio. Addicts performed "sacred rituals, ministering to [their] body's need" because that was the only way they could deal with the humiliation of struggling to provide for their families.

David R. Ruiz, a prisoner in Huntsville Prison, wrote about the barrio in similar terms:

> Chicano! Chicana! Where are you?
> A Voice echoes from the unknown
> Why do you cry, why do you hate so?
> All this Blood mixed with tears,
> Floating from los barrios,
> Jefitas without husbands, Hijos without Jefes,
> Why all this misery?

Justice, that flaunted lady, where is she,
Amerikka for what she stands,
Chicano! Chicana! Where are you? [. . .]
Here, Here!
Echoes my voice, as I awaken from my
NIGHTMARE!"[38]

Barrio cultural nationalism rejected the negative characterizations of the barrio and instead presented it as the front line in the fight against state penetration. In the Chicana/o barrios was where people were working the hardest to provide for their families, struggling to maintain human dignity, and suffering the most at the hands of an Anglo-dominated economic system. Moreover, the barrio was where most people were working the hardest to resist this victimization. Consequently, the barrio had to be the primary site of Chicana/o independence and liberation.

Abelardo Delgado went further, comparing the barrio to a colony: "we hate the colonial conditions where all aspects of control are outside of the community. Even the priests are outsiders."[39] Carlos Guerra likewise believed the barrio was an internal colony. In the article "The Colonization of the Chicano" he wrote

> Chicanos, particularly those that now live in places where they form the majority of the population, create a socioeconomic phenomenon because they perceive every detail as due to *colonialism.* Under the *colonization* system, we have to depend on social forces and economic systems that not only clash culturally [with us] but also are foreign and outside of the community. . . . this brings us to the conclusion that we are a *colony* inside of the United States. That is to say, we are not an independent people, but a people dependent on the gringo and his systems.[40]

Since the barrio was the site of liberation and independence from the state, reformed Chicano batos were proud of where they came from. They performed their bato identity often. Raúl Castillo explained his desire to be recognized as belonging to the barrio in a simple statement:

No quiero ser poeta inteligente,
Quiero ser poeta entre la gente.[41]

Abelardo Delgado wrote similarly that "while we answer 'yes' to the charge of being ill-educated, we must answer 'no' to the charge of being stupid."[42] For his part Ricardo Sánchez chose to perform his bato persona more emphatically. Sánchez resented university-educated and non-barrio Chicana/o activists, believing they were a hindrance to the Chicano Movement due to their position in the US bureaucracy. Sánchez called these people "quasi-movement types," "the new oligarquía," and "poverty pimps," claiming that "now these pendejos are the dangerous ones, for they have lulled the community and co-opted the movement (to them it is movidas, not Movimiento, ¡y que si las muevan!), and they will not hesitate to destroy it if it means their newly acquired status and high salaries (color them pastel brownie and very much self-aggrandizing coconuts)."[43]

Sánchez argued that middle-class and university-educated activists were only pretending to be Chicana or Chicano for their own personal benefit, perceiving "money in their becoming more *barrio-istic* and *bato-loco* than los desmadrados." On one occasion, Sánchez believed he was denied a grant because the better educated reviewers did not respect him. He exclaimed angrily, "I came to find out that the poverty pimps will not allow articulate carnales the opportunity to serve La Raza. . . . Yes, I was too qualified—a bato who was a high school dropout, ex-convict, and could run circles around the bureaucrats. Bull shit!"[44]

Like Sánchez, Armando Cavada also addressed the growing divide between barrio nationalists and university activists who learned their Chicanismo "secondhand": "the students read this in class and so people in college got their political awareness in a roundabout way, by reading, by discussing political activism in an academic setting. . . . There's no identification with activities on a grass-roots level." He added, "The poor people are often suspicious of educated Chicanos, because they act and talk as if they were white instead of brown."[45]

Raza Unida Party state chairman Guadalupe Youngblood agreed with other barrio cultural nationalists that university activists felt entitled to lead the movement because of their education. In a December 1974 interview in *Caracol*, he explained, "Lots of people think that because they have a diploma or something like that, they not only have the obligation and responsibility but the right to take the reins of the movement. That's very presumptuous. People like Mrs. Arévalo [a long-time community organizer] have proven themselves and have taken the opportunity and have developed a political awareness to the point where it's very dumb for a sell-out, student, lawyer, or whoever, to think they are going to win a political argument against her."[46] The antagonism directed toward university activists was perhaps hypocritical: Delgado received a bachelor's degree from the University of Texas–El Paso and, eventually, Sánchez would earn a doctorate.

These antagonisms manifested themselves in a factional disagreement between the MAYO–University of Houston and MAYO–Barrio chapters during the Raza Unida Party state convention in Houston in 1974. The fact that the convention was held in a major urban area hinted at the growing influence of university activists. Tatcho Mindiola, an assistant professor of sociology at the University of Houston and Harris County chairman of Raza Unida, organized the convention at the upscale Whitehall Hotel. A contingent led by former MAYO organizer Daniel Bustamante argued that the convention should be held at a high school in the barrio, a location more in touch with the party's community roots. Mindiola's selection of the hotel was not motivated by ideological reasons but because he could not find adequate facilities in the Mexican barrio. The MAYO–Barrio representatives he consulted did not initially object.[47] Later, the rural-barrio contingent almost boycotted the event, before agreeing at the last moment to meet at the Whitehall Hotel.

Barrio cultural nationalists often romanticized the barrio and idealized traditional gender roles. If the Chicano nation was oppressed, then Chicano men needed to fight for it. Hence, these activists failed to challenge the gendered notions of citizenship. If masculinity was a historical prerequisite for citizenship in the United States, then social subordination and political exclusion was seen—and often described—as emasculation. Misogyny, then, was central to liberation and an expression of full rights.

This led to a strong strain of sexism in barrio cultural nationalism. Batos locos had prided themselves on their manliness in their fights with other gangs.[48] Barrio cultural nationalism directed this masculinist impulse toward Anglos and used masculinity as a trope for liberation. Anybody could be angry, but only a Chicano *man* could stand up and fight for his community and Chicano liberation. Abelardo Delgado wrote many pages on the intricate intertwining between male sexuality and resistance to injustice, as his poem "Macho" illustrates:

> tell, why does an hembra find you attractive?
> [. . .] and why is your anger like a human flood.
> women find my love brutal yet so gentle
> [. . .] my anger cries justice as if I were God.[49]

Ricardo Sánchez also illustrated the melding of sexuality, masculinity, and liberation in barrio cultural nationalism when he wrote "the Chicano, in the main, never did—and still does not—want assimilation; there is no sexualized compulsion for making love to a blue-eyed, blonde gringa."[50] He went further in a poem about his transformation from a bato loco into a Chicano activist, in which he associated assimilation with having sex with white women and true Chicanismo to finding a proper Chicana:

> angustia assailed me until I ran from the putísmo into the
> purefying [*sic*] arms of a [Chicana] woman who gave me her
> nourishing love and purity of spirit and being
> [. . .] es bellísimo ser chicano
> casado con chicana,
> tener hijos hechos
> del hierro de la raza
> de bronce . . .
>
> grito ¡VIVA AZTLÁN!"[51]

Abel Garza, too, exposed the sexism underlying barrio cultural nationalism in his poem "Couplets":

> Brown-eyed women of the sun
> make life easier in Aztlán
> Our Raza is reborn,
> the Chicano Movement is formed
> [. . .] There's a sexy girl named Yvonne;
> she walks down the street turning men on.[52]

Barrio cultural nationalism used Chicano virility, masculinity, and sexuality to argue for equality; as men they could not be denied what was theirs, both women and civil rights.

Barrio cultural nationalism was an important strain of thought in the Chicano Movement because it refocused the energy of bato youth inward, toward their community. The angry masculinity of working-class gang culture was redirected from fighting other Chicanos to fighting gringos and inequality. Many of the problems of the barrio were gendered. For this reason, men—machos and bato locos—needed to take up *la causa.* Unfortunately, this masculinist impulse often reproduced conservative familial, gender, and sexual roles and promoted an equally oppressive patriarchy. Women, or "batas que se dejan" as Ortiz described them, were one-dimensional, serving roles as submissive sex partners and passive wives.

Barrio cultural nationalism reimagined the locus of Chicana/o belonging as the barrio, but not in the sense of being relegated to segregated urban ghettos. Instead, the close-knit and culturally homogenous barrio was a source of strength for the community. The solution was not to let liberal Anglos in but to keep all gringos out. Gringos would only bring with them more state surveillance, violence, and penetration. Anglo economic structures would only continue to extract Chicano resources from the barrio. Only direct community control of barrio resources would bring an end to the Chicana/o plight. The barrio was the location from which Chicanos would push back against the state. Their imagined community was limited to those in their own and other barrios across the Southwest. In sum while barrio cultural nationalism at times portended a greater imaginative vision of the world, it was also limiting.

CULTURAL TRANSNATIONALISM AND A STATE OF INDEPENDENCE

Where barrio cultural nationalism was angry (for good reason) and heavy-handed, cultural transnationalism could be esoteric and abstruse at times. Nationalism is easily defined as an imagined community, often controlled or coerced by the nation-state to coincide with its political boundaries. Transnationalism, in contrast, is a term with myriad meanings, a collection of ideas used to imagine a community transcending the political borders of the nation-state. In the context of Chicano Movement activism, Chicanas and Chicanos used their culture and experiences in the United States to begin to reimagine their connections with people across the globe. They began to see themselves as intimately connected to other oppressed or colonized people in the world, whether they were Vietnamese, Bolivian, or Mexican. Chicana/o cultural transnationalists saw themselves as part of a growing and exploited third world. As this group of ideas developed over the long decade of the 1960s, liberation came to mean an increasingly abstract, philosophical state of independence.

Chicana/o cultural transnationalists began moving away from conceptualizing belonging only in terms of the barrio or their small town by connecting the many Chicana/o barrios and pueblos across the United States. Tino Villanueva, a former migrant worker from San Marcos, Texas, wrote about the connections among Chicanas and Chicanos across the nation as forming "another voice" that needed to speak, but not necessarily forming a separate nation-state. In "Hay Otra Voz" (There Is Another Voice) Villanueva described the Chicana/o connections across Texas, California, and Colorado:

> there is another voice that wants to speak
> there is another profile that has bronze skin
> on knees
> dragging themselves on the ground in the
> Cotton-fields of El Campo and Lubbock, Texas.
> Where am I going?, someone asks
> To the cucumber patches of Joliet
> the vineyards of San Fernando Valley,
> to the beet fields of Colorado?
> There are certain uncertain certainties;
> the bitterness of picking oranges
> the tearfulness of picking onions [. . .]
> There is another voice that wants to speak.[53]

Unlike barrio cultural nationalism, Chicana/o cultural transnationalism connected to issues and themes outside of the barrios and moved past them. In some ways, cultural transnationalism was more philosophical than barrio cultural nationalism. Chicana/o cultural transnationalists described political, economic, and racial connections in sensitive and sympathetically human ways. In the inaugural issue of the Chicana/o journal *Caracol*, the editorial board headed by Cecilio García-Camarillo, described the publication's goal:

> CARACOL is a tool at the disposal of our people. With it we want Chicanos of all ages to question, reinforce, share cultural values. . . . We will not be afraid to dissect our image as Chicanos because at this moment in history it is important for us to know the explanations of how we got to be where we are as a people in relation to ourselves, the United States and the rest of the world. Then we will stand a better chance of carving a path into the future—our future—the way we want it to be.[54]

The editors explained they chose the name "Caracol" (snail shell) because the spiral shell represented the nature of the intellectual, philosophical, and spiritual journeys they wanted readers to experience. They hoped that readers who became aware of themselves in abstract and reflective ways would follow the spiral outwards, becoming politicized and aware of the issues that confronted the Chicana/o community. For readers who were already politicized, the editors hoped they would follow the spiral inward, becoming more introspective and thoughtful.[55]

Other activists hoped that the many Chicanismos would move towards more encompassing understandings of the world. Ralph Cruz Castillo explained in an essay on Chicano thought that "Chicanismo is a philosophy that embraces a wide spectrum of thought, word, and action, that can be thoroughly experienced by the Chicano himself."[56]

Reyes Cárdenas, a poet from Seguin, in central Texas, felt connections to fellow Chicanos in Dallas, as well as to Native American and Indonesian poets. Instead of channeling anger into liberation, Cárdenas flirted with liberation through the absurd. In "William Wordsworth," he waxed philosophical:

The pink and black flowers of the
chinaberry tree fall, or decide to fly.
A Chicano walks somewhere in England.
In Dallas an eleven-year-old Chicanito
is shot to death by a pig.
The pig would rather talk about pancakes.
Countless Indians murdered at Wounded Knee.
Gringos are killing everything.
Let's take the moon away from them.
It wouldn't be much of a revenge.
Revenge is no good.
Chairil Anwar takes a girl into the daffodils.
What's life? What's a tortilla?
Rosa's legs in blue jeans.
The universe crumbles if you run along the beach.
The crabs get out of the way.
They don't care about earth, mankind, starfish [. . .][57]

Bernardo Verastique exemplified the imaginative dimensions of cultural transnationalism that helped push Chicanismo toward a more encompassing imaginary when he described his understanding of his own positionality:

i am not the atlas
though there is a world
of delicate balance
set up on this frame.
i am not ninety pounds of weakness
but my strength is
born of fragile construction.
i am all,
flesh, and water, and bone.
i am an arrangement,

arrangement of the totality,
the totality of living matter.[58]

California Chicanas/os also subscribed to cultural transnationalism. Chicano playwright Luis Valdez described what it meant to be Chicana/o in the larger philosophical vein of cultural transnationalism:

To be CHICANO is not (NOT)
to hate the gabacho or the
gachupín or even the pobre
vendido [. . .]
To be CHICANO is to love yourself
your culture, your
skin, your language
And once you become CHICANO
that way
you begin to love other people
otras razas del mundo.[59]

Cultural transnationalists were thinking about larger relationships among themselves, with people across the globe, and with the world itself, at times placing Chicanas and Chicanos at the center of the world in order to focus on their own spatial, political, and intellectual importance. No longer were Chicanas and Chicanos only aware that they were "Joaquín lost in a world of confusion"; instead, they were increasingly aware that they were "flesh, and water, and bone" and part of a multifaceted world of profoundly connected humans.[60] These activists and artists understood the larger project of forging Aztlán as a philosophical state of independence. Their freedom was profoundly connected to their free expression. Some activists would disregard this collection of ideas for that very reason—it lacked the political realism they wanted Chicana/o cultural productions to have.

CHICANA FEMINIST TRANSNATIONALISM

Although cultural transnationalism tried to move away from the explicit sexism and masculinity of barrio cultural nationalism, it still fell short of gender and sexual equality, as did the Chicano Movement in general. Male-dominated leadership often pressed women into traditional roles of preparing food, cooking meals, and making tortillas while men made decisions.[61] Women who did not conform to gender roles were punished. For example, disgruntled male members of the California State University, Long Beach, chapter of MEChA hung in effigy the elected leader of the group, Anna NietoGomez, in part because of her politics, but also because she was a woman.[62] Across the nation, many emerging Chicana feminists were being called *vendidas* or *malinches* (sellouts, traitors) and lesbians for trying to create a movement that addressed all forms of inequality, including gender. The increasing sexism of Chicano organizations left many women in the movement frustrated and marginalized.

Many of the most popular ideas and images of the Chicano Movement were implicitly sexist or had an underlying reactionary agenda. Concepts like Aztlán and the emphasis on the Mexican family reproduced female subordination. The concept of Aztlán was problematic because it was masculinist in its assertion and encouraged "the association of machismo with domination" and liberation.[63] Chicanos, as a means of asserting their masculinity, conjured romanticized and idealized notions of an imperial society based upon violence and destruction. By transporting and imposing these patriarchal visions upon the cultural geography of the Southwest, some Chicano leaders promoted a male-dominated, male-centered version of racialized citizenship in which women were static cultural conceits.

The trope of the Mexican family was also prevalent but not without its limitations. Chicano barrio cultural nationalists, especially, used the family as a model for a society that presupposed male leadership and female subordination. In consequence, many men romanticized the family, failing to acknowledge the violence acted out upon women in traditional family relationships, including rape or domestic abuse. As Chicanas tried to voice concern over the increasingly patriarchal, alienating, and exclusionary portrayal of the nation-family, many Chicanos reacted harshly and negatively. Conflating family with nation reduced many cultural nationalisms to "patriarchal nationalism." The constraints of the concept of the Chicano family were often used to discipline and silence women in the movement.[64]

Caught between male-centered nationalisms and class-privileged mainstream feminism, Chicanas articulated their position in the world through their own feminist practices.[65] Chicanas found mainstream feminism to be ethnocentric, articulating the political and social aspirations of only white upper-class women. Instead, Chicana feminists sought an understanding of the world that explained the intersections of race and gender: "Chicana organizers were influenced not only by the awakening of racial consciousness and cultural renewal generated by the Chicano movement but also by the struggles over gender and sexuality within it, which together ultimately produced new Chicana political identit[ies]" across the country, explains Chicana scholar Maylei Blackwell.[66]

Texas Chicanas generally avoided the worst backlash—such as the hanging in effigy of NietoGomez—because women were early participants in La Raza Unida Party.[67] In the early 1970s, Chicana members of Raza Unida stormed a meeting in Crystal City and demanded to be included in the decision making, not just the cooking and cleaning.[68] They were successful in gaining leadership positions in Cristal and in the party, but this was just was one of many battles. Women in Raza Unida actively combatted the sexism in the movement and the party at the local, state, and national levels.

In 1972, its first year as an official party, RUP dedicated an entire section of its platform to "la mujer."[69] The platform illustrated the conflicting stances on feminism in the early Chicano Movement: "Raza Unida party declares the belief in the family structure as the basis of development, but also clearly states that it must be a *total* development of the family—men, women, and children."[70] The trope of the family was still evident, but women had pushed for a more coequal vision of the family where men, women, and children were responsible for fighting all forms of inequality. In addition, the platform recognized that fighting for equal rights entailed fighting for women's rights and that women must be included in party decision making.

It was clear that women had won major gains in the party. In 1972, the first Chicana to run for statewide office in the history of Texas, Alma Canales, ran for lieutenant governor on the Raza Unida ticket. By that time 36 percent of all Raza Unida county chairs and 20 percent of precinct chairs were women. On August 4, 1973, the first Conferencia de

Mujeres por la Raza Unida was held in San Antonio. Almost two hundred women from twenty counties across the state attended. Only eight months later, in April 1974, women members of Raza Unida held the Central Texas Conferencia de Mujeres in Temple. Raza Unida member and Chicana activist Evey Chapa concluded that participation in the party had allowed Chicanas in Texas "to develop our own philosophies as women within a minority group—as CHICANAS."[71]

Feminism in the Chicano Movement was not without its conflicts. The differences in Chicana feminist thought were evident as early as May 1971 at the national Conferencia de la Mujer in Houston. More than six hundred Chicanas from twenty-three states attended. On the evening of the third day, the conference broke into two factions over disagreements on the most important resolutions. Some women felt that racism was a more pressing concern than sexism, or that emphasis should be placed on "the gabacho, not the macho."[72] Eventually, the disagreement over strategy led the Chicanas who sought to focus on racism to walk out.[73] Despite the debate over privileging racism over sexism, many Chicanas later noted that both systems of privilege functioned together to exclude and subordinate them.

Chicanas across the Southwest contested and constructed ideologies that explained their position through a framework of multiple insurgencies that laid the early foundations of intersectionality. This emerging Chicana framework understood that gender, race, and class overlapped. Chicanas had to respond both to condescending upper-class feminists and to reactionary Chicanos who claimed that they were *agringadas*.

In a 1973 article Texas Chicana activist Marta Cotera dissected how race and class influenced feminist thought. The feminism of privileged white women did not address Chicanas' needs because it represented the "ideology of an alien culture that actively seeks our continued domination. . . . There has always been feminism in our ranks and there will continue to be as long as Chicanas live and breathe in the Movement, but we must see to it that we specify philosophical direction and that our feminist expression will be our own and coherent with our Raza's goals in cultural areas which are ours."[74]

Evey Chapa similarly described the growing distance between Anglo feminism and an emerging women-of-color feminism. At the 1973

National Women's Political Caucus, Chicanas objected that middle-class Anglo women failed to understand how race and class affected Chicanas. She concluded, "Because of the uniqueness of the problems of the Chicana, we cannot allow anyone or any group to speak for us. We must make the decisions concerning the solutions to our problems."[75]

When the United Nations declared 1975 as International Women's Year, Chicanas chafed under what they felt to be white women's appropriation of the planning. In a letter to a colleague, activist Diana Camacho wrote that the "white liberal women" considered themselves "new world saviors."[76] At the Texas International Women's Year meeting, Chicanas described "white liberal women" as "patronizing," "confident they speak for and represent us, they feel Chicanas never represent them," and "still unwilling to coalesce with us when we are under attack."[77] Because Chicanas understood the intersections among race, class, and gender, they often criticized the Chicano Movement but defended it from outsiders' criticisms. An example is the resolution Elma Teresa Salinas of San Antonio drafted in the Racism, Sexism and Classism workshop:

> Whereas the term [machismo] has been employed by the media and social scientists to describe the degradation of women by men; and that label has created an unfavorable image of the Mexican male in the eyes of the American society,
>
> BE IT RESOLVED that the term "machismo" not be employed to further promote a negative stereotype of the Mexican community.[78]

Despite such defenses, many feminists were still accused of being untrue to the Chicano Movement. Anna NietoGomez defended herself in an article in *Caracol*. Acknowledging that many thought "Chicana feminist" was an oxymoron, she explained this was far from the truth:

> When you say you're Chicana, you mean you come from a particular community, one which is subject to racism and the exploitation of centuries. When you say you are feminist you mean you're a woman who opposes the oppression of not only the group in general, but of women in particular. In fact, the statement is not contradictory at all, it is a very unified statement: I support my

> community and I do not ignore the women in my community (who have been long forgotten).[79]

In response to the gendered biases of barrio cultural nationalism and cultural transnationalism, Chicanas created a feminist transnationalism that reimagined human relationships as the basis for a more equal and just world. One of their strategies was to reimagine sensual and sexual relationships between men and women on a more equal basis. Specifically, in their writings they explored the sensitive and human ways that two lovers could overcome inequality. Whereas the Chicano trope of the family reproduced gendered inequality, Chicanas exposed the gendered, class, and racial biases in heterosexual relationships while maintaining that these relationships could be reworked to forge greater sympathy among people. If two people in love could not find a way to overcome inequality, they believed, then there was little hope for the world.

In order to offer their alternative understandings of sensual and sexual relationships, Chicanas first needed to uproot the sexualized stereotypes of women perpetuated by Chicano and Anglo men. Carmen Tafolla deconstructed multiple eroticized stereotypes of Chicanas in her poem "Soy Chicana" (1975):

> I will not be your Spanish señorita
> I will not be your liberated mod
> I will not curse my 'buela for her role
> I will not be your swingin' ethnic broad
> Nor your echo of cathedral's purity
> Nor your treasure of erotic sensitivity
> Nor anything that you would have me be
> Nor anything at all that is not me.[80]

In a single poem Tafolla attacked the myths of "Spanish" passivity, Anglo feminism, the virgin-whore dichotomy, and the notion that feminist activism was a waist-down affair.

Inés Hernández-Tovar attacked the underlying colonial project behind Anglo-centric US concepts of beauty in "To Other Women Who Were Ugly Once":

Do you remember how we used to panic
when Cosmo, Vogue and Mademoiselle
ladies would Glamour-us out of
existence
[. . .] so lovely their
complexion
their confianza based on
someone else's fashion
and their mascara'd mascaras
hiding their cáscaras that hide
their ser.[81]

Hernández-Tovar begins the poem by expressing how comparing her appearance to white beauty standards made her feel inferior and perpetuated notions of white superiority. Ultimately, however, she concludes that Chicanas' attempts to whiten themselves—whether through their hair, dress, makeup, or cultural ideals—are artificial and threaten their inner beauty and selfhood.

Chicanas also spoke out against Chicanos who criticized them for dating Anglos while behaving no differently themselves. If a Chicana was seen with anybody other than a Chicano, she risked being labeled a traitor or counterrevolutionary. Angela de Hoyos exposed Chicano hypocrisy in no uncertain terms:

No me contestes
si no quieres
but wasn't it you
I saw
yesterday
coming out of that motel
con una gringuita
all smiles . . . ?
No te apenes, amigo
Homogenization
is one good way
to dissolve differences
and besides

what's wrong
with a beautiful race
café con leche?[82]

Underlying this critique is a subtext accusing Chicanos of dating white women for the very reasons Hernández-Tovar wrote about in her poem. That is, Chicanos had internalized colonial constructs of beauty connected to white supremacy.

In "Chicano-Gringa Bump" (1976) Evangelina Vigil described a Chicano, at a dance celebrating Chicana week, dancing with a white woman because it boosted his social capital and self-worth:

chicano
bumping butt
on gringa's ass
chancleando
en el baile
de la semana chicana
hombre
jiving, bumping
getting down
todavía insecure
proving yourself
with a gringa's nalgas."[83]

Vigil also criticized the fact that Chicanas were expected to sleep with Chicano Movement leaders. In "Ay Que Ritmo," describing a Chicano Movement party, Vigil equates the movement with the rhythm of sexism:

Latino salsa music
sonidos de aquellas
pegando
aventando ondas
en el coco loco nightclub
where the cool people go
Y el hermano latino
gyrating hips and butt

and grinding balls
in skin-tight levis
circumcised penis
hanging neatly
Y el hermano latino
in grotesque ego-orgasm
milling high monkey ass
latino style
to el ritmo
del sexismo
While desperate Latina groupies
sip and suck nervously
watching the boring show
trying desperately
but unsuccessfully
to feel and keep the rhythm—
Gagging
but not really comprendiendo why
knowing
but not really understanding
que el ritmo del sexismo
da asco.[84]

Instead of participating in a movement for equality, Chicanas found themselves stuck in a dance that reduced them to "groupies" and sexual objects. Chicanos were using them for their own "ego-orgasm" of political power and sexual pleasure.

Having deconstructed sexual stereotypes and attacked the underlying sexism of the movement, Chicanas envisioned sexual and romantic relationships on a more equal basis that addressed race, class, and gender. In "La Isabela de Guadalupe and El Apache Mio Cid" (1975) Carmen Tafolla explored how two people of different classes, races, and worlds could come together through the metaphor of a Spanish conquistador and an Indian woman falling in love:

I as an India
And you as a Spaniard

How can we ever make love?
[. . .] I, que me gusta andar descalsa,
Y tu, bordado en hilos de oro,
How can we ever make love?

Will I have to crawl inside your armor?
Will you have to paint your feet with dirt?
Will we have to stop the world, take off its reins
And blind its eyes, give it a lump of sugar,
And tell it to go ver si puso la marrana

Have you ever seen mecate elope with chains?

Will we have to meet between the day and night,
enlazados, escondidos, entejidos en amor,
with two masks and jet-way tickets labeled Smith?

Will we make a funny pair—
red dirt floors and chandeliers?

(Did we make that house already?)
Did we already shift the worlds,
blend over blend in prism states,
moving between the mirrors of our many, many lives?[85]

Tafolla's poem exemplifies Chicana feminist transnationalism because she draws on Chicana/o history and culture as a basis to imagine a more just world, while remaining acutely aware of race, class, and gender inequalities. As Tafolla suggests, Spaniards and Indians, conquered and conquerors, poor and rich can "shift the worlds" if they choose to love and accept each other as humans.

Angela de Hoyos contributed to the creation of Chicana feminist transnationalism in writing of the long Chicana history of gendered conquest and ethnocentrism that had displaced her geographically and temporally. In "Hermano" (1975) she explored the history of San Antonio and the future of Chicanas, Chicanos and the world:

I was born too late
in a land

that no longer belongs to me
(so it says, right here in this Texas History)
[. . .] Tu cielo
ya no me pertenece
Ni el Álamo, ni la Villita,
ni el río que a capricho
por tu mero centro corre.
Ni las misiones
[. . .] They belong to a pilgrim
who arrived here only yesterday
whose racist tongue says to me: I hate
Meskins. You're a Meskin. Why don't you
go back to where you came from?
Yes, amigo . . . ! Why don't I? Why don't I
resurrect the Pinta, the Niña and the Santa María
and you can scare up your little 'Flor de Mayo'
so we can all sail back
to where we came from: the motherland womb.
I was born too late
or perhaps I was born too soon: It is not yet my time: this is
    not yet my home.
I must wait for the conquering barbarian
to learn the Spanish word for love.[86]

The erasure of her history threatens to erase her claim to belonging in the present. Yet the physical evidence, the missions and Spanish names in San Antonio, make that erasure incomplete. Whereas mid-century Mexican Americans used those totems and talismans to claim belonging, de Hoyos uses them to make white claims on the land seem ridiculous. Imaginary descendants of British Protestant separatists of the Northeast are claiming ownership of Spanish Catholic missions in the Southwest. Distinct from Mexican Americanism and other cultural nationalisms, Chicana feminist transnationalists like de Hoyos look at belonging through the lens of loving relationships among people. While de Hoyos acknowledges the cruelty of conquest and the legacies of colonization, she believes these forces cannot be overcome until people learn to see each other as humans and love one another. She concludes, sardonically and uncertainly, that she must "wait for the conquering barbarian / to learn the Spanish word for love."

In "La Malinche," (1977), named for the Tlaxcalan woman who became Hernán Cortés's translator and mistress, Tafolla further developed the feminist transnationalist critique of sexism, inequality, and injustice. She engaged the history of conquest but hoped that the future would be free of perpetual cycles of conquest:

I saw our World
And I saw yours
And I saw—
another.
And yes—I helped you—against Emperor Moctezuma
  Xocoyotzin himself!
I became Interpreter, Advisor, and lover.
They could not imagine me dealing on a level with you—
so they said I was raped, used,
chingada
¡Chingada!
But I saw our world
and your world
and another.
No one else could see!
Beyond one world, none existed.
And you yourself cried the night
the city burned,
and burned at your orders.
The most beautiful city on earth
in flames.
You cried broken tears the night you saw your destruction.
My homeland ached within me
(but I saw another!)
Another world—
a world yet to be born.
And our child was born . . .

and I was immortalized Chingada!
Years later, you took away my child (my sweet mestizo new
world child)
to raise him in your world.
You still didn't see.
You still didn't see.
And history would call me
chingada.
But Chingada I was not.
Not tricked, not screwed, not traitor.
For I was not traitor to myself—
I saw a dream
and I reached it.
Another world. . . . .
la raza.[87]

Whereas Mexican public intellectuals like Octavio Paz branded La Malinche as a whore and traitor, Tafolla reconsidered the story from a Chicana perspective. Chicanas recognized the failures of both worlds, the sexist white and Chicano worlds, and believed in another possibility. Sexual inequality and differential power relations between men and women had existed in the past, in the present, and in most relationships, not only romantic ones. Chicanas like Tafolla believed those relations could be remade, changing the world. The imagined Chicana/o homeland and nation could exist. It was known and knowable to her because she was a woman. Her experience as both a Chicana and a woman allowed her to imagine and work toward a better world. As in the poem, women literally and figuratively would give birth to the new world.

For Chicana feminist transnationalists, the solution was a more encompassing empathy that could see past the current state of politics and envision a more just, human, and humane world. Chicana feminist transnationalism created a transnational and transracial imaginary that used very personal relationships—the sexual and sensual—as a basis for building greater equality. If people could overcome injustice and biases in intimate relationships, as Tafolla imagined Malinche did with

Cortés, then people could overcome these in larger political and social relations. Although their imaginary relied on the trope of heterosexual relationships, Chicana feminist transnationalism was not dismissive of queer relationships or people. Indeed, queer studies would pursue similar goals of reimagining sexual and sensual human relationships as a model to rethink the world and belonging.

Chicana feminist thought pushed the Chicano Movement to rethink belonging. No longer could Chicanos frame belonging solely through the masculinist concept of Aztlán as an independent nation or a form of political independence from the state. Chicanas pushed the entire community to think about belonging on a global scale, but without trying to erase racial, ethnic, cultural, or sexual diversity.

Chicana/o protest took many forms, but, importantly, it blurred the line between politics and poetics. Chicana/o art, literature, and poetry helped create Chicana/o consciousness. The arts helped imagine new ways of looking at the world. Barrio batos, Chicana feminists, Raza Unida Party chairs, and other community activists all used Chicana/o arts to recruit supporters and to outline their thoughts. Chicana/o poetry was not just an aesthetic exercise; it articulated complex thoughts, ideas, and imaginaries. Chicano artist César Augusto Martínez expressed this complexity as follows:

> Arte Chicano is not easy to write about because it is heavily laced with controversy. It involves dealing with an emerging and constantly evolving philosophy. . . . Synonymous as it is with activism, it deals not only with our politics but with our culture, our environment, our food, our family, our attitudes, our history, our locura, our position in the cosmos, hunger, poverty, our mejicano origins, our indigenous blood, our Spanish blood, los perros, los tamales, tacos, Tio Taco. . . . Chicano art deals with everything that touches our lives."[88]

Reyes Cárdenas similarly commented, "It is poetry, of course, but a poetics merged with a protest which so upsets the establishment."[89] In order to understand the intellectual history of the Chicano Movement in Texas and across the United States, scholars must understand that

Chicana/o cultural productions and Chicana/o cultural nationalisms were deeply entwined intellectually and ideologically.[90] Barrio cultural nationalism, cultural transnationalism, and Chicana feminist transnationalism were only three of many sets of ideas that were available to Chicana/o activists. The many Chicana/o cultural nationalisms allowed a greater ideological breadth to the US-born Mexican community than ever before.

The intellectual developments of the Chicano Movement were important because Chicana/o intellectuals reimagined belonging and relationships among people of the world. Chicanas and Chicanos saw themselves as political actors with agency who were interconnected with other people around the world. The concept of Aztlán provided an important alternative spatial conceptualization that allowed them to reject limiting American and Mexican nationalisms. The concept of Aztlán was malleable enough that Chicanas and Chicanos could use it to push for an independent state, independence from the state, or a philosophical state of independence. These concepts mapped onto the beliefs of barrio cultural nationalists who found belonging in the barrio and liberation through an aggressive and angry masculinity. Chicano cultural transnationalists tried to reimagine community through more philosophical human connections. In their cultural productions, they remade the world, often putting themselves at the center of it in order to challenge the ethnocentrism of the US nation and global white supremacy. Chicanas confronted gender inequality in politics and poetics. They refused to accept any longer a nation, a world, or a future where sexual and gender inequality existed. Some Chicana feminist transnationalists reimagined sexual and sensual relationships and believed that equality could be reached through an empathetic understanding of humanity. They too built upon the history and experiences of being Chicana and connected these ideas to an imagined global community. An intellectual history of the Chicano Movement reveals how Chicanas and Chicanos throughout the long decade of the 1960s imagined a different world and created a new understanding of belonging.

CONCLUSION
From Workers of the World to Loyal Citizens to Global Consumers
US LATINX BELONGING SINCE 1970

Over most of the twentieth century, citizenship and the rise of the nation-state influenced how ethnic Mexicans in Texas, and the borderlands generally, thought about belonging. Beginning in the 1970s, however, economic ideas and policies started to make borders disappear for materials, goods, and capital, but harden for people. The 1970s were also the beginning of a new epistemological epoch. Historian Daniel T. Rodgers has pointed out that the era was a dramatic "age of fracture" in the United States and the world. Many of the ideas, institutions, and politics of the early twentieth century unwound or became ineffective or irrelevant. Certainty fell apart in a cascade of disaggregation.[1]

Mexican Americans and Chicanas and Chicanos experienced the limitations of liberation through liberalism firsthand. Mexican Americans discovered that recognition as American citizens often did not lead to the gradual economic improvement and incremental social change promised by American liberalism. Historian Benjamin Johnson explains that at the height of racial violence in Texas in 1915, Mexican Americans learned "that it was dangerous to be a people without a state. . . . They needed to be Mexican or American, and it turned out that to be both was impossible and to be neither was unwise."[2] Many threw their lot in with the United States, sure that American principles, practices, and politics would protect them. By the 1960s, as the 1968 US Commission on Civil Rights report showed, the Mexican American community had achieved minimal economic and social gains. It seemed that Mexican Americans had made the wrong choice, but in an age of nation-states other options seemed impossible.

Chicanas and Chicanos and leftists across the world also learned the limitations of nationhood in an era of globalization. National economies were no longer independent and autonomous. As the era of anticolonial movements came to an end, and third world nations won their independence, they found they were not free from the nations they fought against, but rather more indebted to them economically. The World War II vision of postcolonialism turned into neocolonialism. Chicanas and Chicanos and leftists around the world learned the hard way that nationhood did not mean independence. For many, it only left their nations more dependent upon the global north.

The important unifying social metaphors that had harnessed the "power of the central state to fuse the nation into a unified citizenry" during the first half of the twentieth century also collapsed.[3] The pluralistic metaphors of melting pots, forged alloys, social cacophony, and cosmic races, so important across the industrializing world in the early twentieth century came undone in the 1970s. While these symbolic social monoliths did unify nations, they also homogenized and erased group differences in the United States and across the world. Some of these social metaphors needed to be shattered. And shattered they were. But that did not mean that the groups who broke with exclusionary traditions, institutions, politics, and ideas did not try to put back together some of the pieces. Years after the Chicano Movement, the poet Reyes Cárdenas illustrated the uncertainty, the unmoored and insecure nature of social change after the long decade that challenged so much in society:

> If we praise the Aztecs
> or Zapata
> we praise something too far removed.
> If we embrace Guevara
> we must realize
> that revolution
> works only on rare occasions.

If we succumb to the Great White Way
we learn the hard way.
If we try "the middle of the road"
we cross the
dividing line.
If we live for the future
we betray the present.[4]

As Cárdenas lamented, all the avenues for social change seemed foreclosed. Romantic indigeneity, Latin American–style revolution, and American liberalism had all failed and offered little hope for the future. Cárdenas was not alone in his feelings. The 1970s represented a "crisis in ideas and intellectual authority."[5]

The liberal state could not resolve the economic crisis of the 1970s. Conservatives in the United States and abroad took advantage of the stalling and failure of liberalism worldwide, blaming statist interventions for the crises.[6] US President Jimmy Carter identified the problems the nation faced as indicators of a larger "crisis of confidence," stating, "The erosion of our confidence in the future is threatening to destroy the social and the political fabric of America."[7] It was an insufficient explanation. Carter's successor, Ronald Reagan, provided a more satisfactory indictment of the culprit in his 1981 inaugural address: "in this present crisis, government is not the solution to our problem; government is the problem. From time to time we've been tempted to believe that society has become too complex to be managed by self-rule, that government by an elite group is superior to government for, by, and of the people. Well, if no one among us is capable of governing himself, then who among us has the capacity to govern someone else?"[8] Reagan, Margaret Thatcher in the United Kingdom, and a wave of neoclassical economists charged the liberal state as the guilty party for paltry economic growth. Dismantling social programs, cutting tax rates, reducing regulations, lowering tariffs, and unleashing capitalism—unrestrained and unrestricted—would recharge the world economy.

The rise of neoliberalism in the late twentieth century was important for the multiple Latinx communities in the United States. In his 1996 State of the Union address, Democratic president Bill Clinton declared,

"We know big government does not have all the answers. We know there's not a program for every problem. . . . The era of big government is over."[9] He proceeded to disparage welfare assistance and celebrate higher education as the best avenue for upward socioeconomic mobility. For Mexican Americans and other Latinxs, the predominance of neoliberalism and the post-Clintonian strain of liberal neoliberalism in American politics changed the political landscape for the remainder of the twentieth century and into the twenty-first century. Liberal neoliberalism supported mass incarceration, a stronger deportation regime, and the rollback of the social safety net. The only mechanism for socioeconomic advancement offered nationally was higher education. Unfortunately, remaking the Democratic Party in Clinton's image did not protect Latinx communities from conservative policies and rhetoric. Since the 1990s, the Latinx community has also borne the brunt of xenophobia and nativism, from Proposition 187 in California in 1994 to the Minutemen border patrols of the early 2000s, to Donald Trump's denunciation of Latinxs as criminals and rapists. All these events have challenged ethnic Mexican and Latinx belonging in the United States.

As I have shown in this book, the turn of the twenty-first century is far from the first time that ethnic Mexican belonging has been challenged. In the years after the Mexican Revolution, as homelands collided with the rise of the nation-state and regionalisms gave way to nationalisms, ethnic Mexicans debated which group of ideas would best situate belonging in the borderlands. Some believed that their romantic regionalisms perfectly maintained *en el destierro* (in exile) would provide them with sufficient protection once the chaos that shook Mexico subsided. The Revolution did not vanish, however, but became institutionalized, promoting a new Mexican nationalism and state. The Mexican state tried to incorporate its citizens living abroad, and in the process, unwittingly co-opted the Afuerense ideology. Thereby, US-born Mexicans were not only left out of México de Afuera and the nation of Mexico itself, but they were also excluded from Mexican identity. The Mexican anthropologist Manuel Gamio concluded at the end of the 1930s that US-born Mexicans were people without a country.

In response, some decided that US-born Mexicans should attempt to make themselves recognizable to the American state. This was one of the main goals of Mexican Americanism in the mid-twentieth century. Mexican Americans understood that in order to receive the benefits and protections of citizens, they needed to be seen and recognized by the synoptic state. For this reason, they railed against being counted separately as "Mexican" in the 1930 census and complained about directories that labeled them as "colored" or failed to differentiate between US-born and foreign-born Mexican residents. If these documents failed to acknowledge their presence, then the state would overlook their existence. Efforts like these continued until 1980, when Latinx organizations across the nation encouraged their various ethnic groups to mark "Hispanic" on the census.[10] Since then, "Hispanic" has become an identity that many people subscribe to.

Others could not trust the US state to protect workers from the exploitative desires of the international bourgeoisie. The ethnic Mexican left challenged the authority of nation-states and their attendant citizenships, which they viewed as forms of mystification meant to divide workers of the world. Building on their imaginary of a united global working class, the ethnic Mexican left fought against racism and discrimination in workplaces, neighborhoods, and nations. The transformation of the United States from a corporate state into a welfare state in the 1930s and 1940s struck a blow to ethnic Mexican labor internationalism.

As the left declined at the "end of reform" Mexican Americanism became even more confident in the power of American liberalism to cement their belonging in the nation and to include them within the protections and imaginings of the nation-state. Mexican Americans attempted to insert themselves into the historical narratives of development that defined social scientific and liberal thought at the time. By the late 1960s, however, the Mexican American community had not achieved levels of socioeconomic advancement comparable to other white citizens. Social science models would explain this lag in terms of cultural deficiencies and aborted development, but US-born Mexican activists and academics would challenge these explanations. Eventually, the prevailing ideas of liberation through liberalism collapsed, with the help of US-born Mexican intellectuals and activists around the world.

Responding to the shortcomings of liberalism and Mexican Americanism, activists in the 1960s and 1970s adopted a post-national protest using culture and aesthetics—blurring the distinction between poetry and protests—to reimagine the relationships among people of the world. Through the concept of Aztlán, they created an alternative spatial conceptualization that challenged citizenship as the legitimate means of belonging. Barrio cultural nationalists rethought the barrio as a site of independence from the white-dominated state. Chicano cultural transnationalists imagined a global community that transcended the political borders of nation-states. For them, belonging became an increasingly abstract philosophical state of independence, where they often placed themselves at the center of the world in order to focus on their own spatial, political, and intellectual importance. Chicana feminist transnationalists reimagined the sensual and sexual relationships between humans as the basis for a more equal and just world.

Ethnic Mexican and US Latinx belonging is still changing in an era of globalization. Recently, some organizations have changed their approach from soliciting state support to being embraced by corporations. For example, Clinton's Housing and Urban Development secretary Henry B. Cisneros cofounded the nonprofit Latino Donor Collaborative (LDC) in 2010. The LDC directors are almost all chief executive officers of corporations. The LDC's mission and vision sound similar to those of early twentieth-century Mexican American groups like OSA and LULAC; namely, to make sure that "American Latinos are well-regarded as patriotic Americans in all facets of American life." However, the LDC directs its promotion of the Latino community not at government but at "friendly high-level dialogue, with the goal of finding best ways to grow revenue and market share—by targeting and serving the Latino audiences. We do this through a nonpartisan agenda that includes outreach to influential people in media, advertising, politics, corporate America, and civil society by confronting stereotypes with data that brings understanding and appreciation of the actual roles being played by Latinos in society, politics, and commerce."[11] In other words, the LDC considers corporate America, not the US government, as the primary institution of power in the twenty-first century. Indeed, as the government has recently enacted policies to deport or socially ostracize Latinxs, corporations have reached out to this group because of their numbers and potential buying power.

In one of its most ambitious projects, in 2015 the LDC compiled the "Latino Gross Domestic Product (GDP) Report" to show the economic power of US Latinos. The Latino GDP, reflecting the economic activity of US Latinxs alone, was $2.13 trillion. If US Latinos/as were an independent country, they would be the seventh largest economy and the third fastest-growing GDP in the world. Therefore, "the common perception of Latinos being a burden to U.S. society is utterly wrong. To the contrary, Latinos are the element most needed to fuel the growth of this economy."[12] This understanding of the Latinx contribution to the United States as primarily economic indicates an important political and ideological shift from previous understandings of belonging. In addition, the Latino GDP, which measures Latinx economic contribution as a nation within a nation differs greatly from the Chicana/o understanding of their community as an internal colony (Aztlán).

The Latino GDP illustrates how ideas of belonging continue to transform in the twenty-first century. No longer are Latinxs in the United States a people without a country, citizens seeking the embrace of a liberal state, or colonized subjects. Instead they are a large conglomerate of consumers with trillions of dollars to spend and a large workforce that will continue growing in the future. The amount of money at stake gives corporations reasons to protect Latinxs from deportation or political scapegoating. In the era of neoliberalism, the institution that must recognize and embrace the Latinx community is corporations, not the state.

Yet, despite the optimistic picture the LDC paints, the resurgence of right-wing nationalism in the United States has targeted the Latinx population, once again throwing their belonging into question. Increasingly punitive, deportation-centered policies have disproportionately affected young US-born children whose families live in heightened fear.[13] President Donald Trump's rhetoric attacks all Latinxs in the United States, regardless of their citizenship. His attacks on "Mexican" Judge Gonzalo Curiel, calls for building a border wall, and policies aimed at restricting immigration make very little distinction between US-born and foreign-born Latinxs. In his vision, the nation is a landscape of "American carnage," for which all Latinxs are to blame.[14] The moment has left many in the community once again questioning their belonging to this nation.

In 2019, the first Latino US Poet Laureate, Richard Blanco, published a poetry collection centered around the question of belonging. The title, *How to Love a Country*, dealt directly with the election of Donald Trump and the changes occurring subsequently. In many of the poems the poet struggles to recognize his neighbors, let alone his country. But he is not ready to abandon his belonging in this nation. In "Mother Country," Blanco uses his mother's story of fleeing from Cuba to the United States to tell his own story of belonging to the nation. Instead of abdicating his allegiance, he decides:

> To love a country as if you've lost one [. . .]
> To love a country as if I was my mother last spring
> hobbling, insisting I help her climb all the way up
> to the US Capitol, as if she were here before you today
> instead of me, explaining her tears, cheeks pink
> as the cherry blossoms coloring the air that day when
> she stopped, turned to me, and said: You know, *mijo*,
> it isn't where you're born that matters, it's where
> you choose to die—that's your country.[15]

Yet, later in the collection he equivocates on his bold declaration:

> I write: country—
> end it with a question mark.[16]

This history of ethnic Mexican belonging since 1900 has shown belonging to be a complex web of ideas that composes the architecture of human interconnectedness. Ethnic Mexicans have been in conversation with many of the most important "communities of discourse" of the twentieth century.[17] Ethnic Mexicans have constructed and contested their belonging between the Wilsonian moment and the age of fracture. Ethnic Mexican intellectual history has transformed the history of ethnic Mexicans from a minor addendum or afterthought to the overarching liberal story of American progress since the mid-twentieth century. In fact, they were informed by changes across the globe and transformed the world in response. From workers of the world to proud and loyal American citizens, to global consumers, US Latinx belonging continues to change.

Notes

NOTE ON TERMINOLOGY

1. For examples see David G. Gutiérrez, *Walls and Mirrors: Mexican Americans, Mexican Immigrants, and the Politics of Ethnicity* (Berkeley: University of California Press, 1995), 217n1, 218n3; Lorena Oropeza, *¡Raza Sí! ¡Guerra No! Chicano Protest and Patriotism during the View Nam War Era* (Berkeley: University of California Press, 2005), xvii–xiii; Gabriela González, *Redeeming La Raza: Transborder Modernity, Race, Respectability, and Rights* (New York: Oxford University Press, 2018), xv–xvi. For an example of the increasing complexity of using "Chicana/o" and "Chicano Movement," see Alan Eladio Gómez, *The Revolutionary Imaginations of Greater Mexico: Chicana/o Radicalism, Solidarity Politics, and Latin American Social Movements* (Austin: University of Texas Press, 2016), 213n1.
2. Eric D. Weitz, *A World Divided: The Global Struggle for Human Rights in the Age of Nation-States* (Princeton, NJ: Princeton University Press, 2019), 6.

INTRODUCTION

1. John Chávez, *Beyond Nations: Evolving Homelands in the North Atlantic World, 1400–2000* (New York: Cambridge University Press, 2009), 8, 6.
2. Richard L. Nostrand, *The Hispano Homeland* (Norman: University Oklahoma Press, 1992), 214.
3. Richard L. Nostrand and Lawrence E. Estaville, *Homelands: A Geography of Culture and Place across America* (Baltimore, MD: Johns Hopkins University Press, 2001).
4. Chavez, *Beyond Nations*, 14–38, 66–94.
5. Weitz, *World Divided*, 1–11.
6. Catherine E. Kelly, *In the New England Fashion: Reshaping Women's Lives in the Nineteenth Century* (Ithaca, NY: Cornell University Press, 1999), 6, 7.
7. Compare Donald R. Kelley, "What Is Happening to the History of Ideas?" *Journal of the History of Ideas* 51, no. 1 (1990): 4, 13–15; and Dominick LaCapra, "Intellectual History and Its Ways," *American Historical Review* 97, no. 2 (April 1992): 436–37.
8. Kelley, "What Is Happening to the History of Ideas?" 25.
9. For an excellent example of transnational intellectual history, see Ruben Flores, *Backroad Pragmatists: Mexico's Melting Pot and Civil Rights in the*

United States (Philadelphia: University of Pennsylvania Press, 2014). For an example of cultural/intellectual history, see Eric Avila, *Popular Culture in the Age of White Flight: Fear and Fantasy in Suburban Los Angeles* (Berkeley: University of California Press, 2004). Richard A. García approaches intellectual history at moments in his work. See García, "Class, Consciousness, and Ideology—The Mexican Community of San Antonio, Texas: 1930–1940," *Aztlán* 9, nos. 1–2 (1978): 23–69; *The Rise of the Mexican American Middle Class, San Antonio, 1929–1941* (College Station: Texas A&M University Press, 1991), 221–99; and "The Origins of Chicano Cultural Thought: Visions and Paradigms: Romano's Culturalism, Alurista's Aesthetics, and Acuña's Communalism," *California History* 74 no. 3 (Fall 1995): 290–305. Another early example is Mario T. García, "La Frontera: The Border as Symbol and Reality in Mexican-American Thought," in *Between Two Worlds: Mexican Immigrants in the United States*, ed. David G. Gutiérrez (Wilmington, DE: Scholarly Resources, 1996). See also Ignacio M. García, *Chicanismo: The Forging of a Militant Ethos among Mexican Americans* (Tucson: University of Arizona Press, 1997).

10. José David Saldívar, *Border Matters: Remapping American Cultural Studies* (Berkeley and Los Angeles: University of California Press, 1997); Ramón Saldívar, *Chicano Narrative: The Dialectics of Difference* (Madison: University of Wisconsin Press, 1990); Sonia Saldívar-Hull, *Feminism on the Border: Chicana Gender Politics and Literature* (Berkeley and Los Angeles: University of California Press, 2000); Benjamin V. Olguín, *La Pinta: Chicana/o Prisoner Literature, Culture, and Politics* (Austin: University of Texas Press, 2010); José F. Aranda, *When We Arrive: A New Literary History of Mexican America* (Tucson: University of Arizona Press, 2003); Ellie D. Hernández, *Postnationalism in Chicana/o Literature* (Austin: University of Texas Press, 2009); George Mariscal, *Brown-Eyed Children of the Sun: Lessons from the Chicano Movement, 1965–1975* (Albuquerque: University of New Mexico Press, 2005); John Morán González, *Border Renaissance: The Texas Centennial and the Emergence of Mexican American Literature* (Austin: University of Texas Press, 2009); Leticia M. Garza-Falcón, *Gente Decente: A Borderlands Response to the Rhetoric of Dominance* (Austin: University of Texas Press, 1998); Raúl Coronado, *A World Not to Come: A History of Latino Writing and Print Culture* (Cambridge, MA: Harvard University Press, 2012).
11. John E. Toews, "Intellectual History after the Linguistic Turn: The Autonomy of Meaning and Irreducibility of Experience," *American Historical Review* 92, no. 4 (October 1987): 883.
12. Sarah Maza, "Stephen Greenblatt, New Historicism, and Cultural History, or, What We Talk About When We Talk about Interdisciplinarity," *Modern Intellectual History* 1, no. 2 (August 2004): 263, 258–61.

13. See Mario T. García, *Mexican Americans: Leadership, Ideology, and Identity, 1930–1960* (New Haven, CT: Yale University Press, 1989); Gutiérrez, *Walls and Mirrors*; Benjamin H. Johnson, *Revolution in Texas: How a Forgotten Rebellion and Its Bloody Suppression Turned Mexicans into Americans* (New Haven, CT: Yale University Press, 2003); Emilio Zamora, *Claiming Rights and Righting Wrongs in Texas: Mexican Workers and Job Politics during World War II* (College Station: Texas A&M University Press, 2009); Cynthia Orozco, *No Mexicans, Women, or Dogs Allowed: The Rise of the Mexican American Civil Rights Movement* (Austin: University of Texas Press, 2009); José A. Ramírez, *To the Line of Fire! Mexican Texans and World War I* (College Station: Texas A&M University Press, 2009); George J. Sánchez, *Becoming Mexican American: Ethnicity, Culture, and Identity in Chicano Los Angeles, 1900–1945* (Oxford: Oxford University Press, 1993).
14. Daniel A. Wickberg distinguishes between social and intellectual history as follows: "Whereas the historian of thought is interested in written texts for the patterns of meaning they reveal, the social historian is interested in them as registers of experience. Where the historian of thought looks at texts, ideas, cultural representations in relationship to other texts, ideas, and cultural representations, the social historian of intellectuals looks at them in relationship to social institutions, concrete experiences, and immediate 'contexts.' One is concerned with ideas, the other with persons." Wickberg, "Intellectual History vs. the Social History of Intellectuals," *Rethinking History* 5, no. 3 (2001): 384.
15. See García, *Mexican Americans*; Carlos Kevin Blanton, *George I. Sánchez: The Long Fight for Mexican American Integration* (New Haven, CT: Yale University Press, 2014); Vicki L. Ruiz, *Cannery Women, Cannery Lives: Mexican Women, Unionization, and the California Food Processing Industry, 1930–1959* (Albuquerque: University of New Mexico Press, 1987); Félix D. Almaráz Jr., "The Making of a Boltonian: Carlos E. Castañeda of Texas—The Early Years," *Red River Valley Historical Review* 1 (Winter 1974), 329–50; Almaráz, *Knight without Armor: Carlos Eduardo Castañeda, 1896–1958* (College Station: Texas A&M University Press, 1999); Michael Olivas, *In Defense of My People: Alonso S. Perales and the Development of Mexican-American Public Intellectuals* (Houston, TX: Arte Público Press, 2013); Juanita Luna Lawhn, "The Mexican Revolution and the Women of El México de Afuera, the Pan American Round Table, and the Cruz Azul Mexicana," in *War along the Border: The Mexican Revolution and Tejano Communities*, ed. Arnoldo De León (College Station: Texas A&M University Press, 2012), 156–75; Sonia Hernández, "Women's Labor and Activism in the Greater Mexican Borderlands, 1910–1930," in *War along the Border: The Mexican Revolution and Tejano Communities*, ed. Arnoldo De León (College Station: Texas A&M University Press, 2012), 176–204.

16. See John Torpey, *The Invention of the Passport: Surveillance, Citizenship, and the State* (Cambridge: Cambridge University Press, 2000).
17. See Andrés Reséndez, *Changing Identities at the Frontier: Texas and New Mexico, 1800–1850* (New York: Cambridge University Press, 2004).
18. On the notion of extensive versus intensive development see Christopher Clark, *Social Change in America: From the Revolution through the Civil War* (Chicago: Ivan R. Dee, 2006), x–xi; also Charles Sellers, *The Market Revolution: Jacksonian America, 1815–1846* (New York: Oxford University Press, 1991).
19. Randolph B. Campbell, *Gone to Texas: A History of the Lone Star State* (New York: Oxford University Press, 2003), 131–33, 186.
20. Lawrence A. Cardoso, *Mexican Emigration to the United States, 1897–1931* (Tucson: University of Arizona Press, 1980), 1; Douglas S. Massey et al., *Return to Aztlan: The Social Process of International Migration from Western Mexico* (Berkeley and Los Angeles: University of California Press, 1987), 40.
21. John Mason Hart, *Revolutionary Mexico: The Coming and Process of the Mexican Revolution* (Berkeley: University of California Press, 1997), 84–92; Alan Knight, *The Mexican Revolution: Porfirians, Liberals and Peasants* (Cambridge: Cambridge University Press, 1986), 1:36.
22. Hart, *Revolutionary Mexico*, 255.
23. Colin M. MacLachlan and William H. Beezley, *El Gran Pueblo: A History of Greater Mexico* (Upper Saddle River, NJ: Prentice Hall, 1994), 274.
24. See Flores, *Backroads Pragmatists*.
25. Gabriela F. Arredondo, *Mexican Chicago: Race, Identity, and Nation, 1916–1939* (Urbana: University of Illinois Press, 2008), 146.
26. David Montejano, "Frustrated Apartheid: Race, Repression, and Capitalist Agriculture in South Texas, 1920–1930," in *The World-System of Capitalism: Past and Present*, ed. Walter L. Goldfrank (Beverly Hills, CA: Sage, 1979), 132. For more on the "semi-periphery," see Dennis N. Valdés, "Region, Nation, and World-System: Perspectives on Midwestern Chicana/o History," in *Voices of a New Chicana/o History*, ed. Refugio I. Rochín and Dennis N. Valdés (East Lansing: Michigan State University, 2000), 131.
27. Emilio Zamora, *The World of the Mexican Worker in Texas* (College Station: Texas A&M University Press, 1993), 92.
28. James C. Scott, *Seeing Like a State: How Certain Schemes to Improve the Human Condition Have Failed* (New Haven, CT: Yale University Press, 1998), 9–53.
29. "Respetable Radio-Auditorio," Andrés de Luna Collection, Box 1, Folder 9, Benson Library, University of Texas at Austin. Original text: "pedir patria dentro de su propia patria."

CHAPTER 1

1. Nemesio García Naranjo, "La obra del destierro," *La Prensa*, July 13, 1920. Original text: "El presidente ha abierto de par en par las puertas de la Patria y no van a tardar muchas semanas sin que regresen al terruño casi todos los desterrados. Podrá haber algunos que permanezcan en el extranjero por tiempo indefinido, pero la emigración como entidad colectiva esta ya a punto de desaparecer."
2. Lawhn, "Women of El México de Afuera," 156; Nicolás Kanellos, "Cronistas and Satire in Early Twentieth Century Hispanic Newspapers," *MELUS* 23, no. 1 (Spring 1998): 6.
3. García, *Rise of the Mexican American Middle Class*, 221–23.
4. Nora E. Riós McMillan, "Lozano, Ignacio E.," in *Handbook of Texas Online*, accessed September 9, 2019, http://www.tshaonline.org/handbook/online/articles/fl047; Kanellos, "Cronistas and Satire," 8.
5. García, *Rise of the Mexican American Middle Class*, 223–23; Kanellos, "Cronistas and Satire," 11.
6. Lawhn, "Women of El México de Afuera," 158.
7. González, *Redeeming La Raza*, 51–52.
8. On the role of US investors in Mexico, see Hart, *Revolutionary Mexico*.
9. Cardoso, *Mexican Emigration to the United States*; Juan Mora-Torres, *The Making of the Mexican Border: The State, Capitalism, and Society in Nuevo Leon, 1848–1910* (Austin: University of Texas Press, 2001); Rodolfo Acuña, *Corridors of Migration: The Odyssey of Mexican Laborers, 1600–1933* (Tucson: University of Arizona Press, 2007). Although Acuña does not study Texas, the long history of economic connections that brought Mexican workers to the United States have similar parallels in Texas.
10. See Julie Leininger Pycior, *Democratic Renewal and the Mutual Aid Legacy of US Mexicans* (College Station: Texas A&M University Press, 2014).
11. Zamora, *World of the Mexican Worker*, 86.
12. González, *Redeeming La Raza*, 27–50; Garza-Falcón, *Gente Decente*, 88–91.
13. See Oscar J. Martínez, *Border Boomtown: Ciudad Juárez since 1848* (Austin: University of Texas Press, 1978); Gilberto Hinojosa, *A Borderlands Town in Transition: Laredo, 1755–1870* (College Station: Texas A&M University Press, 1983); Albert Camarillo, *Chicanos in a Changing Society: From Mexican Pueblos to American Barrios in Santa Barbara and Southern California, 1848–1930* (Dallas, TX: Southern Methodist University Press, 2005); Carlos G. Vélez-Ibañez, *Border Visions: Mexican Cultures in the Southwest United States* (Tucson: University of Arizona Press, 1996).
14. US Bureau of the Census, 1930 Census, vol. 2, p. 72. The census numbers are clearly imperfect, but the data nonetheless helps establish broad historical patterns.

15. 1930 US Census, 2:72.
16. García, *Rise of the Mexican American Middle Class*, 35–36.
17. 1930 US Census, 2:68, 69.
18. Nicolás Kanellos, *Hispanic Periodicals in the United States, Origins to 1960: A Brief History and Comprehensive Bibliography* (Houston, TX: Arte Público Press, 2000), 28–59.
19. Kanellos, "Cronistas and Satire," 4–9; Kanellos, *Hispanic Periodicals*, 34–41; García, *Rise of the Mexican American Middle Class*, 223–45.
20. Raúl A. Ramos, "Understanding Greater Revolutionary Mexico: The Case for a Transnational Border History," in *War along the Border: The Mexican Revolution and Tejano Communities*, ed. Arnoldo De León (College Station: Texas A&M University Press, 2012), 311–16.
21. Zamora, *World of the Mexican Worker*, 86, 92. Whereas Zamora associates "homeland politics" closely with the exile politics of the Mexican Revolution, I would like to expand his idea to include the transnational conversation regarding ethnic Mexican belonging.
22. John Chávez, *The Lost Land: The Chicano Image of the Southwest* (Albuquerque: University of New Mexico Press, 1984), 84.
23. "Patria ausente" appears in "Nuestro Celo Patrio," *El Cronista del Valle* (Brownsville, TX), November 19, 1924. See also Aaron E. Sánchez, "Of Patriots and Pochos: Ethnic Mexicans and the Politics and Poetics of Changing Nationalisms, Texas, 1910–1940," *Journal of the West* 54, no. 1 (Winter 2015): 30–31.
24. For a discussion on patria and *nación* see Coronado, *A World Not to Come*, 63–71.
25. Omar S. Valerio-Jiménez, *River of Hope: Forging Identity and Nation in the Rio Grande Borderlands* (Durham, NC: Duke University Press, 2013), 92–128, 230–31.
26. Nicolás Kanellos, *Hispanic Immigrant Literature: El sueño del retorno* (Austin: University of Texas Press, 2011), 53.
27. Coronado, *World Not to Come*, 68.
28. Chávez, *Beyond Nations*, 6–8.
29. The eminent Chicano historian F. Arturo Rosales has called this "Mexico Lindo cultural nationalism," drawing on the themes of a beautiful place of origin and the necessity of return expressed in the song "México Lindo." This song was popularized by Mexican singer Jorge Negrete in the 1940s, so I have chosen not to use Rosales's term, even though his research has influenced my study. For more on Rosales's "Mexican Lindo cultural nationalism," see Rosales, *¡Pobre Raza! Violence, Justice, and Mobilization among México Lino Immigrants, 1900–1936* (Austin: University of Texas Press, 1999), 22–33.
30. Manuel Bonilla Jr., "El silencio de los desterrados," *Revista Mexicana* (San Antonio, TX), May 28, 1916. Original text: "nosotros no somos traidores. Los

que vivimos refugiados a la sombra de una extraña bandera . . . los traidores no somos nosotros . . . los traidores en todo caso, son otros."

31. For a discussion on the cooperation and difference between liberal, masonic, and Magonista reformers, see González, *Redeeming la Raza*, 51–81.
32. Ignacio Valdespino, "Sin Patria," *Revista Mexicana* (San Antonio, TX), June 4, 1916. Original text: "¿Cómo cantar en tierra ajena? . . . / porque mi canto / No puede más que ser triste gemido, / La segura señal de mi quebranto, / El eco del dolor de un pecho herido."
33. Guadalupe Anchando, "Oh, Dulce Patria," *La Patria* (El Paso, TX), September 15, 1919. Original text: "todo la tierra de galas viste / todo la llena de luz y amor; / pero mi alma la encuentra triste / porque está triste mi corazón . . . / cuando suspiro sin esperanza, / ¡oh dulce Patria! Lejos de ti."
34. Vicente Osillo, "A México, mi Patria," *La Patria* (El Paso, TX), September 15, 1919.
35. On the consequences of Porfirian policies on Mexican workers see Douglas S. Massey et al., *Return to Aztlan: The Social Process of International Migration from Western Mexico* (Berkeley and Los Angeles: University of California Press, 1987), 40–44; Hart, *Revolutionary Mexico*, 84–92; Mora-Torres, *Making of the Mexican Border*, 129; Cardoso, *Mexican Emigration to the United States*.
36. I am borrowing heavily from postcolonial scholar Homi K. Bhabha's works *Nation and Narration* and *The Location of Culture*. Bhabha builds upon Benedict Anderson's concept that nations are imagined communities by arguing that what gives the nation-state its coherence is largely the ubiquitous discourse it perpetuates about itself; that is, the imaginations of community are largely underwritten by narratives.
37. For more on the "crustacean type of nation," see Torpey, *Invention of the Passport*, 93–121.
38. Juan Sintierra (pseudonym), "Pensando en la Patria," *La Época* (San Antonio, TX), August 11, 1918. Original text:

> Si existimos nosotros y tenemos alguna realidad en la vida es porque llevamos en nuestro ser todos los atributos esenciales de la patria. Nuestra sangre nos la dio ella: sabemos, porque en su ciencia nos alimentamos, hablamos palabras que la patria nos enseño a hablar; el aire de la patria modeló nuestro carácter; sus desgracias nos lastimaron, sus triunfos nos enorgullecieron . . . la patria nos pertenece entera, puesto que de ella somos en absoluto, mientras la humanidad no averigüe una nueva forma de existir y relacionarse, el patriotismo es un sentimiento tan positivo y necesario como el del amor filial.

39. "México emigrado y México esclavo: El regreso a la patria," *Revista Mexicana* (San Antonio, TX), August 6, 1916. Original text: "la patria no es únicamente

el territorio: es fundamentalmente el pensamiento, las instituciones, la historia, el hogar."

40. "El patriotismo," *La Prensa* (San Antonio, TX), February 13, 1913. Original text: "la patria no es solo el territorio en que hemos visto la luz: hay algo mas, que unido al territorio constituye lo que debemos amar como patria."
41. "México emigrado y México esclavo: El regreso a la patria," *Revista Mexicana* (San Antonio, TX), August 6, 1916. Original text:

    Y comparando nuestra tristeza con la de aquellos que se han quedado en México, tenemos que confesar que si nosotros sufrimos la nostalgia del terruño, ellos en cambio sufren la nostalgia inconsolable del espíritu nacional. Son desterrados en su propio suelo, y esperan dentro de sus aldeas y ciudades, el retorno del alma de la Patria. Aún viven en México; pero fuera, enteramente fuera. . . . Y aquellas pobres gentes piden a Dios que el alma de la Patria vuelva a la Patria. Hacen bien aquellas pobres gentes en esperar que México retorne a México. Nosotros, por nuestra parte, debemos considerar nuestro regreso a la Patria, como un deber y no como un deseo. Representamos el pensamiento patrio en su esencia y por tanto, nuestra obligación urgente consiste en unificarnos para luego ir a unificar las energías y las aspiraciones incoherentes de una nacionalidad que espera nuestras vuelta como una salvación . . . el México emigrado va a redimir al México esclavo.

42. "México emigrado y México esclavo." Original text: "los desterrados volverán a reconstruir a la Patria. Si no lo hicieren [*sic*] merecerían . . . la maldición de la Historia por no haber legado a sus hijos la herencia de una patria intacta y autónoma que recibieron de sus Padres."
43. "El día de la patria," *Revista Mexicana* (San Antonio, TX), September 15, 1918. Original text: "El 16 de Septiembre, será para los desterrados un día de dolor; para los habitantes de las grandes ciudades de México será un día de profanación." And "No es tiempo de cantar; pero tampoco hay que entregarse a vanas lamentaciones. Preparemos el regreso al terruño; restauremos los altares profanados; reconquistemos la Patria."
44. Historian F. Arturo Rosales has touched on the subject of early formations of cultural nationalism in the ethnic Mexican community in the United States, referring to it as "México Lindo cultural nationalism." Rosales did not develop his concept in depth, but suggested that this form of Mexico-centric cultural nationalism was a precursor to Chicanismo. See Rosales, *¡Pobre Raza!*, 5; and *Chicano! The History of the Mexican American Civil Rights Movement* (Houston, TX: Arte Público Press, 1996), 56–71.
45. For histories of long-established ethnic Mexican communities in the United States, see Camarillo, *Chicanos in a Changing Society*; Richard Griswold del

Castillo, *The Los Angeles Barrio, 1850–1890: A Social History* (Berkeley and Los Angeles: University of California Press, 1979); Ricardo Romo, *East Los Angeles: History of a Barrio* (Austin: University of Texas Press, 1983).

46. Conrado Espinoza, *Sol de Texas/Under the Texas Sun* (Houston, TX: Arte Público Press, 2007), 48. Original text: "familias que . . . han perdido su catalogación Mexicana y son, por el lenguaje (pésimo español, pésimo ingles), por las costumbres (groseras y licenciosas), por los anhelos (ambiciones fútiles o necias), grupo hibrido que no se acomoda ni entre los elementos de este país ni entre los nuestros [México]."
47. Santiago G. Guzmán, "En Edinburg no hay mexicanos," *El Defensor* (Edinburg, TX), May 2, 1930. Original text: "Nosotros que vergüenza! Hasta negamos que nuestros padres son o fueron mexicanos, y aunque hasta la manera de pararnos se conozca al mexicano este lo niega cobardemente y con mas ganas si sabe tartamudear el ingles (a medias)."
48. Manuel Gamio, *The Mexican Immigrant: His Life-Story* (Chicago: University of Chicago Press, 1931), 58.
49. "Una campaña en pro del idioma español," *El Cronista del Valle* (Brownsville, TX), February 15, 1927.
50. A. C. Tato, "Vamos aprendiendo ingles," *La Época* (San Antonio, TX), October 6, 1918. Original text: "ya no debemos ser burros, / no lo debemos ya ser / vámonos poniendo changos, / ¡vamos aprendiendo ingles! / Caray ¿no te da vergüenza / cuando por la callas ves / a chiquillos de nueve años / que te dicen de corrido / cualquiera cosa en inglés? / Dime, ¿no te da vergüenza? / y eso que tiene que ver—/ Ellos nacieron aquí . . . / Tenemos aquí cuatro años que los he contado bien, y del idioma sabemos / solamente el 'veri güel' / y eso por casualidad. / ¿No es vergonzoso, mujer? / Casilda, por Dios, Casilda: / ¡Vamos aprendiendo inglés! / Bueno, y ultimadamente, / ¿por qué no lo aprendes, pues? / Porque tu no quieres que ande con gringas / Qué he de querer!"
51. Américo Paredes, *A Texas-Mexican Cancionero: Folksongs of the Lower Border* (Urbana: University of Illinois Press, 1976), 164.
52. Arthur L. Campa, *Spanish Folk-Poetry in New Mexico* (Albuquerque: University of New Mexico Press, 1946), 9, quoted in García, *Mexican Americans*, 285. Original text: "Los pochis de California / No saben comer tortillas / Porque solo en la mesa / Usan pan con mantequilla. // Me casé con una pochi / Para aprender inglés / Y al los tres días de casado / Yo ya le decía yes.
53. For a discussion of gender among borderland reformers see González, *Redeeming La Raza*, 36–43, 76–81, 103–7.
54. Paredes, *Texas-Mexican Cancionero*, 163.
55. Gamio, *Mexican Immigrant*, 45, 46.
56. Gamio, *Mexican Immigrant*, 53.
57. González, *Redeeming La Raza*, 53, 84.

58. Marjorie (pseudonym), "Caridad! Especial para *La Patria*." *La Patria* (El Paso, TX), January 31, 1920. Original text: "divinamente elegida para compadecer y para sentir; que está llamada para anidar en su alma Caridad: que ha nacido para amar, y para amar puramente, por mas que el hombre llene de asechanzas su camino, no acude a la voz de la desgracia, y no escucha el eco de dolor de nuestros hermanos infortunados." And "¿de quien es entonces la obligación? De la mujer, y precisamente de la mujer mexicana depende en estos amargos momentos el auxilio que debe impartirse a los millares de huérfanos de infortunados que sin pan, sin abrigo, sin familia, sin hogar, cuentan sólo con sus lagrimas y su dolor!"
59. Guadalupe S. de García Hidalgo, "Todo, menos la ignominia: carta de una valiente mujer mexicana," *La República* (El Paso, TX), November 30, 1919. Original text: "La mujer está llamada a desempeñar un importante papel en la sociedad y especialmente en el hogar donde deben hacerse sentir sus virtudes y su benéfica influencia. Ella debe ser modelo de abnegación; heroína que sin cesar se inmole en el ara del deber, alentando a su compañero en las luchas diarias, y confortando su alma con las muestras comprobadas de su energía moral, que no vencerán las privaciones, ni las múltiples penas que acompañan al destierro." And "Poco podremos laborar por la Patria: pero contribuyamos todas las mujeres mexicanas, a endulzar las penas de nuestros esposos, de nuestros hijos, de nuestros hermanos; para no restarles energías, si contemplan en nuestras huellas demasiado visibles de pesares no bien soportados."
60. Manuel Gamio, *Mexican Immigration to the United States: A Study of Human Migration and Adjustment* (Chicago: University of Chicago Press, 1930), 129.
61. Gamio, *Mexican Immigration to the United States*, 89. Original text: "Los paños colorados / Los tengo Aborrecidos / Ya hora las pelonas / Los usan de vestidos / Las muchachas de S. Antonio / Son flojas pa'l metate / Quieren andar pelonas / Con sombreros de petate. / Se acabaron las pizcas, / Se acabo el algodón / Ya andan las pelonas / De puro vacilón."
62. Benjamín Padilla, "Las que tienen novios gringos," *La Evolución* (Laredo, TX), June 15, 1919. Original text: "El peligro yanke, una vez que ha invadido nuestro campo minero, mercantil e industrial, amenaza algo que debía ser exclusivamente nuestro, algo íntimo y que nos pertenece a los del país, los corazones vírgenes de nuestras pollas: el amor inefable de nuestras muchachas mexicanas."
63. For more on ethnic Mexican chaperonage and women, see Vicki L. Ruiz, *From Out of the Shadows: Mexican Women in Twentieth-Century America* (New York: Oxford University Press, 1998), 51–71.
64. Padilla, "Las que tienen novios gringos." Original text: "Oh muchachas partidarias de los gringos! En el pecado llevan la penitencia!"

65. Gamio, *Mexican Immigrant*, 169.
66. Espinoza, *Sol de Texas*, 97. Original text:

> QUICO: aquí hemos de encontrar todas las perdidas.
> CUCA: O perder todas las halladas.

67. Espinoza, *Sol de Texas*, 110. Original text: "ellos no volverán. . . . Aquí perdieron la honra, aquí se quedarían para no morir de vergüenza al llegar a su tierra, al volver entre sus conocidos que, muy rancheros, muy simples, sabían afrontar la miseria a cambio de conservar el honor. Seria un México-texano mas." And "Váyanse, dígales a los paisanos que se aguanten como hombres, que se queden en su tierra . . . aquí se encuentra mas fácilmente la muerte y la deshonra que el dinero."
68. Daniel Venegas, *Las aventuras de don Chipote, o cuando los pericos mamen* (Houston, TX: Arte Público Press, 1999), 159. Original text: "Y pensando en esto, llegó a la conclusión de que los mexicanos se harán rico en Estados Unidos: CUANDO LOS PERICOS MAMEN."
69. Jorge Ainslie, *Los pochos: novela* (Los Angeles: Latin Publishing Co., 1934), 151. Original text: Ahora vivimos en un país, donde con el pretexto de la civilización, los muchachos han confundido la libertad con el libertinaje . . . ¡Cuantas familias han sufrido como nosotros los rigores del destierro, sin embargo no se van, ni quieren volverse . . . [pero] ya volverán cuando se convenzan de que es mas sabroso una tortilla comida entre amigos, que una tajada de jamón entre enemigos."
70. "México emigrado y México esclavo."
71. Ismael M. Vázquez, "Mexicanos! Es la tierra que guarda las cenizas veneradas de nuestros abuelos donde os espera el porvenir de nuestros hijos," *El Defensor* (Edinburg, TX), February 27, 1931. Original text: "queridos compatriotas, es allá (México) en la tierra que guarda las cenizas verdaderas de nuestros abuelos donde os espera el porvenir de nuestros hijos; es allá donde está la tierra de promisión, la que os espera con los brazos abiertos a semejanza de la madre que espera a sus hijos amados, donde tendréis todas las garantías a que sois acreedores, donde vuestros hijos no tendrán que sufrir humillaciones en donde viviréis contentos y felices."
72. Torpey, *Invention of the Passport*, 92.
73. Mora-Torres, *Making of the Mexican Border*; Cardoso, *Mexican Emigration to the United States*.
74. Torpey, *Invention of the Passport*, 5, 6.
75. Arredondo, *Mexican Chicago*, 145.
76. Manuel Gamio, *Forjando patria* (Mexico City: Editorial Porrúa, 1960), 7. Original text: "Exceptuando muy pocos países latinoamericanos, en los demás no se observan las características inherentes a la nacionalidad definida

e integrada, ni hay concepto único ni sentimiento unánime de lo que es la Patria. Existen pequeñas patrias y nacionalismos locales."

77. Gamio, *Forjando Patria*, 6. Original text: "toca hoy a los revolucionarios de México empuñar el mazo y ceñir el mandil del forjador para hacer que surja del yunque milagroso la nueva patria hecha de hierro y de bronce confundidos. . . . Ahí está el hierro. . . . Ahí ésta el bronce. . . . Batid hermanos!"
78. Historical sociologist John Torpey explains that "the idea of belonging that is at the root of the concept of citizenship is threatened when people cross borders, leaving spaces where they 'belong' and entering those where they do not." Torpey, *Invention of the Passport*, 12.
79. Rosales, *¡Pobre Raza!*, 41, 42.
80. Lawhn, "Women of El México de Afuera," 168.
81. Arredondo, *Mexican Chicago*, 172.
82. Gamio, *Mexican Immigrant*, 49.
83. Arredondo, *Mexican Chicago*, 88–92.
84. Paul S. Taylor, *Mexican Labor in the United States: Chicago and the Calumet Region*, University of California Publications in Economics 7, no. 2 (Berkeley: University of California Press, 1932), 217, quoted in Arredondo, *Mexican Chicago*, 88.
85. Santiago G. Guzmán, "En Edinburg no hay mexicanos," *El Defensor* (Edinburg, TX), May 2, 1930. Original text: "Hemos oído decir . . . [que] mi patria es donde la paso mejor. Además [que] yo soy México-Texano. Para terminar diré que los que no aman a su patria, no aman a Dios y a su hogar, son seres venidos de las más recónditos avernos."
86. C. R. Escudero, "Americanización y mexicanización," *El Continental* (El Paso, TX), December 25, 1935. Original text: "¿Como puede ser buen ciudadano si . . . [no] puede apoyarse en la rica tradición de su patria porque no la conoce?"
87. Gamio, *Mexican Immigrant*, 126.
88. Gamio, *Mexican Immigrant*, 148.
89. Gamio, *Mexican Immigration to the United States*, 65, 129.
90. Gamio, *Mexican Immigration to the United States*, 177.
91. Enrique Santibáñez, *Ensayo acerca de la inmigración mexicana en los Estados Unidos* (San Antonio, TX: Clegg, 1930), 90. Original text: "Algunos [U.S.-born Mexicans] viven muy envanecidos de esa superioridad y de que son ciudadanos americanos. Yo creo que mas lo demuestran que lo sienten."
92. *La Prensa*, editorial, April 24, 1930, quoted in Johnson, *Revolution in Texas*, 191.
93. Gamio, *Mexican Immigrant*, 166.
94. Gamio, *Mexican Immigrant*, 151.
95. Gamio, *Mexican Immigrant*, 151.

96. Paul S. Taylor, *A Spanish-Mexican Peasant Community: Arandas in Jalisco, Mexico* (Berkeley: University of California Press, 1933), 50.
97. Gamio, *Mexican Immigrant*, 45.
98. "Mexican Spies and Their Work in El Paso," *El Paso Herald*, September 18, 1912. Quoted in David Dorado Romo, *Ringside Seat to a Revolution: An Underground Cultural History of El Paso and Juarez: 1893–1923* (El Paso, TX: Cinco Puntos Press, 2005), 211.
99. C. R. Escudero, "Americanización y mexicanización." Original text: "una raza de mirlos blancos o patitos feos de habla de sangre de nombre y de herencia." And "a quienes los [Anglos] siguen considerando mexicanos a pesar de que son ciudadanos de Estados Unidos y los mexicanos consideran renegados feos porque ni su propio idioma conocen."
100. Ainslie, *Pochos*, 143. Original text: "¿Y tu que eres? Una pocha infeliz que ni a 'bolilla' llegas."

CHAPTER 2

1. "Constitución y leyes de la Orden Hijos de America," Oliver Douglas Weeks Collection, Box 1 Folder 1, Benson Library, University of Texas at Austin. Original text: "Es una sincera opinión nuestra, que, la Orden Hijos de America [*sic*] ha surgido en el campo de la civilización norte-americana para colocar un lindero en la senda de los procesos evolutivos en que nosotros hemos venido desenvolviendo nuestro destino como ciudadanos de los Estados Unidos de Norte America. Casi cien años han transcurrido desde los tiempos en que nuestro antepasados eran los primeros laborantes [*sic*], semi-civilizados por el ambiente en que vivían, hasta este día de hoy en que nos proclamamos a si mismos, ciudadanos conscientes, amantes, y devotos de nuestro patrio suelo."
2. Paul S. Taylor, *An American-Mexican Frontier: Nueces County, Texas* (Chapel Hill: University of North Carolina Press, 1934), 241.
3. Oropeza, *¡Raza Sí! ¡Guerra No!*, 74.
4. Of course this was not the only force that did so. Benjamin H. Johnson has written about how the Plan de San Diego and the violence that ensued in 1915 shaped Mexican American identity in *Revolution in Texas*. José A. Ramírez wrote about the important influences of World War I on the ethnic Mexican community in *To the Line of Fire!*
5. Chicana/o scholars disagree on whether changes in politics, ideas, and behaviors during this time were assimilationist, accommodationist, or activist in nature. Two historiographical schools have formed regarding what Chicano historian Mario T. García called the "Mexican American generation" (García, *Mexican Americans*). Even though García's generational schema has been debated, it has become a defining feature of Chicana/o history due to its usefulness.

For scholars who see Mexican Americans and organizations such as LULAC and the American GI Forum as generally assimilationist/accommodationist see David Montejano, *Anglos and Mexicans in the Making of Texas, 1836–1986* (Austin: University of Texas Press, 1987); and *Quixote's Soldiers: A Local History of the Chicano Movement, 1966–1981* (Austin: University of Texas Press, 2010); García, *Rise of the Mexican American Middle Class*; Benjamin Márquez, *LULAC: The Evolution of a Mexican American Political Organization* (Austin: University of Texas Press, 1993); Manuel Peña, *The Mexican American Orquesta: Music, Culture, and the Dialectic of Conflict* (Austin: University of Texas Press, 1999); Mariscal, *Brown-Eyed Children of the Sun*; Oropeza, *¡Raza Sí! ¡Guerra No!*

For scholars who see the Mexican American generation as leading an important and admirable movement that created a more respected and useful political and civic tradition, see Chávez, *"¡Mi raza primero!" (My People First): Nationalism, Identity, and Insurgency in the Chicano Movement in Los Angeles, 1966–1978*. Berkeley and Los Angeles: University of California Press, 2002); Orozco, *No Mexicans, Women, or Dogs*; Johnson, *Revolution in Texas* and "The Cosmic Race in Texas: Racial Fusion, White Supremacy, and Civil Rights Politics," *Journal of American History* 98, no. 2 (September 2011): 404–19.

Historians Ignacio García and Mario T. García are examples of scholars who offer a middle-ground reading of the Mexican American generation. See Mario T. García, *Mexican Americans*; and Ignacio García, *Viva Kennedy: Mexican Americans in Search of Camelot* (College Station: Texas A&M Press, 2000). More recent studies have reassessed the activism and ideas of the Mexican American generation, balancing some of the shortcomings of their ideas with their political activism and success. See González, *Redeeming La Raza*; Olivas, *In Defense of My People.*

6. Torpey, *Invention of the Passport*, 57, 71.
7. Torpey, *Invention of the Passport*, 93 (quotation), 108.
8. Scott, *Seeing Like a State*, 1–11, 32.
9. Torpey, *Invention of the Passport*, 108–18, 122.
10. Torpey, *Invention of the Passport*, 95, 96.
11. Erika Lee, *At America's Gates: Chinese Immigration during the Exclusion Era, 1882–1943* (Chapel Hill: University of North Carolina Press, 2003), 4, 6, 7.
12. Mae M. Ngai, *Impossible Subjects: Illegal Aliens and the Making of Modern America* (Princeton, NJ: Princeton University Press, 2004), 2.
13. Ngai, *Impossible Subjects*, 8.
14. Ngai, *Impossible Subjects*, 3, 25.
15. See Natalia Molina, *How Race Is Made in America: Immigration, Citizenship, and the Historical Power of Racial Scripts* (Berkeley: University of California Press, 2014).

16. See John Chávez, *Lost Land* and *Beyond Nations.*
17. For a description of the synoptic view of the state see Scott, *Seeing Like a State*, 9–53.
18. Quoted in Ngai, *Impossible Subjects*, 229.
19. "Ritual of Order of Sons of America: Council No. 1. San Antonio, Texas," Oliver Douglas Weeks Collection, Box 1, Folder 1, Benson Library, University of Texas at Austin.
20. Cynthia Orozco, "Order of Knights of America," in *Handbook of Texas Online*, accessed December 14, 2010, http://www.tshaonline.org/handbook/online/articles/veo02.
21. *OKA News* 1, no. 2 (December 1927), Oliver Douglas Weeks Collection, Box 1, Folder 2, Benson Library, University of Texas at Austin. Original text: "se constituye exclusivamente con individuos de origen Mexicano, y que laborará por la educación de sus miembros, respecto a sus deberes y derechos, ya sea como ciudadanos de este país."
22. *Manual for Use by the League of Latin American Citizens*, Oliver Douglas Weeks Collection, Box 1, Folder 3, Benson Library, University of Texas at Austin. For an English translation, see "Objective and Aims of the Latin American Citizens League," in Orozco, *No Mexicans, Women, or Dogs*, 235–36.
23. "Constitution, League of United Latin American Citizens," in Orozco, *No Mexicans, Women, or Dogs*, 237–39.
24. Gutiérrez, *Walls and Mirrors*, 74–78.
25. Orozco, *No Mexicans, Women, or Dogs*, 67.
26. "Constitución y leyes de la Orden Hijos de America," Weeks Collection. Original text: "que hasta hoy y nunca en los pasado han tenido algún ideal bien definido de lo que intentan hacer en su posición presente y dentro del cartabón de sus deberes, derechos, y prerrogativas como ciudadanos de los Estados Unidos."
27. "Constitución y leyes de la Orden Hijos de America," Weeks Collection.
28. "Constitución y leyes de la Orden Hijos de America," Weeks Collection.
29. Andrés de Luna, "Orden Hijos de America," Clemente N. Idar Papers, Box 8, Folder 4, Benson Library, University of Texas at Austin. Original text: "pues de una vez por todas queremos dejar de ser mendigos de nacionalidad, hombres sin patria, elemento racial inconsciente, y desorientado, o peregrinos que al través de varias generaciones, viven en un estado de incompleta incertidumbre en cuanto se relaciona con sus intereses de patria y ciudadanía."
30. *El Paladín*, February 22, 1929, Weeks Collection, Box 1, Folder 10, Benson Library, University of Texas at Austin.
31. *El Paladín*, April 12, 1929, Weeks Collection,
32. *El Paladín*, May 24, 1929, Weeks Collection.
33. *El Paladín*, April 12, 1929, Weeks Collection.

34. "Para los que no conocen nuestra [institución]," circa 1930, Ben Garza Collection, Box 1, Folder 2, Benson Library, University of Texas at Austin. Original text: "Si las demás razas obraran como nosotros sería este país un conglomerado de patrias de afuera: Alemania de afuera, Inglaterra de afuera, Suecia de afuera, etc., etc., ni más ni menos como nosotros en la actualidad formamos un México de afuera."
35. "Para los que no conocen nuestra [institución]." Original text: "Mientras no nos elevemos al nivel de ciudadanos no seremos mas que conquistados."
36. "Respetable radio-auditorio," Andrés de Luna Collection, Box 1, Folder 9, Benson Library, University of Texas at Austin. Original text: "en este giron [*sic*] de tierra de los estados fronterizos de la Union Americana, a donde el pabellón tricolor, insigna [*sic*] gloriosa de la patria de nuestros antepasados no nos alcansa [*sic*] a cubrir." And "pedir patria dentro de su propia patria."
37. "Proceedings at San Diego, Texas," February 16, 1930, Oliver Douglas Weeks Collection, Box 1, Folder 6, Benson Library, University of Texas at Austin.
38. "Editorial: nobles propósitos," *El Defensor* (Edinburg, TX), November 21, 1930. Original text: "Demostremos que deveras [*sic*] tenemos patria y que esta la amamos y procuraremos engrandecerla y así podremos borrar las fortísimas barreras que nos separan de nuestros conacionales los anglo americanos."
39. Oropeza, *¡Raza Sí! ¡Guerra No!*, 49.
40. The historian Benjamin Johnson offers a somewhat more sympathetic view of the middle-class Mexican American imaginary that evolved in the 1920s and 1930s. The internationalization of the borderlands meant that transnational ways of coping could no longer offer protection for borderland residents. As he explains it, "What many Tejanos discovered during the plan de San Diego, however, was that it was dangerous to be a people without a state. A people could combine cultural elements of the two nations that served their own interests, but in crises they had to be able to call on the power of a central state to protect themselves. They needed to be Mexican or American, and it turned out that to be both was impossible and to be neither was unwise." Johnson, *Revolution in Texas*, 209.
41. Chávez, *Lost Land*, 114.
42. Richard García, *Rise of the Mexican American Middle Class*, 4–7. See also Mario García, *Mexican Americans*, 25–113.
43. "Encino, Texas, Survey," "Falfurrias Texas Survey," and "San Antonio, Texas, Survey," all in Oliver Douglas Weeks Collection, Box 1, Folder 8, Benson Library, University of Texas at Austin.
44. J. Montiel Olvera, *Primer anuario de los habitantes hispano-americanos de Texas/First Year Book of the Latin-American Population of Texas*, 1939, 29, Recovering the U.S. Hispanic Heritage Project Archives, University of Houston.

45. Olvera, *Primer anuario de los habitantes hispano-americanos*. Original text: "constituye una demostración de que la inteligencia y la pericia, no son patrimonio exclusive de algunos grupos étnicos."
46. Douglas Monroy, *Rebirth: Mexican Los Angeles from the Great Migration to the Great Depression* (Berkeley: University of California Press, 1999), 259.
47. Oropeza, *¡Raza Sí! ¡Guerra No!*, 19–21.
48. "Constitución y leyes de la Orden Hijos de America," Weeks Collection. Original text: "para mejorar su condición moral, social e intelectual" and "la Orden Hijos de América ha sido creada con el fijo propósito de cambiar el cauce de los acontecimientos, combatiendo la negligencia y morosidad de los ciudadanos de este país—mexicanos o españoles por el origen racial."
49. *OKA News* 1, no. 2 (December 1927), Oliver Douglas Weeks Collection, Box 1, Folder 2, Benson Library, University of Texas at Austin. Original text: "busca, ante todo, la elevación moral y material de los elementos nuestros que solo necesitan una preparación razonable para poder ocupar su sitio en el concurso de la civilización moderna."
50. Mauro Machado, "An Answer to Our Critics," *OKA News* 1, no. 3 (January 1928), Oliver Douglas Weeks Collection, Box 1, Folder 2, Benson Library, University of Texas at Austin.
51. Alonso S. Perales to Ben Garza, June 22, 1928, Andrés De Luna Collection, Box 1, Folder 3, Benson Library, University of Texas at Austin.
52. J. T. Canales, speech, *El Paladín*, February 22, 1929, Oliver Douglas Weeks Collection, Box 1, Folder 10, Benson Library, University of Texas at Austin.
53. J. Luz Saenz, speech, *El Paladín*, May 17, 1929, Oliver Douglas Weeks Collection, Box 1, Folder 10, Benson Library, University of Texas at Austin.
54. Alonso S. Perales, "The Unification of the Mexican-Americans," *La Prensa* (San Antonio, TX), September 4, 1929.
55. M. C. González, "President General of the LULAC Gives Views as to What Is Meant by 'True and Loyal Citizen of the United States of America,'" *El Defensor* (Edinburg, TX), June 5, 1931.
56. "Ritual of Order Sons of America: Council No. 1, San Antonio, Texas, Oliver Douglas Weeks Collection, Box 1, Folder 1, Benson Library, University of Texas at Austin.
57. "Constitución y leyes de la Orden Hijos de America," Weeks Collection.
58. Canales, speech, *El Paladín*, February 22, 1929, Weeks Collection.
59. Cynthia E. Orozco, "Ladies LULAC," in *Handbook of Texas Online*, accessed September 16, 2019, https://tshaonline.org/handbook/online/articles/wel06.
60. Cynthia E. Orozco, "Alice Dickerson Montemayor," in *Handbook of Texas Online*, accessed September 23, 2019, http://www.tshaonline.org/handbook/online/articles/fmobl and Cynthia E. Orozco, "Esther Nieto Machuca," in *Handbook of Texas Online*, accessed September 16, 2019, http://www.tshaonline.org/handbook/online/articles/fmadb.

61. Orozco, *No Mexicans, Women, or Dogs*, 211.
62. Monica Perales, "'Who Has a Greater Job Than a Mother?' Defining Mexican Motherhood on the U.S.-Mexico Border in the Early Twentieth Century," in *On the Borders of Love and Power: Families and Kinship in the Intercultural American Southwest*, ed. David Wallace Adams and Crista DeLuzio (Berkeley and Los Angeles: University of California Press, 2012), 165.
63. See González, *Redeeming La Raza* for her discussion on the role of Mexican motherhood and *marianismo* as a corollary to "Republican Motherhood."
64. See Orozco, *No Mexicans, Women, or Dogs*, 196–219.
65. For this idea I am indebted to the historian Willard B. Gatewood. See Gatewood, *Aristocrats of Color: The Black Elite, 1880–1920* (Bloomington: Indiana University Press, 1990), 23; also Preston H. Smith II, "The Chicago School of Human Ecology and the Ideology of Black Civic Elites," in *Renewing Black Intellectual History: The Ideological and Material Foundations of African American Thought*, ed. Adolph Reed Jr. and Kenneth W. Warren (Boulder, CO: Paradigm, 2010), 137.
66. Gatewood, *Aristocrats of Color*, 344.
67. Touré F. Reed, "The Educational Alliance and the Urban League in New York: Ethnic Elites and the Politics of Americanization and Racial Uplift, 1903–1932," in *Renewing Black Intellectual History: The Ideological and Material Foundations of African American Thought*, ed. Adolph Reed Jr. and Kenneth W. Warren (Boulder, CO: Paradigm, 2010), 97.
68. *El Paladín*, April 12, 1929, May 17, 1929 (article by J. Luz Saenz), and May 24, 1929, Oliver Douglas Weeks Collection, Box 1, Folder 10, Benson Library, University of Texas at Austin.
69. Carl N. Degler, *In Search of Human Nature: The Decline and Revival of Darwinism in American Social Thought* (New York: Oxford University Press, 1991), 13.
70. Gail Bederman, *Manliness and Civilization: A Cultural History of Gender and Race in the United States, 1880–1917* (Chicago: University of Chicago Press, 1995), 25.
71. "Problemas de actualidad: americanismo," *La Evolución* (Laredo, TX), November, 19, 1919. Original text: "la razas no retroceden, sino al contrario, avanzan incesantemente."
72. "Constitución y leyes de la Orden Hijos de America," Weeks Collection. Original text, quotation 1: "queremos una oportunidad amplia, completa y sin cortapisas para nuestra evolución social, económica y política. Nos adaptaremos al fenómeno de la evolución, a medida que vayamos progresando, a medida que vayamos aprendiendo a ser prósperos . . . a medida que vayamos emergiendo de las incertidumbres del pasado." Quotation 2: "por medio del cultivo moral y mental de nuestro elemento racial, podremos colocarnos en el sendero de una marcha de progreso y engrandecimiento substancialmente

benéfica para la sociedad y para la civilización de nuestra grande amada República Americana." Quotation 3: "Nosotros estamos resueltos a continuar avantes en nuestra marcha de progreso con la mirada fija en los horizontes del porvenir. . . . Confiaremos mas en las enseñanzas elocuentes de la evolución."

73. "El Fruto del Esfuerzo," *El Defensor* (Edinburg, TX), February 20, 1931. Original text: "la revolución en todos los países del mundo significa una evolución rápida y violenta . . . la revolución es un movimiento ascensional de progreso que pasa sutilmente a través de todos los obstruccionismos . . . la revolución en fin, no la detienen, en su incesante marcha."
74. Report by the Committee on Organization, 1929, Oliver Douglas Weeks Collection, Box 1, Folder 6, Benson Library, University of Texas at Austin.
75. *El Paladín*, February 22, 1929, Oliver Douglas Weeks Collection, Box 1, Folder 10, Benson Library, University of Texas at Austin.
76. J. Luz Saenz, *El Paladín*, May 17, 1929, Weeks Collection.
77. *El Paladín*, June 14, 1929, Weeks Collection.
78. Eduardo Idar, "Nuestros grandes problemas: colaboración especial para 'El Defensor,'" *El Defensor* (Edinburg, TX), June 19, 1931. Original text: "el sajón es materialista y positivista por que es ésta la escuela filosófica de que procede, nosotros somos románticos y soñadores por que procedemos de una filosofía que tiene en esto otro sus raigambres . . . no procede en los indoamericanos poder ser como los sajones y como ellos no nos entienden tampoco. . . . Nuestras esencia le parece al sajón una norma de impreparacion [*sic*], de notable falta de criterio para ver las cosas en un aspecto utilitario y practico."
79. "Wages of whiteness" is the historian David R. Roediger's adaptation of W. E. B. Du Bois's words. See Roediger, *The Wages of Whiteness: Race and the Making of the American Working Class* (London: Verso, 1991).
80. Historians disagree on the periodization of whiteness. For example, in *The Wages of Whiteness* David R. Roediger periodizes the rise in importance of whiteness as 1830–60 because "the systematic development of a sense of whiteness went hand in hand for the US white working class" (8). That is, whiteness was born of anxiety over the market revolution and fears of economic dependency. Whiteness became significant as the late eighteenth-century prediction of economic independence gave way to lifelong realities of wage labor in the nineteenth century. See Roediger, *The Wages of Whiteness*. Neil Foley's periodization is closely attached to the rise and fall of agriculture in the United States, from the early republic through the New Deal. See Foley, *The White Scourge: Mexicans, Blacks and Poor Whites in Texas Cotton Culture* (Berkeley: University of California Press, 1997). In the "Old South" "whiteness" was a surrogate for the traditional American idea of the political economy. Landownership and citizenship became interchangeable with whiteness, although agricultural consolidation in the late nineteenth

century began to threaten this ideal. Mexican migrant farm labors exacerbated the crisis of whiteness because many became sufficiently affluent to claim whiteness. White workers, increasingly in competition with Mexican workers, began to lose the entitlement to landownership that had defined their status for many years. New notions of scientific management, eugenicist science, and New Deal agricultural policy essentially ended the association and national obsession with agrarian whiteness and yeoman manhood. No longer social institutions that provided the means for citizenship and a particular form of "American" living, farms instead became factories in the field whose goal was to produce profit. Thus, the white farmer was stripped of his social value and replaced by racialized wage labor. Foley argues the Bracero Program marked the end of agrarian whiteness because the "public's concern" for white farmers ceased, and they tacitly accepted racialized wage labor and the factory model of farming. Matthew Frye Jacobson periodizes whiteness from the 1840s through the 1920s and places it within the context of evolutionary thought. According to Jacobson, whiteness had three great epochs: 1790 to 1840 corresponded to the republican convergence of race and fitness for self-government. From the 1840s to 1924, in the period of mass European migrations, "whiteness" fractured into multiple hierarchies of races, ostensibly with scientific backing. From 1924 on, whiteness was reconsolidated through immigration restrictions and increased African American populations in the US North and West. Jacobson, *Whiteness of a Different Color: European Immigrants and the Alchemy of Race* (Cambridge, MA: Harvard University Press, 1998).

81. Foley, *White Scourge*, 5.
82. Jacobson, *Whiteness of a Different Color*, 7, 34; quotation on p. 33.
83. Jacobson, *Whiteness of a Different Color*, 86–88; Ngai, *Impossible Subjects*, 15–55.
84. "Variegated whiteness" is Jacobson's term. See *Whiteness of a Different Color*, 52, 95.
85. Ian F. Haney López, *White by Law: The Legal Construction of Race* (New York: New York University Press, 1996), 1.
86. "Constitución y leyes de la Orden Hijos de America," Weeks Collection. Original text: "nuestra raza . . . debe considerarse, como lo es, raza Blanca."
87. Rodolfo A. de la Garza, "Who Are You?," *LULAC News*, 2, no. 1 (September 1932), quoted in Frances Jerome Woods, *Mexican Ethnic Leadership in San Antonio, Texas* (Washington, DC: Catholic University of America Press, 1949), 30.
88. Gregory R. Salinas to Louis Wilmot, August 13, 1936, Andrés de Luna Collection, Box 1, Folder 6, Benson Library, University of Texas at Austin.
89. Robert Meza to Jeff Bell, November 24, 1939, Andrés de Luna Collection, Box 1, Folder 6, Benson Library, University of Texas at Austin.

90. Meza to Bell.
91. Meza to Bell.
92. Manuel C. González, "No Segregation!" in J. Montiel Olvera, *Primer anuario de los habitantes hispano-americanos de Texas/First Year Book of the Latin-American Population of Texas*, 1939. Recovering the U.S. Hispanic Heritage Project Archives, University of Houston.
93. The historian Alexandra Minna Stern shows that even though US scientists were embarrassed by similarities between their racial and genetic ideas and those of the Nazis, those ideas did not suddenly disappear. Socially, they were replaced by cultural deficiency theories. But in the sciences, eugenics continued into the late twentieth century. Stern, *Eugenic Nation: Faults and Frontiers of Better Breeding in Modern America* (Berkeley: University of California Press, 2005).
94. Jacobson, *Whiteness of a Different Color*, 99.
95. George H. Roeder Jr., "Censoring Disorder: American Visual Imagery of World War II," in *The War in American Culture: Society and Consciousness during World War II*, ed. Lewis A. Erenberg and Susan E. Hirsch (Chicago: University of Chicago Press, 1996), 47.
96. Gary Gerstle, "The Working Class Goes to War," in *The War in American Culture: Society and Consciousness during World War II*, ed. Lewis A. Erenberg and Susan E. Hirsch (Chicago: University of Chicago Press, 1996), 114.
97. Ian Haney López and Michael A. Olivas, "Jim Crow, Mexican Americans, and the Anti-Subordinate Constitution: The Story of *Hernandez v. Texas*," in *Race Law Stories*, ed. Rachel F. Moran and Devon Wayne Carbado (New York: Foundation Press), 2008, 297.
98. Haney López and Olivas, "*Hernandez v. Texas*," 299, 280–81, quotation on 300.
99. Haney López and Olivas, "*Hernandez v. Texas*," 284.
100. Haney-López, *White by Law*, 35.

CHAPTER 3

1. "La raza mexicana del estado de Texas," *La Crónica* (Laredo, TX), October 1, 1910. Original text: "En el Estado de Texas nunca ha habido *tramps* mexicanos, ni aun entre los mas indigentes. No importa la edad, condición social o grado de instrucción: el mexicano siempre trabaja para ganarse el pan que se come." And "que es buen obrero, lo demuestra el hecho de que su trabajo es preferido en los ferrocarriles, en los minas de carbón, en las haciendas de agricultura y en los campos como vaqueros."
2. Montejano, *Anglos and Mexicans in the Making of Texas*, 103–78.
3. Zamora, *World of the Mexican Worker*, 213.
4. Juan Gómez-Quiñones, *Mexican American Labor, 1790–1990* (Albuquerque: University of New Mexico Press, 1994), 74.

5. Zamora, *World of the Mexican Worker*, 213.
6. Zamora, *World of the Mexican Worker*, 213–14.
7. For more on the dual wage market, see Mario Barrera, *Race and Class in the Southwest: A Theory of Racial Inequality* (Notre Dame, IN: University of Notre Dame Press, 1979); and Camarillo, *Chicanos in a Changing Society*.
8. Zaragosa Vargas, *Labor Rights Are Civil Rights: Mexican American Workers in Twentieth-Century America* (Princeton, NJ: Princeton University Press, 2005), 19, 18.
9. Selden C. Menefee and Orin C. Cassmore, *The Pecan Shellers of San Antonio: The Problem of Underpaid and Unemployed Mexican Labor* (Washington, DC: Government Printing Office, Division of Research Work Projects Administration, 1940), x, xvi, xvii, 26.
10. Menefee and Cassmore, *Pecan Shellers of San Antonio*, 26.
11. Vargas, *Labor Rights Are Civil Rights*, 19–21.
12. Menefee and Cassmore, *Pecan Shellers of San Antonio*, 28.
13. Vargas, *Labor Rights Are Civil Rights*, 21.
14. Gómez-Quiñones, *Mexican American Labor*, 131.
15. Emilio Zamora, "Chicano Socialist Labor Activity in Texas, 1900–1920," *Aztlán* 6, no. 2 (Summer 1975): 221.
16. See Bederman, *Manliness and Civilization*; Montejano, *Anglos and Mexicans in the Making of Texas*; David R. Roediger, *Towards the Abolition of Whiteness: Essays on Race, Politics, and Working Class History* (London: Verso, 1994); Foley, *White Scourge*; William D. Carrigan, *The Making of a Lynching Culture: Violence and Vigilantism in Central Texas, 1836–1916* (Urbana: University of Illinois Press, 2004); Jacobson, *Whiteness of a Different Color*.
17. For the changing economic foundations of racism see Montejano, *Anglos and Mexicans in the Making of Texas*. For the changing epistemological foundations of race, see Jacobson, *Whiteness of a Different Color*, 31–38.
18. See Foley, *White Scourge*, 118–40, 204–6. For the rise of middle-class managers and scientific management, see Alfred D. Chandler, *The Visible Hand: The Managerial Revolution in American Business* (Cambridge, MA: Harvard University Press, 1977).
19. Foley, *White Scourge*, 66.
20. Vargas, *Labor Rights Are Civil Rights*, 39; Robert S. McElvaine, *The Great Depression: America, 1929–1941* (New York: Times Books, 1984), 149–51; Foley, *White Scourge*, 164–69.
21. Foley, *White Scourge*, 65–69, 73, 88–89.
22. James R. Green, *Grass-Roots Socialism: Radical Movements in the Southwest, 1895–1943* (Baton Rouge: Louisiana State University Press, 1978), xi.
23. James R. Green, "Tenant Farmer Discontent and Socialist Protest in Texas, 1901–1917," *Southwestern Historical Quarterly* 81, no. 2 (1977): 135.

24. Alwyn Barr, "Socialist Party," in *Handbook of Texas Online*, accessed June 14, 2012, http://www.tshaonline.org/handbook/online/articles/was01.
25. Foley, *White Scourge*, 93.
26. Green, "Tenant Farmer Discontent," 147–49.
27. Green, *Grass-Roots Socialism*, 9.
28. Regarding how working-class whites came to see meaning in whiteness during an earlier period see Roediger, *Wages of Whiteness*. For a study of how white supremacy and male superiority fused during the Progressive Era to form a gendered racism, see Bederman, *Manliness and Civilization*, 1–44.
29. Roediger, *Towards the Abolition of Whiteness*, 23.
30. Foley, *White Scourge*, 97.
31. Roediger, *Towards the Abolition of Whiteness*, 141.
32. Foley, *White Scourge*, 47.
33. Foley, *White Scourge*, 95.
34. Tom Hickey, quoted in Foley, *White Scourge*, 95.
35. Roediger, *Towards the Abolition of Whiteness*, 148.
36. Johnson, *Revolution in Texas*, 64.
37. "Conflict and the Race Problem," Box 2E306, Folder 5, Labor Movement in Texas Collection, 1845–1954, Dolph Briscoe Center for American History, University of Texas at Austin.
38. "Conflict and the Race Problem" Dolph Briscoe Center for American History.
39. "Mexican Labor and Longshoremen," Box 2E306, Folder 5, Labor Movement in Texas Collection, 1845–1954, Dolph Briscoe Center for American History, University of Texas at Austin.
40. Zamora, "Chicano Socialist Labor Activity," 221, 222.
41. Gómez-Quiñones, *Mexican American Labor*, 69.
42. Johnson, *Revolution in Texas*, 60.
43. Justin Akers Chacón, *Radicals in the Barrio: Magonistas, Socialists, Wobblies, and Communists in the Mexican-American Working Class* (Chicago: Haymarket Books, 2018), 195, 207–8.
44. Johnson, *Revolution in Texas*, 61.
45. Chacón, *Radicals in the Barrio*, 207, 195, 196.
46. Hernández, "Women's Labor and Activism," 177–80.
47. Chacón, *Radicals in the Barrio*, 153.
48. Zamora, *World of the Mexican Worker*, 133.
49. Zamora, *World of the Mexican Worker*, 136.
50. Chacón, *Radicals in the Barrio*, 214.
51. For a deeper discussion of the connections between the PLM and ethnic Mexican labor in the United States see Zamora, *World of the Mexican Worker*, 139–61.
52. Zamora, *World of the Mexican Worker*, 133.

53. Zamora, *World of the Mexican Worker*, 133; and "Chicano Socialist Labor Activity," 228–29.
54. See Chacón, *Radicals in the Barrio*, 181–205.
55. Vargas, *Labor Rights Are Civil Rights*, 64.
56. Chacón, *Radicals in the Barrio*, 251, 259–60.
57. García, *Mexican Americans*, 146, 145.
58. Ruiz, *Cannery Women*, 41.
59. Chacón, *Radicals in the Barrio*, 536–38.
60. Ruiz, *Cannery Women*, 42.
61. "Official Proceedings of the First National Convention of the United Cannery, Agricultural, Packing and Allied Workers of America," p. 15, Box 1, Folder 11, Food, Tobacco, Agricultural, and Allied Workers Union of America, CIO Texas Locals Collections, University of Texas at Arlington.
62. "Official Proceedings of UCAPAWA," 3.
63. "Official Proceedings of UCAPAWA," 59–60.
64. "Official Proceedings of UCAPAWA," 74–75.
65. "Official Proceedings of UCAPAWA," 75.
66. Menefee and Cassmore, *Pecan Shellers of San Antonio*, 17–18.
67. "A Resolution from Pecan Workers Union, Local #172," Box 1, Folder 13, Food, Tobacco, Agricultural, and Allied Workers Union of America, CIO Texas Locals Collections, University of Texas at Arlington.
68. "Bulletin," Box 1, Folder 6, Food, Tobacco, and Allied Workers Union of America, CIO Texas Locals Collection, University of Texas at Arlington.
69. United Cannery, Agricultural, Packing and Allied Workers of America, C.I.O Weslaco Local #223 and Donna Local #180 to the Mexican Methodist Church, July 8, 1938, Box 27, Folder 9, George and Latane Lambert Papers, University of Texas at Arlington.
70. George Lambert to Norman Thomas, February 6, 1940, Box 1, Folder 3, Food, Tobacco, Agricultural, and Allied Workers Union of America CIO Texas Locals Collection, University of Texas at Arlington.
71. George Lambert to Herb ?, August 6, 1938, Box 27, Folder 9, George and Latane Lambert Papers, University of Texas at Arlington.
72. Vargas, *Labor Rights Are Civil Rights*, 65, 144.
73. Chacón, *Radicals in the Barrio*, 472, 483–83.
74. Emma Tenayuca and Homer Brooks, "The Mexican Question in the Southwest," in *Herencia: The Anthology of Hispanic Literature of the United States*, ed. Nicolás Kanellos (Oxford: Oxford University Press, 2002), 158, 159.
75. Tenayuca and Brooks, "Mexican Question," 161; Vargas, *Labor Rights Are Civil Rights*, 116.
76. "Interview with Mrs. Zappone of San Antonio, Member of the ILGWU, October 5, 1936," Box 2E308, Folder 9, Labor Movement in Texas Collection,

1845–1954, Dolph Briscoe Center for American History, University of Texas at Austin.

77. "Interview with Miss Rebecca Taylor, Ladies Garment Workers, San Antonio, October 6, 1936," Box 2E308, Folder 9, Labor Movement in Texas Collection.
78. "The International Ladies Garment Workers Union Comes to Texas," Box 2E308, Folder 9, Labor Movement in Texas Collection.
79. "Interview with Miss Rebecca Taylor."
80. Vargas, *Labor Rights Are Civil Rights*, 117–18, 119.
81. "José Jacobs, Jacobs' Studio, Laredo, Texas, October 15, 1936," Box 2E309, Folder 12, Labor Movement in Texas Collection.
82. García, *Mexican Americans*, 196; George N. Green, "Texas State Industrial Union Council," in *Handbook of Texas Online*, accessed June 19, 2012, http://tshaonline.org/handbook/online/articles/octbg.
83. Vargas, *Labor Rights Are Civil Rights*, 166, 168.
84. Chacón, *Radicals in the Barrio*, 545, 549–51, 542–45.
85. "Resolution from the Meeting of the Fort Worth Local #37 of the International Association of Oil Field, Gas Well and Refinery Workers of America," Box 2E309, Folder 13, Labor Movement in Texas Collection.
86. Menefee and Cassmore, *Pecan Shellers of San Antonio*, 40–43.
87. George Lambert to the Executive Board of the Pecan Workers Union Local #172, March 23, 1939, Box 27, Folder 9, George and Latane Lambert Papers.
88. Chacón, *Radicals in the Barrio*, 442.
89. See John Weber, *From South Texas to the Nation: The Exploitation of Mexican Labor in the Twentieth Century* (Chapel Hill: University of North Carolina Press, 2015).
90. See Ruiz, *Cannery Women*.
91. See Foley, *White Scourge*, 118–40.
92. See Francisco E. Balderrama and Raymond Rodríguez, *Decade of Betrayal: Mexican Repatriation in the 1930s* (Albuquerque: University of New Mexico Press, 1995).
93. Chacón, *Radicals in the Barrio*, 455–58, 548.
94. Sánchez, *Becoming Mexican American*, 222, 261.
95. See, by Dennis Valdés, *Barrios norteños: St. Paul and Midwestern Mexican Communities in the Twentieth Century* (Austin: University of Texas Press, 2000); *Al Norte: Agricultural Workers in the Great Lakes Region, 1917–1970* (Austin: University of Texas Press, 1991); and *Mexicans in Minnesota* (St. Paul: Minnesota Historical Society Press, 2005); as well as Zaragosa Vargas, *Proletarians of the North: A History of Mexican Industrial Workers in Detroit and the Midwest, 1917–1933* (Berkeley: University of California Press, 1993).
96. Américo Paredes, *George Washington Gómez: A Mexicotexan Novel* (Houston, TX: Arte Público Press, 1990), 195.

97. Alan Brinkley, *The End of Reform: New Deal Liberalism in Recession and War* (New York: Vintage Books, 1995), 1–30.
98. For more on the exploitative effects of the "Mexican Miracle" and its attendant political suppression see Gómez, *Revolutionary Imaginations of Greater Mexico*, 40–66.
99. Garcia, *Mexican Americans*, 145–230; Douglas C. Rossinow, *Visions of Progress: The Left-Liberal Tradition in America* (Philadelphia: University of Pennsylvania Press, 2008).

CHAPTER 4

1. "Staff Report: The Mexican American Population of Texas," in US Commission on Civil Rights, *Hearing before the United States Commission on Civil Rights: Hearing Held in San Antonio, Texas, December 9–14, 1968* (Washington, DC: Government Printing Office, 1969), 22, 767–93.
2. Selden C. Menefee, *Mexican Migratory Workers of South Texas* (Washington DC: Government Printing Office 1941), 37, 38.
3. I calculated for inflation using the Bureau of Labor Statistics inflation calculator, accessed March 27, 2019, https://data.bls.gov/cgi-bin/cpicalc.pl?cost1=561.00&year1=193801&year2=196002.
4. Pauline R. Kibbe, *Latin Americans in Texas* (Albuquerque: University of New Mexico Press, 1946), 131, 126.
5. Erez Manela, *The Wilsonian Moment: Self-Determination and the International Origins of Anticolonial Nationalism* (Oxford: Oxford University Press, 2007), 6.
6. Manela, *Wilsonian Moment*, 42, 10.
7. Manela, *Wilsonian Moment*, 217.
8. Eric Helleiner, *Forgotten Foundations of Bretton Woods: International Development and the Making of the Postwar Order* (Ithaca, NY: Cornell University Press, 2014), 16.
9. Helleiner, *Forgotten Foundations*, 44, 50 (quotation), 52–60.
10. "Atlantic Charter," *The Avalon Project: Documents in Law, History, and Diplomacy*, accessed March 28, 2019, http://avalon.law.yale.edu/wwii/atlantic.asp.
11. See Weitz, *World Divided*.
12. "Charter of the United Nations," chapter 1, *The Avalon Project: Documents in Law, History, and Diplomacy*, accessed March 28, 2019, https://www.un.org/en/sections/un-charter/chapter-i/index.html.
13. "Charter of the Organization of American States," article 9, *The Avalon Project: Documents in Law, History, and Diplomacy*, accessed March 29, 2019, http://avalon.law.yale.edu/20th_century/decad062.asp#art9.
14. Michael E. Latham, *Modernization as Ideology: American Social Science and "Nation Building" in the Kennedy Era* (Chapel Hill: University of North Carolina Press, 2000), 34, 4.

15. Quotation from Walter W. Rostow, *The Stages of Economic Growth: A Non-Communist Manifesto* (Oxford: Oxford University Press, 1991). See also Latham, *Modernization as Ideology*, 45.
16. Latham, *Modernization as Ideology*, 53.
17. Nils Gilman, *Mandarins of the Future: Modernization Theory in Cold War America* (Baltimore, MD: Johns Hopkins University Press, 2003), 65; see also 62–67.
18. Postcolonial theorist Homi K. Bhabha explains that the nation is made coherent and readable through narrations—or stories the nation tells about itself. See "Narrating the Nation," in *Nation and Narration*, ed. Homi K. Bhabha (New York: Routledge, 1990), 1–3.
19. M. C. Gonzalez, "President General of the LULAC Gives Views as to What Is Meant by 'True and Loyal Citizen of the United States of America,'" *El Defensor* (Edinburg, TX), June 5, 1931.
20. Santiago G. Guzman, "One Flag, One Nation Indivisible with Liberty and Justice for All," *El Defensor* (Edinburg, TX), June 19, 1931.
21. Order of Sons of America, "Opening Hymn 'America,'" Oliver Douglas Weeks Collection, Box 1, Folder 1, Benson Library, University of Texas at Austin.
22. Guzman, "One Flag, One Nation."
23. John M. González has written that Lozano's historiographical interventions radically revised the narrative of the nation. See González, *Border Renaissance*, 110–19.
24. Rubén Rendon Lozano, *Viva Tejas: The Story of the Mexican-Born Patriots of the Republic of Texas* (San Antonio, TX: Southern Literary Institute, 1936), 21, 19.
25. Lozano, *Viva Tejas*, 26.
26. Lozano, *Viva Tejas*, 49, 50.
27. J. C. Machuca to Alicia Dickerson Montemayor, January 26, 1938, Alicia Dickerson Montemayor Papers, Box 3, Folder 3, Benson Library, University of Texas at Austin.
28. J. C. Machuca to Mrs. O. N. Lightner, February 2, 1938, Alicia Dickerson Montemayor Papers, Box 3, Folder 6.
29. Carlos E. Castañeda, "La aportación del mexicano al desarrollo de Texas," in *Primer anuario de los habitantes hispano-americanos de Texas/First Year Book of the Latin-American Population of Texas*, ed. J. Montiel Olvera (1939), 13, Recovering the US Hispanic Heritage Project Archives, University of Houston. Original text: "no hay grupo racial en la cosmopolita población del estado de Texas que haya contribuido más a su historia, su desarrollo físico, y material y su cultura que el Mexicano." And "es necesario recordar que a medida que se hacía inevitable el conflicto con México, muchos de los mexicanos en Texas no solamente concedían la razón a los nuevos colonos sino que hicieron propia su causa."

30. Zamora, *Claiming Rights and Righting Wrongs*.
31. For "double victory," see Ronald Takaki, *Double Victory: A Multicultural History of America in World War II* (New York: Little and Brown, 2000), 22–57.
32. Zamora, *Claiming Rights and Righting Wrongs*, 63–96.
33. Blanton, *George I. Sánchez*, 73–76.
34. Natalie Mendoza, "The Good Neighbor in the American Historical Imagination: Boltonians, Mexican Americans, and the Creation of a Common American Heritage," *Western Historical Quarterly*, forthcoming.
35. Jerry Thompson, "Juan Nepomuceno Cortina," in *Handbook of Texas Online*, accessed February 3, 2012, https://tshaonline.org/handbook/online/articles/fco73.
36. J. T. Canales, *Juan N. Cortina, Bandit or Patriot?* (San Antonio, TX: Artes Gráficas, 1951), 5, 7 (quotation).
37. Canales, *Juan N. Cortina*, 10–11.
38. Canales, *Juan N. Cortina*, 6.
39. Gus C. García, "Address Delivered before the Convention," in *Minutes of a State Convention of Latin American Leaders Creating a Texas Pro Human Relations Fund*, July 29, 1951, 11–12, Albert Peña Collection, Box 3, Folder 9, University of Texas at San Antonio.
40. González, *Border Renaissance*, 120.
41. V. Carl Allsup, "American G.I. Forum of Texas," in *Handbook of Texas Online*, accessed February 3, 2011, http://www.tshaonline.org/handbook/online/articles/voa01.
42. Jose Antonio Villarreal, *Pocho* (New York: Anchor Books, 1959), 3.
43. Villarreal, *Pocho*, 146, 147.
44. Villarreal, *Pocho*, 175.
45. Eduardo Quevedo et al., Open Resolution Directed to the President of the United States and Executive Departments and Agencies, by National Hispanic and Mexican-American Organizations on Civil Disobedience and Riot Investigations, in "The History of Political Organizations among Mexican-Americans in Los Angeles since the Second World War," by Kay Lynn Briegel (master's thesis, University of Southern California, 1967), 64.
46. García, "Address Delivered before the Convention," Peña Collection.
47. Kibbe, *Latin Americans in Texas*, 134.
48. Kibbe, *Latin Americans in Texas*, 91.
49. Kibbe, *Latin Americans in Texas*, 228.
50. Mario T. García, *Mexican Americans*, 113. See also García, *The Making of a Mexican American Mayor: Raymond L. Telles of El Paso and the Origins of Latino Political Power* (Tucson: University of Arizona Press, 2018).
51. Martin Donell Kohout, "González, Henry Barbosa," in *Handbook of Texas Online*, accessed March 29, 2019, http://www.tshaonline.org/handbook/online/articles/fgo76.

52. García, *Mexican Americans*, 136.
53. Mary L. Dudziak, *Cold War Civil Rights: Race and the Image of American Democracy* (Princeton, NJ: Princeton University Press, 2000), 13, 6–12.
54. José Ángel Gutiérrez, *Albert A. Peña Jr.: Dean of Chicano Politics* (East Lansing: Michigan State University Press, 2017), 70, 76.
55. Albert Peña, interview by José Ángel Gutiérrez, San Antonio, TX, July 2, 1996, Tejano Voices: University of Texas at Arlington Center for Mexican American Studies Oral History Project.
56. García, *Viva Kennedy*, 10, 53, 51.
57. Albert Peña to Tommy Powers, October 17, 1961, Albert Peña Collection, Box 1, Folder 11, University of Texas at San Antonio.
58. García, *Chicanismo*, 25.
59. Albert Peña, "Address to State PASO Convention," Austin, TX, August 26, 1962, Albert Peña Collection, Box 28, Folder 3, University of Texas at San Antonio.
60. Robert O. Self, *American Babylon: Race and the Struggle for Postwar Oakland* (Princeton, NJ: Princeton University Press, 2003), 93–94.
61. Albert Peña, "Speech at the University of Texas," September 23, 1971, Albert Peña Collection, Box 26, Folder 3, University of Texas at San Antonio.
62. Peña, "Speech at the University of Texas."
63. "Crystal City Gave PASO Pilot Project It Needed," *Dallas Morning News*, May 7, 1963, Albert Peña Collection, Box 1, Folder 14, University of Texas at San Antonio. On the divisions between the liberal and conservative factions within the Texas Democratic Party see Sean P. Cunningham, *Cowboy Conservatism: Texas and the Rise of the Modern Right* (Lexington: University Press of Kentucky, 2010).
64. "Crystal City Gave PASO Pilot Project It Needed."
65. García, *Viva Kennedy*, 148.
66. Albert Peña, interview by José Ángel Gutiérrez, Tejano Voices.
67. "Crystal City Gave PASO Pilot Project It Needed."
68. "Crystal City Gave PASO Pilot Project It Needed."
69. Albert Fuentes Jr. to Membership of PASO, March 14, 1963, Albert Peña Collection, Box 22, Folder 2, University of Texas at San Antonio.
70. García, *Viva Kennedy*, 150–52.
71. García, *Viva Kennedy*, 153.
72. Peña, interview by José Ángel Gutiérrez, Tejano Voices.
73. Peña, interview by José Ángel Gutiérrez, Tejano Voices.
74. Albert Peña to Héctor P. García, July 21, 1967, Albert Peña Collection, Box 22, Folder 2, University of Texas at San Antonio.
75. Albert Peña, "Speech to McAllen PASO," August 9, 1964, Albert Peña Collection, Box 22, Folder 8, University of Texas at San Antonio.
76. Albert Peña, "Speech to McAllen PASO," Albert Peña Collection.

77. Albert Peña, "County Comment," April 30, 1965, Albert Peña Collection, Box 28, Folder 4, University of Texas at San Antonio.
78. Albert Peña, "PASO Speech," 1966, Albert Peña Collection, Box 22, Folder 8, University of Texas at San Antonio.
79. Ignacio M. García, *United We Win: The Rise and Fall of La Raza Unida Party* (Tucson: University of Arizona Press, 1989), 11; José Ángel Gutiérrez, *The Making of a Chicano Militant: Lessons from Cristal* (Madison: University of Wisconsin Press, 1998), 64–70.
80. José Ángel Gutiérrez, *La Raza and Revolution: The Empirical Conditions of Revolution in Four South Texas Counties* (San Francisco: R and E Research Associates, 1971), 67.
81. Gutiérrez, *Raza and Revolution*, 1–2, 5, 6, 7, 9.
82. Gutiérrez, *Raza and Revolution*, 25.
83. Gutiérrez, *Raza and Revolution*, 42.
84. Montejano, *Sancho's Journal*, 14.
85. Montejano, *Sancho's Journal*, 9.
86. The phrase "science of society" comes from Latham, *Modernization as Ideology*, 53.
87. Montejano, *Sancho's Journal*, 16; see also the culmination of his search in *Anglos and Mexicans in the Making of Texas*.
88. Montejano, "Frustrated Apartheid," 132.
89. Helleiner, *Forgotten Foundations*, 54, 74.
90. George N. Green, "The Good Neighbor Commission," in *Handbook of Texas Online*, accessed October 22, 2019, https://tshaonline.org/handbook/online/articles/mdg02; see also Zamora, *Claiming Rights and Righting Wrongs*, 78–89; 117–18.
91. Gilman, *Mandarins of the Future*, 234–35; see also Immanuel Wallerstein, *The Modern World-System* (New York: Academic Press, 1974).
92. Immanuel Wallerstein, "Immanuel Wallerstein's Thousand Marxisms," *Jacobin*, August 31, 2019.
93. Gilman, *Mandarins of the Future*, 237.
94. See Carlos Muñoz Jr., "On the Cause and Tension in the Chicano Community," *Aztlán* 1 (Fall 1970); Tomás Almaguer, "Toward the Study of Chicano Colonialism," *Aztlán* 2 (Spring 1971): 7–21; Mario Barrera, Carlos Muñoz, and Charles Ornelas, "The Barrio as Internal Colony," in *People and Politics in Urban Society*, ed. Harlan Hahn (Beverly Hills, CA: Sage, 1972); Rodolfo Acuña, *Occupied America: The Chicano's Struggle toward Liberation* (San Francisco, CA: Canfield Press, 1972); and John R. Chávez, "Aliens in Their Native Lands: The Persistence of Internal Colonial Theory," *Journal of World History* 22, no. 4: 785–809; Chávez, "When Borders Cross Peoples: The Internal Colonial Challenge to Borderlands Theory," *Journal of Borderlands Studies* 28, no. 1 (2013): 33–46.

95. Chávez, "Aliens in Their Native Lands," 789, 786.
96. Almaguer, "Toward the Study of Chicano Colonialism," 11, 12.
97. Jacob I. Rodríguez, "Mexican? Mexican-American? Chicanos? All Wrong!!" Jacob I. Rodríguez Collection, Box 7, Folder 12, Benson Library, University of Texas at Austin.
98. Montejano, *Quixote's Soldiers*, 87–98, 228–33.
99. Henry B. González, *The New Racism: Speeches of U.S. Rep. Henry B. González which Appeared in the Congressional Record April 3, 15, 16, 22, 28, 29, May 1, 1969*, Joe J. Bernal Papers, Box 18, Henry B. González Folder, Benson Library, University of Texas at Austin.
100. Gilman, *Mandarins of the Future*, 6.
101. Gilman, *Mandarins of the Future*, 3.
102. Guadalupe San Miguel Jr., "In the Midst of Radicalism: Mexican American Liberals during the Early Years of the Chicano Movement—The Case of Vicente T. Ximenes and the Interagency Committee on Mexican American Affairs, 1965–1968," *Journal of South Texas* 31, no. 2. (Spring 2018), 21.

CHAPTER 5

1. See John R. Chávez, *Eastside Landmark: A History of the East Los Angeles Community Union, 1968–1993* (Stanford, CA: Stanford University Press, 1998).
2. Abelardo Delgado, *Chicano: 25 Pieces of a Chicano Mind* (El Paso, TX: Barrio Publications, 1972), 4.
3. Ricardo Sánchez, *Canto y grito mi liberación: The Liberation of a Chicano Mind* (Grand City, NY: Anchor Press/Doubleday, 1973), 14.
4. Armando Cavada, "Raza Unida Party and the Chicano Middle Class," *Caracol*, September 1974, 17.
5. "Z" [pseudonym], "The Dilemma of the Assimilated Mexican," *Magazín*, September 1973, 13.
6. José Ángel Gutiérrez, "The Mexican-American Político," *Caracol*, February 1975, 17.
7. Angela de Hoyos, "The Missing Ingredient," in *Arise, Chicano! and Other Poems* (San Antonio, TX: M&A Editions, 1980), 24.
8. Montejano, *Quixote's Soldiers*, 80–98, 228–33.
9. La mano negra de Aztlán, "un canto de amor por henry b.," Joe J. Bernal Papers, Box 38, Henry B. González Folder, Benson Library, University of Texas at Austin.
10. Rene Abelardo González, "Como," *Tejidos* (Summer 1977), 46.
11. George Mariscal explains "at the heart of the diverse collective projects that arose in the United States was a critique of traditional liberalism that exposed the contradictions and hypocrisies of a system that had promised equality to all groups but had refused to deliver it." Mariscal, *Brown-Eyed Children of the Sun*, 9.

12. Angela de Hoyos, "Gracias, mees-ter . . . !," in *Arise, Chicano!*, 22.
13. Angela de Hoyos, "The Final Laugh," in *Arise, Chicano!*, 32.
14. Mariscal, *Brown-Eyed Children of the Sun*, 9.
15. Rosales, *Chicano*!, 184–86.
16. "List of Demands from Edcouch-Elsa Walkout," Joe J. Bernal Papers, Box 7, MAUC Folder, Benson Library, University of Texas at Austin.
17. Bradley Galloway, "Sick at Heart: The Latino Boycott of the Abilene Independent School District" (master's thesis, Abilene Christian University, 2001), 13–17.
18. Gutiérrez, *Making of a Chicano Militant*, 142, 97–121, 178, 153.
19. Carlos Muñoz Jr., *Youth, Identity, Power: The Chicano Movement* (New York: Verso, 1989), 65; Guadalupe San Miguel, *Brown, Not White: School Integration and the Chicano Movement in Houston* (College Station: Texas A&M University Press, 2001), xii, 196, 197–201.
20. Delgado, "La Raza," in *Chicano*, 6.
21. On Chávez's distance from the Chicano Movement see Muñoz, *Youth Identity, Power*, 59–60.
22. Mariscal, *Brown-Eyed Children of the Sun*, 142.
23. Delgado, "La Huelga," in *Chicano*, 7.
24. Joe J. Bernal, "Boycott Si—Lettuce No," *Chicano Times*, August 17–31, 1973, Joe J. Bernal Papers, Box 38, *Chicano Times* Folder, Benson Library, University of Texas at Austin.
25. For an overview of how Chicanas/os in different southwestern states deployed the concept of Aztlán, see "Aztlán Rediscovered" in Chávez, *Lost Land*, 129–55.
26. Rosales, *Chicano*!, 181.
27. "Plan Espiritual de Aztlán," in *Literatura chicana: texto y contexto/Chicano Literature: Text and Context*, ed. Antonia Castañeda Shular, Tomás Ybarra-Frausto, and Joseph Sommers (Englewood Cliffs, NJ: Prentice-Hall, 1972), 84.
28. The concept of Aztlán and its role in the Chicano Movement is not without controversy. For some scholars, Aztlán was a call for separatism and regression into a narrowly focused and nearly myopic nationalism. See, for example, Rosales, *Chicano*!, 181; and Chávez, *¡Mi Raza Primero*! Some scholars view the notion of Aztlán in a more positive light. In *Brown-Eyed Children of the Sun*, literary scholar George Mariscal argues that "Chicano humanism" is more about the "important principle of foundational Movement documents like the 'Plan Espiritual de Aztlán' than narrow forms of ethnic nationalism" (57). Historian John R. Chávez sees Aztlán as one of many perceptions that US-born Mexicans have of the Southwest, one that has a long intellectual history. See Chávez, *Lost Land*, 129–55.
29. García, *United We Win*, 55.

30. Juan Tejeda, interview by the author, San Antonio, TX, September 13, 2011.
31. Cecilio García-Camarillo, Reyes Cárdenas, and Carmen Tafolla, *Nahuallian-doing: Español/Nahuatl/English* (San Antonio, TX: Caracol, 1977), 5–6.
32. Carmen Tafolla, interview by the author, San Antonio, TX, September 12, 2011.
33. Montejano, *Quixote's Soldiers*, 30, 41.
34. Montejano, *Quixote's Soldiers*, 45.
35. Interview with Lalo Martínez, April 2, 1975, quoted in Montejano, *Quixote's Soldiers*, 54.
36. Rudy Ortiz, "Bits and Pieces," *Caracol*, April 1975, 19.
37. Raúl Salinas, "El Tecato," *Tejidos*, Fall 1975, 9.
38. David R. Ruiz, "Chicano," *Caracol*, September 1976, 13.
39. Donald Urioste, "Entrevista a Abelardo Lalo Delgado," *Caracol*, April 1976, 9. Original text: "hay un poco de odio por las condiciones de 'colonia' donde todo aspecto de autoridad es extraño albarrio [*sic*]. Son extranjeros hasta los mismos padres de la Iglesia."
40. Carlos Rene Guerra, "Colonización del Chicano," *Caracol*, February 1975, 7. Original text: "los Chicanos, particularmente los que hoy viven en sitios donde formamos la mayoría de la población, crean un fenómeno socio-económico porque se parece detalladamente al *colonialismo*. Bajo el sistema de *colonialismo* tenemos que depender en fuerzas sociales y sistemas económicos que no solamente forman choques culturales, sino que también son ajenas y no están situadas en la comunidad. . . . [esto] nos llevan a concluir que somos una *colonia* dentro de los Estados Unidos. Es decir, no somos una gente independiente sino una gente que depende del gringo y sus sistemas."
41. Raúl Castillo, "Yo," *Caracol*, March 1975, 20. Original text: "I do not want to be an intelligent poet / I want to be a poet among the people.
42. Abelardo Delgado, *The Chicano Movement: Some Not Too Objective Observations* (Denver, CO: Totinem Publications, 1971), 10.
43. Sánchez, *Canto y grito mi liberación*, 12, 13, 4.
44. Both quotations from Sánchez, *Canto y grito mi liberación*, 14.
45. Cavada, "Raza Unida Party and the Chicano Middle Class," 18.
46. Guadalupe Youngblood, "An Interview with Guadalupe Youngblood," *Caracol*, December 1974, 17. Original text: "Mucha gente cree que porque tienen una diploma o algo así, tienen no nomás el deber, responsabilidad y el derecho y todo, de tomar las riendas de toda la onda. Eso ya es presumir mucho. Personas como la Sra. Arévalo han comprobado que han tomado la oportunidad y han desarrollado una conciencia política a tal punto que está muy cabrón pa' que un vendido, estudiante, o abogado o lo que sea, les vaya a ganar en un argumento político."
47. Tatcho Mindiola, interview by the author, Houston, TX, September 6, 2012.

48. Montejano, *Quixote's Soldiers*, 50.
49. Delgado, "El macho," in *Chicano: 25 Pieces of a Chicano Mind*, 9.
50. Ricardo Sánchez, "Demadrazgo," in *Canto y grito mi liberación*, 37.
51. Sánchez, "Stream," in *Canto y grito mi* liberación, 77–78, 83.
52. Abel Garza, "Couplets," *Caracol*, August 1975, 23.
53. Tino Villanueva, "Hay otra voz," in *Hay otra voz: Poems* (1968–1971) (Staten Island, NY: Editorial Mensaje, 1979), 34–35. Original text: "que hay otra voz que quiere hablar; / que hay un perfil de tez bronceada / que de rodillas / arrastrándose camina por los / *Cotton-fields* de *El Campo* y *Lubbock, Texas.* /—¿A dónde voy?—, pregunta. / ¿A los *cucumber patches* de *Joliet*, / a las *vineyards* de *San Fernando Valley*, / a los *beet fields* de *Colorado*? / Hay ciertas incertidumbres ciertas: / lo amargo de piscar naranjas / lo lloroso de cortar cebollas [. . .] / Hay otra voz que quiere hablar."
54. *Caracol*, September 1974, 2.
55. *Caracol*, September 1974, 2.
56. Ralph Cruz Castillo, "An Essay Concerning Chicano Philosophy," *Caracol*, July 1975, 3.
57. Reyes Cárdenas, "William Wordsworth," *Caracol*, July 1975, 15.
58. Bernardo Verastique, "Some Conclusions," in *Yellow Luna* (San Antonio, TX: n.p., 1977), 22.
59. Luis Valdez, "Pensamiento serpentino," in *Luis Valdez—Early Works: Actos, Bernabé, and Pensamiento Serpentino* (Houston: Arte Público Press, 1990), 175.
60. Rodolfo "Corky" Gonzales, "I Am Joaquín," in *Message to Aztlán: Selected Writings* of Rodolfo "Corky" Gonzales, comp. Antonio Esquibel (Houston, TX: Arte Público Press, 2001), 16; Verastique, "Some Conclusions," 22.
61. Oropeza, *¡Raza Sí! ¡Guerra No!*, 111, 110.
62. Maylei Blackwell, *¡Chicana Power! Contested Histories of Feminism in the Chicano Movement* (Austin: University of Texas Press, 2011), 80.
63. Elizabeth Martínez, *De Colores Means All of Us: Latina Views for a Multi-Colored Century* (Cambridge, MA: South End Press, 1998), 175.
64. Rosa Linda Fregoso, *MeXicana Encounters: The Making of Social Identities on the Borderlands* (Berkeley and Los Angeles: University of California Press, 2003), 86, 85.
65. Denise A. Segura and Beatriz M. Pesquera, "Beyond Indifference and Antipathy: The Chicana Movement and Chicana Feminist Discourse," *Aztlán* 19, no. 2 (1990): 69.
66. Blackwell, *¡Chicana Power!*, 24–26, 1 (quotation).
67. Discussion with Marta Cotera, Maylei Blackwell, and Anna NietoGomez, CMAS Plática, University of Texas at Austin, October 10, 2011.
68. Montejano, *Quixote's Soldiers*, 162–63.

69. Montejano, *Quixote's Soldiers*, 167.
70. Evey Chapa, "Mujeres por la Raza Unida," *Caracol*, October 1974, 3; emphasis in original.
71. Chapa, "Mujeres Por la Raza Unida," 4, 5 (quotation).
72. Montejano, *Quixote's Soldiers*, 165, see also 164.
73. Some scholars have tried to condense the walkout into simple dichotomies, usually biased ones, but Chicana historian Maylei Blackwell has urged multiple understandings of the differences and conflicts. This was not an event of tejanas versus californias, real feministas versus vendidas, etc., but a group of women, a generation of activists, who were working to make meaning of the conditions that affected them. Multiple issues were involved, all of them resisting simple categorization. The conflicts at the Houston conference should be viewed not as the limitations of the many Chicana feminisms but as evidence of the depth of thought Chicanas had developed. See Blackwell, *¡Chicana Power!*, 160–91.
74. Marta Cotera, "Mexicano Feminism," *Magazín*, September 1973, 30, 32 (quotation), José Ángel Gutiérrez Collection, Box 1, Folder 8, University of Texas at San Antonio.
75. Evey Chapa, "Report from the National Women's Political Caucus," *Magazín*, September 1973, 37 in José Ángel Gutiérrez Collection, Box 1, Folder 8, University of Texas at San Antonio.
76. Diana Camacho to Pat Vasquez, 1975?, Marta Cotera Papers, Box 9, Folder 3, Benson Library, University of Texas at Austin.
77. "Chicanas Change Course of Texas IWY," Marta Cotera Papers, Box 9, Folder 3, Benson Library, University of Texas at Austin.
78. Elma Teresa Salinas, "Resolution," Marta Cotera Papers, Box 9, Folder 10, Benson Library, University of Texas at Austin.
79. Anna NietoGomez, "Chicana Feminism," *Caracol*, January 1976, 3.
80. Carmen Tafolla, "Soy Chicana," Carmen Tafolla Papers, Box 1, Folder 1, Benson Library, University of Texas at Austin.
81. Inés Hernández-Tovar, "To Other Women Who Were Ugly Once," *Tejidos* 5, no. 1 (1978): 12.
82. Angela de Hoyos, "Café con Leche" in *Chicano Poems: For the Barrio* (San Antonio: M&A Editions, 1977), 26.
83. Evangelina Vigil, "The Chicano-Gringa Bump," *Caracol*, September 1976, 5.
84. Evangelina Vigil, "Ay Que Ritmo," *Caracol*, September 1976, 5.
85. Carmen Tafolla, "La Isabela de Guadalupe and El Apache Mio Cid," Carmen Tafolla Papers, Box 1, Folder 1, Benson Library, University of Texas at Austin.
86. Angela de Hoyos, "Hermano," in *Chicano Poems*, 12–13.
87. Carmen Tafolla, "La Malinche," *Tejidos*, Winter 1977, 2.
88. César Augusto Martínez, "Arte Chicano," *Caracol*, December 1974, 8.

89. Reyes Cárdenas, "Poetry Review," *Caracol*, March 1975, 15.
90. Historian Juan Gómez-Quiñones has condemned cultural nationalism as "bogus" and dismissed the powerful Chicana/o cultural productions of the era as nothing more than artists' desperate and selfish attempts to gain notoriety. See Gómez-Quiñones, *Chicano Politics: Reality and Promise, 1940–1990* (Albuquerque: University of New Mexico Press, 1990), 146.

CONCLUSION

1. Daniel T. Rodgers, *Age of Fracture* (Cambridge, MA: Harvard University Press, 2011), 198.
2. Johnson, *Revolution in Texas*, 209.
3. Flores, *Backroads Pragmatists*, 36. For a discussion of the transnational dimension and interconnection of these social metaphors see pp. 19–41.
4. Reyes Cárdenas, "If We Praise the Aztecs," in *Reyes Cárdenas: Chicano Poet, 1970–2010* (San Antonio, TX: Aztlán Libre Press, 2013), 123.
5. Rodgers, *Age of Fracture*, 49.
6. See Rodgers, *Age of Fracture*, 41–76; Gilman, *Mandarins of the Future*, 250–53.
7. Jimmy Carter, "Malaise Speech," *The American Presidency Project*, accessed March 30, 2019, https://www.presidency.ucsb.edu/documents/address-the-nation-energy-and-national-goals-the-malaise-speech.
8. Ronald Reagan, "1981 Inaugural Address," *The American Presidency Project*, accessed March 30, 2019, https://www.presidency.ucsb.edu/documents/inaugural-address-11).
9. Bill Clinton, "1996 Address Before a Joint Session of the Congress on the State of the Union," *The American Presidency Project*, accessed October 28, 2019, https://www.presidency.ucsb.edu/documents/address-before-joint-session-the-congress-the-state-the-union-10.
10. See G. Cristina Mora, *Making Hispanics: How Activists, Bureaucrats, and Media Constructed a New American* (Chicago: University of Chicago Press, 2014); Clara E. Rodríguez, *Changing Race: Latinos, the Census, and the History of Ethnicity in the United States* (New York: New York University Press, 2000).
11. Latino Donor Collaborative, "About," accessed March 30, 2019, http://latinodonorcollaborative.org/who-we-are/).
12. Werner Schink and David Hayes-Bautista, "Latino Gross Domestic Product (GDP) Report: Quantifying the Impact of American Hispanic Economic Growth," p. 4, *Latino Donor Collaborative*, accessed March 30, 2019, http://latinodonorcollaborative.org/latino-gdp-report.
13. See Aaron E. Sánchez, "The Real Health Cost of Living in a Deportation State," *Latino Rebels*, accessed October 29, 2019, http://www.latinorebels

.com/2018/05/03/healthcostdeportionstate; Edward D. Vargas, Gabriel R. Sánchez, and Melina D. Juárez, "The Impact of Punitive Immigrant Laws on the Health of Latina/o Populations," *Politics & Policy* 45, no. 3 (2017): 312–37; and Vargas, Sánchez, and Juárez, "Fear by Association: Perception of Anti-Immigrant Policy and Health Outcomes," *Journal of Health Politics, Policy, and Law* 42, no. 3 (June 2017): 459–83.

14. Donald J. Trump, "2017 Inaugural Address," *White House Website*, accessed October 20, 2019, https://www.whitehouse.gov/briefings-statements/the-inaugural-address.
15. Richard Blanco, "Mother Country," in *How to Love a Country* (Boston, MA: Beacon Press, 2019), 27.
16. Blanco, "Using Country in a Sentence," in *How to Love a Country*, 31.
17. David A. Hollinger, "Historians and the Discourse of Intellectuals," in *In the American Province: Studies in the History and Historiography of Ideas* (Bloomington: Indiana University Press, 1985), 130–51.

Bibliography

ARCHIVAL COLLECTIONS

Joe J. Bernal Papers, Benson Library, University of Texas at Austin.

Marta Cotera Papers, Benson Library, University of Texas at Austin.

Food, Tobacco, Agricultural and Allied Workers Union of America, CIO Texas Locals Collections, University of Texas at Arlington.

Ben Garza Collection, Benson Library, University of Texas at Austin.

José Ángel Gutiérrez Collection, University of Texas at San Antonio.

Clemente N. Idar Papers, Benson Library, University of Texas at Austin.

Labor Movement in Texas Collection, 1845–1954, Dolph Briscoe Center for American History, University of Texas at Austin.

George and Latane Lambert Papers, University of Texas at Arlington.

Andrés de Luna Collection, Benson Library, University of Texas at Austin.

Alicia Dickerson Montemayor Papers, Benson Library, University of Texas at Austin.

Albert Peña Collection, University of Texas at San Antonio.

Alonso S. Perales Collection, M. D. Anderson Library, University of Houston.

Recovering the U.S. Hispanic Literary Heritage Project Archives, University of Houston.

Jacob I. Rodríguez Collection, Benson Library, University of Texas at Austin.

Carmen Tafolla Papers, Benson Library, University of Texas at Austin.

Tejano Voices: University of Texas at Arlington Center for Mexican American Studies Oral History Project.

Oliver Douglas Weeks Collection, Benson Library, University of Texas at Austin.

LITERARY JOURNALS, MAGAZINES, AND NEWSPAPERS

Caracol (San Antonio, TX)

El Continental (El Paso, TX)

La Crónica (Laredo, TX)

El Cronista del Valle (Brownsville, TX)

El Defensor (Edinburg, TX)

La Época (San Antonio, TX)

La Evolución (Laredo, TX)

La Patria (El Paso, TX)

La Prensa (San Antonio, TX)
La República (El Paso, TX)
Magazín (San Antonio, TX)
Revista Mexicana (San Antonio, TX)
Tejidos (Austin, TX)

BOOKS AND JOURNAL ARTICLES

Acuña, Rodolfo. *Corridors of Migration: The Odyssey of Mexican Laborers, 1600–1933*. Tucson: University of Arizona Press, 2007.

———. *Occupied America: The Chicano's Struggle toward Liberation*. San Francisco, CA: Canfield Press, 1972.

Almaráz, Félix D. Jr. *Knight without Armor: Carlos Eduardo Castañeda, 1896–1958*. College Station: Texas A&M University Press, 1999.

———. "The Making of a Boltonian: Carlos E. Castañeda of Texas—The Early Years." *Red River Valley Historical Review* 1 (Winter 1974): 329–50.

Anderson, Benedict. *Imagined Communities: Reflections on the Origin and Spread of Nationalism*. London: Verso, 1983.

Aranda, José F. *When We Arrive: A New Literary History of Mexican America*. Tucson: University of Arizona Press, 2003.

Arredondo, Gabriela F. *Mexican Chicago: Race, Identity, and Nation, 1916–1939*. Urbana: University of Illinois Press, 2008.

Avila, Eric. *Popular Culture in the Age of White Flight: Fear and Fantasy in Suburban Los Angeles*. Berkeley: University of California Press, 2004.

Balderrama, Francisco E., and Raymond Rodríguez. *Decade of Betrayal: Mexican Repatriation in the 1930s*. Albuquerque: University of New Mexico Press, 1995.

Barrera, Mario. *Race and Class in the Southwest: A Theory of Racial Inequality*. Notre Dame, IN: University of Notre Dame Press, 1979.

Bederman, Gail. *Manliness and Civilization: A Cultural History of Gender and Race in the United States, 1880–1917*. Chicago: University of Chicago Press, 1995.

Bhabha, Homi K. *The Location of Culture*. New York: Routledge, 1994.

———. *Nation and Narration*. New York: Routledge, 1990.

Blackwell, Maylei. *¡Chicana Power! Contested Histories of Feminism in the Chicano Movement*. Austin: University of Texas Press, 2011.

Blanton, Carlos Kevin. *George I. Sánchez: The Long Fight for Mexican American Integration*. New Haven, CT: Yale University Press, 2014.

Brinkley, Alan. *The End of Reform: New Deal Liberalism in Recession and War*. New York: Vintage Books, 1995.

Camarillo, Albert. *Chicanos in a Changing Society: From Mexican Pueblos to American Barrios in Santa Barbara and Southern California, 1848–1930*. Dallas, TX: Southern Methodist University Press, 2005.

Campbell, Randolph B. *Gone to Texas: A History of the Lone Star State.* New York: Oxford University Press, 2003.

Canales, J. T.. *Juan N. Cortina, Bandit or Patriot?* San Antonio, TX: Artes Gráficas, 1951.

Cardoso, Lawrence A. *Mexican Emigration to the United States, 1897–1931.* Tucson: University of Arizona Press, 1980.

Carrigan, William D. *The Making of a Lynching Culture: Violence and Vigilantism in Central Texas, 1836–1916.* Urbana: University of Illinois Press, 2004.

Castañeda Shular, Antonia, Tomás Ybarra-Frausto and Joseph Sommers. *Literatura chicana: texto y contexto/Chicano Literature: Text and Context.* Englewood Cliffs, NJ: Prentice-Hall, 1972.

Chacón, Justin Akers. *Radicals in the Barrio: Magonistas, Socialists, Wobblies, and Communists in the Mexican American Working Class.* Chicago: Haymarket Books, 2018.

Chandler, Alfred D. *The Visible Hand: The Managerial Revolution in American Business.* Cambridge, MA: Harvard University Press, 1977.

Chávez, Ernesto. *"¡Mi raza primero!" (My People First): Nationalism, Identity, and Insurgency in the Chicano Movement in Los Angeles, 1966–1978.* Berkeley and Los Angeles: University of California Press, 2002.

Chávez, John R. "Aliens in Their Native Lands: The Persistence of Internal Colonial Theory." *Journal of World History* 22, no. 4: 785–809.

———. *Beyond Nations: Evolving Homelands in the North Atlantic World, 1400–2000.* New York: Cambridge University Press, 2009.

———. *Eastside Landmark: A History of the East Los Angeles Community Union, 1968–1993.* Stanford, CA: Stanford University Press, 1998.

———. *The Lost Land: The Chicano Image of the Southwest.* Albuquerque: University of New Mexico Press, 1984.

———. "When Borders Cross Peoples: The Internal Colonial Challenge to Borderlands Theory." *Journal of Borderlands Studies* 28, no. 1 (2013): 33–46.

Clark, Christopher. *Social Change in America: From the Revolution through the Civil War.* Chicago: Ivan R. Dee, 2006.

Coronado, Raúl. *A World Not to Come: A History of Latino Writing and Print Culture.* Cambridge, MA: Harvard University Press, 2012.

Cunningham, Sean P. *Cowboy Conservatism: Texas and the Rise of the Modern Right.* Lexington: University Press of Kentucky, 2010.

Degler, Carl N. *In Search of Human Nature: The Decline and Revival of Darwinism in American Social Thought.* New York: Oxford University Press, 1991.

Dudziak, Mary L. *Cold War Civil Rights: Race and the Image of American Democracy.* Princeton, NJ: Princeton University Press, 2000.

Erenberg, Lewis A., and Susan E. Hirsch. *The War in American Culture: Society and Consciousness during World War II.* Chicago: University of Chicago Press, 1996.

Flores, Ruben. *Backroads Pragmatists: Mexico's Melting Pot and Civil Rights in the United States*. Philadelphia: University of Pennsylvania Press, 2014.

Foley, Neil. *The White Scourge: Mexicans, Blacks and Poor Whites in Texas Cotton Culture*. Berkeley: University of California Press, 1997.

Fregoso, Rosa Linda. *MeXicana Encounters: The Making of Social Identities on the Borderlands*. Berkeley and Los Angeles: University of California Press, 2003.

Gamio, Manuel. *Forjando patria*. Mexico City: Editorial Porrúa, 1960.

———. *The Mexican Immigrant: His Life-Story*. Chicago: University of Chicago Press, 1931.

———. *Mexican Immigration to the United States: A Study of Human Migration and Adjustment*. Chicago: University of Chicago Press, 1930.

García, Ignacio M. *Chicanismo: The Forging of a Militant Ethos among Mexican Americans*. Tucson: University of Arizona Press, 1997.

———. *United We Win: The Rise and Fall of La Raza Unida Party*. Tucson: University of Arizona Press, 1989.

———. *Viva Kennedy: Mexican Americans in Search of Camelot*. College Station: Texas A&M University Press, 2000.

García, Mario T. "La Frontera: The Border as Symbol and Reality in Mexican-American Thought." In *Between Two Worlds: Mexican Immigrants in the United States*, edited by David G. Gutiérrez (Wilmington, DE: Scholarly Resources, 1996).

———. *The Making of a Mexican American Mayor: Raymond L. Telles of El Paso and the Origins of Latino Political Power*. Tucson: University of Arizona Press, 2018.

———. *Mexican Americans: Leadership, Ideology, and Identity, 1930–1960*. New Haven, CT: Yale University Press, 1989.

García, Richard A. "Class, Consciousness, and Ideology—The Mexican Community of San Antonio, Texas: 1930–1940," *Aztlán* 9, nos. 1–2 (1978): 23–69.

———. "The Origins of Chicano Cultural Thought: Visions and Paradigms: Romano's Culturalism, Alurista's Aesthetics, and Acuña's Communalism," *California History* 74 no. 3 (Fall 1995): 290–305.

———. *The Rise of the Mexican American Middle Class, San Antonio, 1929–1941*. College Station: Texas A&M University Press, 1991.

Garza-Falcón, Leticia M. *Gente Decente: A Borderlands Response to the Rhetoric of Dominance*. Austin: University of Texas Press, 1998.

Gatewood, Willard B. *Aristocrats of Color: The Black Elite, 1880–1920*. Bloomington: Indiana University Press, 1990.

Gerstle, Gary. "The Working Class Goes to War." In *The War in American Culture: Society and Consciousness during World War II*, edited by Lewis A. Erenberg and Susan E. Hirsch, 105–27. Chicago: University of Chicago Press, 1996.

Gilman, Nils. *Mandarins of the Future: Modernization Theory in Cold War America*. Baltimore, MD: Johns Hopkins University Press, 2003.

Gómez, Alan Eladio. *The Revolutionary Imaginations of Greater Mexico: Chicana/o Radicalism, Solidarity Politics, and Latin American Social Movements*. Austin: University of Texas Press, 2016.

Gómez-Quiñones, Juan. *Chicano Politics: Reality and Promise, 1940–1990*. Albuquerque: University of New Mexico Press, 1990.

———. *Mexican American Labor, 1790–1990*. Albuquerque: University of New Mexico Press, 1994.

González, Gabriela. *Redeeming La Raza: Transborder Modernity, Race, Respectability, and Rights*. New York: Oxford University Press, 2018.

González, John Morán. *Border Renaissance: The Texas Centennial and the Emergence of Mexican American Literature*. Austin: University of Texas Press, 2009.

Green, James R. *Grass-Roots Socialism: Radical Movements in the Southwest, 1895–1943*. Baton Rouge: Louisiana State University Press, 1978.

———. "Tenant Farmer Discontent and Socialist Protest in Texas, 1901–1917." *Southwestern Historical Quarterly* 81, no. 2 (1977): 133–54.

Griswold del Castillo, Richard. *The Los Angeles Barrio, 1850–1890: A Social History*. Berkeley and Los Angeles: University of California Press, 1979.

Gutiérrez, David G. *Walls and Mirrors: Mexican Americans, Mexican Immigrants, and the Politics of Ethnicity*. Berkeley: University of California Press, 1995.

Gutiérrez, José Ángel. *Albert A. Peña Jr.: Dean of Chicano Politics*. East Lansing: Michigan State University Press, 2017.

———. *La Raza and Revolution: The Empirical Conditions of Revolution in Four South Texas Counties*. San Francisco: R and E Research Associates, 1971.

———. *The Making of a Chicano Militant: Lessons from Cristal*. Madison: University of Wisconsin Press, 1998.

Haney López, Ian F. *White by Law: The Legal Construction of Race*. New York: New York University Press, 1996.

Haney López, Ian, and Michael A. Olivas, "Jim Crow, Mexican Americans, and the Anti-Subordinate Constitution: The Story of *Hernandez v. Texas*." In *Race Law Stories*, edited by Rachel F. Moran and Devon Wayne Carbado, 274–309. New York: Foundation Press, 2008.

Hart, John Mason. *Revolutionary Mexico: The Coming and Process of the Mexican Revolution*. Berkeley: University of California Press, 1997.

Helleiner, Eric. *Forgotten Foundations of Bretton Woods: International Development and the Making of the Postwar Order*. Ithaca, NY: Cornell University Press, 2014.

Hernández, Ellie D. *Postnationalism in Chicana/o Literature*. Austin: University of Texas Press, 2009.

Hernández, Sonia. "Women's Labor and Activism in the Greater Mexican Borderlands, 1910–1930," in *War along the Border: The Mexican Revolution and Tejano Communities*, edited by Arnoldo De León, 176–204. College Station: Texas A&M University Press, 2012.

Hinojosa, Gilberto. *A Borderlands Town in Transition: Laredo, 1755–1870*. College Station: Texas A&M University Press, 1983.

Hollinger, David A. *In the American Province: Studies in the History and Historiography of Ideas*. Bloomington: Indiana University Press, 1985.

Jacobson, Matthew Frye. *Whiteness of a Different Color: European Immigrants and the Alchemy of Race*. Cambridge, MA: Harvard University Press, 1998.

Johnson, Benjamin H. "The Cosmic Race in Texas: Racial Fusion, White Supremacy, and Civil Rights Politics." *Journal of American History* 98, no. 2 (September 2011): 404–19.

———. *Revolution in Texas: How a Forgotten Rebellion and Its Bloody Suppression Turned Mexicans into Americans*. New Haven, CT: Yale University Press, 2003.

Kanellos, Nicolás. "Cronistas and Satire in Early Twentieth Century Hispanic Newspapers." *MELUS* 23, no. 1 (Spring 1998): 3–25.

———. *Hispanic Immigrant Literature: El sueño del retorno*. Austin: University of Texas Press, 2011.

———. *Hispanic Periodicals in the United States, Origins to 1960: A Brief History and Comprehensive Bibliography*. Houston, TX: Arte Público Press, 2000.

Kelley, Donald R. "What Is Happening to the History of Ideas?" *Journal of the History of Ideas* 51, no. 1 (1990): 3–25.

Kelly, Catherine E. *In the New England Fashion: Reshaping Women's Lives in the Nineteenth Century*. Ithaca, NY: Cornell University Press, 1999.

Kibbe, Pauline R. *Latin Americans in Texas*. Albuquerque: University of New Mexico Press, 1946.

Knight, Alan. *The Mexican Revolution: Porfirians, Liberals and Peasants*, vol 1. Cambridge: Cambridge University Press, 1986.

LaCapra, Dominick. "Intellectual History and Its Ways." *American Historical Review* 97, no. 2 (April 1992): 425–39.

Latham, Michael E. *Modernization as Ideology: American Social Science and "Nation Building" in the Kennedy Era*. Chapel Hill: University of North Carolina Press, 2000.

Lawhn, Juanita Luna. "The Mexican Revolution and the Women of El México de Afuera, the Pan American Round Table, and the Cruz Azul Mexicana," in *War along the Border: The Mexican Revolution and Tejano Communities*, edited by Arnoldo De León, 156–75. College Station: Texas A&M University Press, 2012.

Lee, Erika. *At America's Gates: Chinese Immigration during the Exclusion Era, 1882–1943*. Chapel Hill: University of North Carolina Press, 2003.

MacLachlan, Colin M., and William H. Beezley. *El Gran Pueblo: A History of Greater Mexico*. Upper Saddle River, NJ: Prentice Hall, 1994.

Manela, Erez. *The Wilsonian Moment: Self-Determination and the International Origins of Anticolonial Nationalism*. Oxford: Oxford University Press, 2007.

Mariscal, George. *Brown-Eyed Children of the Sun: Lessons from the Chicano Movement, 1965–1975*. Albuquerque: University of New Mexico Press, 2005.

Márquez, Benjamin. *LULAC: The Evolution of a Mexican American Political Organization*. Austin: University of Texas Press, 1993.

Martínez, Elizabeth. *De Colores Means All of Us: Latina Views for a Multi-Colored Century*. Cambridge, MA: South End Press, 1998.

Martínez, Oscar J. *Border Boomtown: Ciudad Juárez since 1848*. Austin: University of Texas Press, 1978.

Massey, Douglas S., Rafael Alarcon, Jorge Durand, and Humberto González. *Return to Aztlan: The Social Process of International Migration from Western Mexico*. Berkeley and Los Angeles: University of California Press, 1987.

Maza, Sarah. "Stephen Greenblatt, New Historicism, and Cultural History, or, What We Talk About When We Talk About Interdisciplinarity," *Modern Intellectual History* 1, no. 2 (August 2004): 249–65.

McElvaine, Robert S. *The Great Depression: America, 1929–1941*. New York: Times Books, 1984.

Menefee, Selden C. *Mexican Migratory Workers of South Texas*. Washington, DC: Government Printing Office, 1941.

Menefee, Selden C., and Orin C. Cassmore, *The Pecan Shellers of San Antonio: The Problem of Underpaid and Unemployed Mexican Labor*. Washington DC: Government Printing Office, 1940.

Mendoza, Natalie. "The Good Neighbor in the American Historical Imagination: Boltonians, Mexican Americans, and the Creation of a Common American Heritage." *Western Historical Quarterly*, forthcoming.

Molina, Natalia. *How Race Is Made in America: Immigration, Citizenship, and the Historical Power of Racial Scripts*. Berkeley: University of California Press, 2014.

Monroy, Douglas. *Rebirth: Mexican Los Angeles from the Great Migration to the Great Depression*. Berkeley: University of California Press, 1999.

Montejano, David. *Anglos and Mexicans in the Making of Texas*. Austin: University of Texas Press, 1987.

———. "Frustrated Apartheid: Race, Repression, and Capitalist Agriculture in South Texas, 1920–1930." In *The World-System of Capitalism: Past and Present*, edited by Walter L. Goldfrank, 131–68. Beverly Hills, CA: Sage, 1979.

———. *Quixote's Soldiers: A Local History of the Chicano Movement, 1966–1981*. Austin: University of Texas Press, 2010.

———. *Sancho's Journal: Exploring the Political Edge with the Brown Berets*. Austin: University of Texas Press, 2012.

Mora, G. Cristina. *Making Hispanics: How Activists, Bureaucrats, and Media Constructed a New American.* Chicago: University of Chicago Press, 2014.

Mora-Torres, Juan. *The Making of the Mexican Border: The State, Capitalism, and Society in Nuevo Leon, 1848–1910.* Austin: University of Texas Press, 2001.

Muñoz, Carlos Jr.. *Youth, Identity, Power: The Chicano Movement.* New York: Verso, 1989.

Ngai, Mae M. *Impossible Subjects: Illegal Aliens and the Making of Modern America.* Princeton, NJ: Princeton University Press, 2004.

Nostrand, Richard L. *The Hispano Homeland.* Norman: University Oklahoma Press, 1992.

Nostrand, Richard L., and Lawrence E. Estaville. *Homelands: A Geography of Culture and Place across America.* Baltimore, MD: Johns Hopkins University Press, 2001.

Olguín, Benjamin V. *La Pinta: Chicana/o Prisoner Literature, Culture, and Politics.* Austin: University of Texas Press, 2010.

Olivas, Michael. *In Defense of My People: Alonso S. Perales and the Development of Mexican-American Public Intellectuals.* Houston, TX: Arte Público Press, 2013.

Oropeza, Lorena. *¡Raza Sí! ¡Guerra No!: Chicano Protest and Patriotism during the Viet Nam War Era.* Berkeley: University of California Press, 2005.

Orozco, Cynthia. *No Mexicans, Women, or Dogs Allowed: The Rise of the Mexican American Civil Rights Movement.* Austin: University of Texas Press, 2009.

Paredes, Américo. *A Texas-Mexican Cancionero: Folksongs of the Lower Border.* Urbana: University of Illinois Press, 1976.

Peña, Manuel. *The Mexican American Orquesta: Music, Culture, and the Dialectic of Conflict.* Austin: University of Texas Press, 1999.

Perales, Monica. "'Who Has a Greater Job Than a Mother?' Defining Mexican Motherhood on the U.S.-Mexico Border in the Early Twentieth Century." In *On the Borders of Love and Power: Families and Kinship in the Intercultural American Southwest*, edited by David Wallace Adams and Crista DeLuzio, 163–84. Berkeley and Los Angeles: University of California Press, 2012.

Pycior, Julie Leininger. *Democratic Renewal and the Mutual Aid Legacy of US Mexicans.* College Station: Texas A&M University Press, 2014.

Ramírez, José A. *To the Line of Fire! Mexican Texans and World War I.* College Station: Texas A&M University Press, 2009.

Ramos, Raúl A. "Understanding Greater Revolutionary Mexico: The Case for a Transnational Border History," in *War along the Border: The Mexican Revolution and Tejano Communities*, edited by Arnoldo De León, 310–17. College Station: Texas A&M University Press, 2012.

Reed, Adolph Jr., and Kenneth W. Warren. *Renewing Black Intellectual History: The Ideological and Material Foundations of African American Thought.* Boulder, CO: Paradigm, 2010.

Reséndez, Andrés. *Changing Identities at the Frontier: Texas and New Mexico, 1800–1850*. New York: Cambridge University Press, 2004.

Rodríguez, Clara E. *Changing Race: Latinos, the Census, and the History of Ethnicity in the United States*. New York: New York University Press, 2000.

Roeder, George H. Jr. "Censoring Disorder: American Visual Imagery of World War II." In *The War in American Culture: Society and Consciousness during World War II*, edited by Lewis A. Erenberg and Susan E. Hirsch, 46–70. Chicago: University of Chicago Press, 1996.

Roediger, David R *Towards the Abolition of Whiteness: Essays on Race, Politics, and Working Class History*. London: Verso, 1994.

———. *The Wages of Whiteness: Race and the Making of the American Working Class*. London: Verso, 1991.

Rodgers, Daniel T. *Age of Fracture*. Cambridge, MA: Harvard University Press, 2011.

Romo, David Dorado. *Ringside Seat to a Revolution: An Underground Cultural History of El Paso and Juarez: 1893–1923*. El Paso, TX: Cinco Puntos Press, 200.

Romo, Ricardo. *East Los Angeles: History of a Barrio*. Austin: University of Texas Press, 1983.

Rosales, F. Arturo. *Chicano! The History of the Mexican American Civil Rights Movement*. Houston, TX: Arte Público Press, 1996.

———. *¡Pobre Raza! Violence, Justice, and Mobilization among México Lindo Immigrants, 1900–1936*. Austin: University of Texas Press, 1999.

Rossinow, Douglas C. *Visions of Progress: The Left-Liberal Tradition in America*. Philadelphia: University of Pennsylvania Press, 2008.

Rostow, Walt W. *The Stages of Economic Growth: A Non-Communist Manifesto*. Oxford: Oxford University Press, 1991.

Ruiz, Vicki L. *Cannery Women, Cannery Lives: Mexican Women, Unionization, and the California Food Processing Industry, 1930–1950*. Albuquerque: University of New Mexico Press, 1987.

———. *From Out of the Shadows: Mexican Women in Twentieth-Century America*. New York: Oxford University Press, 1998.

Saldívar, José David. *Border Matters: Remapping American Cultural Studies*. Berkeley and Los Angeles: University of California Press, 1997.

Saldívar, Ramón. *Chicano Narrative: The Dialectics of Difference*. Madison: University of Wisconsin Press, 1990.

Saldívar-Hull, Sonia. *Feminism on the Border: Chicana Gender Politics and Literature*. Berkeley and Los Angeles: University of California Press, 2000.

Sánchez, Aaron E. "Of Patriots and Pochos: Ethnic Mexicans and the Politics and Poetics of Changing Nationalisms, Texas, 1910–1940." *Journal of the West* 54, no. 1 (Winter 2015): 29–38.

Sánchez, George J. *Becoming Mexican American: Ethnicity, Culture, and Identity in Chicano Los Angeles, 1900–1945*. New York: Oxford University Press, 1993.

San Miguel, Guadalupe Jr. *Brown, Not White: School Integration and the Chicano Movement in Houston*. College Station: Texas A&M University Press, 2001.

———. "In the Midst of Radicalism: Mexican American Liberals during the Early Years of the Chicano Movement—The Case of Vicente T. Ximenes and the Interagency Committee on Mexican American Affairs, 1965–1968." *Journal of South Texas* 31, no. 2 (Spring 2018): 8–27.

Santibáñez, Enrique. *Ensayo acerca de la inmigración mexicana en los Estados Unidos*. San Antonio, TX: Clegg, 1930.

Scott, James C. *Seeing Like a State: How Certain Schemes to Improve the Human Condition Have Failed*. New Haven, CT: Yale University Press, 1999.

Segura, Denise A., and Beatriz M. Pesquera. "Beyond Indifference and Antipathy: The Chicana Movement and Chicana Feminist Discourse." *Aztlán* 19, no. 2 (1990): 69–92.

Self, Robert O. *American Babylon: Race and the Struggle for Postwar Oakland*. Princeton, NJ: Princeton University Press, 2003.

Sellers, Charles. *The Market Revolution: Jacksonian America, 1815–1846*. New York: Oxford University Press, 1991.

Stern, Alexandra Minna. *Eugenic Nation: Faults and Frontiers of Better Breeding in Modern America*. Berkeley: University of California Press, 2005.

Takaki, Ronald. *Double Victory: A Multicultural History of America in World War II*. New York: Little, Brown, 2000.

Taylor, Paul S. *An American-Mexican Frontier: Nueces County, Texas*. Chapel Hill: University of North Carolina Press, 1934.

———. *Mexican Labor in the United States: Chicago and the Calumet Region*. University of California Publications in Economics 7, no. 2. Berkeley: University of California Press, 1932.

———. *A Spanish-Mexican Peasant Community: Arandas in Jalisco, Mexico*. Berkeley: University of California Press, 1933.

Tenayuca, Emma, and Homer Brooks. "The Mexican Question in the Southwest," in *Herencia: The Anthology of Hispanic Literature of the United States*, edited by Nicolás Kanellos, 156–62. Oxford: Oxford University Press, 2002.

Toews, John E. "Intellectual History after the Linguistic Turn: The Autonomy of Meaning and Irreducibility of Experience." *American Historical Review* 92, no. 4 (October 1987): 879–907.

Torpey, John. *The Invention of the Passport: Surveillance, Citizenship, and the State*. Cambridge: Cambridge University Press, 2000.

United States Commission on Civil Rights. *Hearing before the United States Commission on Civil Rights: Hearing Held in San Antonio, Texas, December 9–14, 1968*. Washington, DC: Government Printing Office, 1969.

Valdés, Dennis N. *Al Norte: Agricultural Workers in the Great Lakes Region, 1917–1970*. Austin: University of Texas Press, 1991.

———. *Barrios norteños: St. Paul and Midwestern Mexican Communities in the Twentieth Century*. Austin: University of Texas Press, 2000.

———. *Mexicans in Minnesota*. St. Paul: Minnesota Historical Society Press, 2005.

———. "Region, Nation, and World-System: Perspectives on Midwestern Chicana/o History." In *Voices of a New Chicana/o History*, edited by Refugio I. Rochín and Dennis N. Valdés, 115–40. East Lansing: Michigan State University, 2000.

Valerio-Jiménez, Omar S. *River of Hope: Forging Identity and Nation in the Rio Grande Borderlands*. Durham, NC: Duke University Press, 2013.

Vargas Edward D., Gabriel R. Sánchez, and Melina D. Juárez. "Fear by Association: Perception of Anti-Immigrant Policy and Health Outcomes." *Journal of Health Politics, Policy, and Law* 42, no. 3 (June 2017): 459–83.

———. "The Impact of Punitive Immigrant Laws on the Health of Latina/o Populations." *Politics & Policy* 45, no. 3 (2017): 312–37.

Vargas, Zaragosa. *Labor Rights Are Civil Rights: Mexican American Workers in Twentieth-Century America*. Princeton, NJ: Princeton University Press, 2005.

———. *Proletarians of the North: A History of Mexican Industrial Workers in Detroit and the Midwest, 1917–1933*. Berkeley: University of California Press, 1993.

Vélez-Ibañez, Carlos G. *Border Visions: Mexican Cultures in the Southwest United States*. Tucson: University of Arizona Press, 1996.

Wallerstein, Immanuel. *The Modern World-System*. New York: Academic Press, 1974.

Weber, John. *From South Texas to the Nation: The Exploitation of Mexican Labor in the Twentieth Century*. Chapel Hill: University of North Carolina Press, 2015.

Weitz, Eric D. *A World Divided: The Global Struggle for Human Rights in the Age of the Nation-States*. Princeton, NJ: Princeton University Press, 2019.

Wickberg, Daniel A. "Intellectual History vs. the Social History of Intellectuals." *Rethinking History* 5, no. 3 (2001): 383–95.

Woods, Frances Jerome. *Mexican Ethnic Leadership in San Antonio, Texas*. Washington, DC: Catholic University of America Press, 1949.

Zamora, Emilio. "Chicano Socialist Labor Activity in Texas, 1900–1920." *Aztlán* 6, no. 2 (Summer 1975): 221–38.

———. *Claiming Rights and Righting Wrongs in Texas: Mexican Workers and Job Politics during World War II*. College Station: Texas A&M University Press, 2009.

———. *The World of the Mexican Worker in Texas*. College Station: Texas A&M University Press, 1993.

LITERATURE AND POETRY COLLECTIONS AS PRIMARY SOURCES

Ainslie, Jorge. *Los pochos: novela.* Los Angeles: Latin Publishing, 1934.

Blanco, Richard. *How to Love a Country.* Boston, MA: Beacon Press, 2019.

Cárdenas, Reyes. *Reyes Cárdenas: Chicano Poet, 1970–2010.* San Antonio, TX: Aztlán Libre Press, 2013.

De Hoyos, Angela. *Arise, Chicano! and Other Poems.* San Antonio, TX: M&A Editions, 1980.

———. *Chicano Poems: For the Barrio.* San Antonio, TX: M&A Editions, 1977.

Delgado, Abelardo. *Chicano: 25 Pieces of a Chicano Mind.* El Paso, TX: Barrio Publications, 1972.

———. *The Chicano Movement: Some Not Too Objective Observations.* Denver, CO: Totinem Publications, 1971.

Espinoza, Conrado. *Sol de Texas/Under the Texas Sun.* Houston, TX: Arte Público Press, 2007.

García-Camarillo, Cecilio, Reyes Cárdenas, and Carmen Tafolla. *Nahualliando-ing: Español/Nahuatl/English.* San Antonio, TX: Caracol, 1977.

Gonzales, Rodolfo "Corky." *Message to Aztlán: Selected Writings of Rodolfo "Corky" Gonzales,* comp. Antonio Esquibel (Houston, TX: Arte Público Press, 2001).

Lozano, Rubén Rendon. *Viva Tejas: The Story of the Mexican-Born Patriots of the Republic of Texas.* San Antonio, TX: Southern Literary Institute, 1936.

Paredes, Américo. *George Washington Gómez: A Mexicotexan Novel.* Houston, TX: Arte Público Press, 1990.

Sánchez, Ricardo. *Canto y grito mi liberación: The Liberation of a Chicano Mind.* Grand City, NY: Anchor Press/Doubleday, 1973.

Valdez, Luis. *Early Works: Actos, Bernabé, and Pensamiento Serpentino.* Houston, TX: Arte Público Press, 1990.

Venegas, Daniel. *Las aventuras de don Chipote, o cuando los pericos mamen.* Houston, TX: Arte Público Press, 1999.

Verastique, Bernardo. *Yellow Luna.* San Antonio: n.p., 1977.

Villanueva, Tino. *Hay otra voz: Poems* (1968–1971). Staten Island, NY: Editorial Mensaje, 1979.

Villarreal, José Antonio. *Pocho.* New York: Anchor Books, 1959.

Index

References to illustrations appear in italic type.